THE MUSIC PARENTS' SURVIVAL GUIDE

D1367756

The Music Parents' Survival Guide

A PARENT-TO-PARENT CONVERSATION

Amy Nathan

OXFORD
UNIVERSITY PRESS

OXFORD
UNIVERSITY PRESS

Oxford University Press is a department of the
University of Oxford. It furthers the University's objective
of excellence in research, scholarship, and education
by publishing worldwide.

Oxford   New York
Auckland   Cape Town   Dar es Salaam   Hong Kong   Karachi
Kuala Lumpur   Madrid   Melbourne   Mexico City   Nairobi
New Delhi   Shanghai   Taipei   Toronto

With offices in
Argentina   Austria   Brazil   Chile   Czech Republic   France   Greece
Guatemala   Hungary   Italy   Japan   Poland   Portugal   Singapore
South Korea   Switzerland   Thailand   Turkey   Ukraine   Vietnam

Oxford is a registered trade mark of Oxford University Press
in the UK and certain other countries.

Published in the United States of America by
Oxford University Press
198 Madison Avenue, New York, NY 10016

Library of Congress Cataloging-in-Publication Data
Nathan, Amy.
The music parents' survival guide : a parent-to-parent conversation / Amy Nathan.
pages   cm
Includes bibliographical references and index.
ISBN 978-0-19-983714-4 (pbk. : alk. paper)—ISBN 978-0-19-983712-0 (hardcover : alk. paper)
1. Music—Instruction and study—Parent participation.   I. Title.
MT1.N279   2014
780.71—dc23   2013035236

9 8 7 6 5 4 3 2 1

Printed in the United States of America
on acid-free paper

For Noah, Eric, and Carl

Contents

THE MUSIC PARENTS' SURVIVAL GUIDE

The author's sons pretending to be in a marching band (top), using toy instruments at about age seven for Eric (left) and age four for Noah. Several years later, they're playing a real trumpet and saxophone in an informal Fourth of July neighborhood marching band. As adults, her older son has become a composer; her younger son has chosen to pursue a non-musical career, but music is still an important part of his life.

1 Parent-to-Parent—The Conversation Begins

THIS BOOK IS AN ENSEMBLE PRODUCTION. Its theme comes from a frustrated music parent who sounded an alarm, calling for a new work to be created to encourage, support, and bolster the morale of one of music's most important backup sections—music parents. More than 150 other music parents have answered that call, contributing their experiences, reflections, warnings, and helpful suggestions. Also chiming in are dozens of professional musicians and music educators. I serve as orchestrator and conductor, pulling together the myriad responses to create a production that we hope will resonate with our audience of readers.

The clarion call that launched this collective performance arrived by e-mail in early 2010. New York–based visual artist Theresa Chong, mother of two young musicians, wrote: "Have you ever thought about writing a book for parents who struggle with daily practice with their kids? It is very much needed, a book on surviving through the first years and forming a daily routine to get the kids to practice."

I knew Ms. Chong from an earlier book I wrote for young people about the New York Philharmonic, *Meet the Musicians*. It includes a photo of her son, cellist Chase Park, as a five-year-old beginner taking part in a master class with the Philharmonic's principal cellist, Carter Brey. Ms. Chong had also seen my other book for kids, *The Young Musician's Survival Guide*, which offers practice and performing tips from professional musicians. Ms. Chong felt that music parents could use a "survival guide" of their own, filled with strategies on how to walk the music-parenting tightrope—how to be supportive but not overbearing, how to encourage excellence but not become bogged down in fruitless battles of wills.

When I followed up with Ms. Chong, she explained that she had a special kind of advice book in mind—a parent-to-parent one. She envisioned a book that would be written "on behalf of mothers like me who are just dying to hear what other parents may be doing to help their kids with practice. I think this could really help many parents, who have the best desires to give their children the gift of music only to find out how hard it really is. I would love to give all my input from my past experiences. Every mother I sit down with and talk with about practice goes through the same thing. You would have more than enough mothers who would tell their side. I'm sure you could interview musicians who have kids themselves and have issues with their practice."

Around that same time, I was invited to talk about my two music books for kids with members of the Parents' Association of the Pre-College Division of Manhattan School of Music (MSM). Several of those parents expressed an interest in having a survival guide similar to the one Ms. Chong suggested.

A parent-to-parent advice book for music parents—that's something my husband and I could have used when we found ourselves unprepared for how to be good music parents for our first child. At eighteen months, our son Eric fell in love with an episode of *Mr. Rogers' Neighborhood* that featured the Empire Brass Quintet. By chance, we videotaped the show. Eric watched the tape so often that he memorized the dialogue and would pretend to be in the quintet himself.

Not being musicians nor having any professional musicians in the family, my husband and I had no one to guide us on how to follow up on our son's interest. We made a lot of mistakes, including one at the very beginning that was almost a game ender: We signed our toddler up for formal lessons when he was way too young and much too shy to focus on serious instruction. Not only that, but the lessons were for an instrument he wasn't really interested in—violin. What were we thinking? Luckily, as pianist (and music dad) Emanuel Ax told me years later, "When you're a parent, you make a mistake every day. At least one. Parents can make mistakes and still things will work out. Absolutely. Otherwise nobody would ever be successful."

Gradually, all three of us bounced back from that mistake. My husband and I began to ask for advice from other parents and teachers. Slowly, we learned how to be better music parents both for Eric (who found his way to shine musically later on with piano, trumpet, and composing) and also for our saxophone-playing younger son. It was a step-by-step process of picking up a good tip here, a useful suggestion there, bolstered along the way by the research I did when I wrote those two music books for kids.

How much more helpful it would have been if there had been a book that would have let us learn from music-parenting veterans. How great it would have been to discover other parents' strategies for dealing with such vexing issues as monitoring practicing and taming performance jitters. What a relief it would have been to find out how they located good teachers, coped with the high cost of music instruction, handled the prickly mood swings of teen musicians, and figured out what kind of guidance to offer a youngster whose passion for music has turned serious, with college and career concerns looming on the horizon. How reassuring also to have heard some answers to that gnawing question: "Can my kid possibly earn a living from music? And if not, is it still worth all the time and effort?"

That is why I accepted the challenge that Theresa Chong placed before me and set out to create a parent-to-parent book that would present useful, parent-tested advice. There are, of course, other advice books out there that give pointers on raising musical kids (the Bibliography lists several), but none of them takes the parent-to-parent approach that Ms. Chong, the MSM parents, and I all thought would be especially helpful. I began looking for experienced music parents to serve as advice givers.

The rest of this chapter describes the team I assembled and explains the book's structure. This chapter also features sidebar boxes in which two musicians on our advice team say "Thanks" to their parents for terrific music parenting.

Team of Advisors

Altogether 265 individuals—including Theresa Chong—serve as volunteer advisors for this book. Music parents are on the team. So are professional musicians, music educators, and other experts who share not only their insights on various issues but also often describe their own music-parenting experiences because many are music parents themselves. In fact, more than 75 percent of the book's advice panelists have had experience raising their own musical kids.

To find the parent advisors, I contacted music schools and music programs around the country, asking them to distribute questionnaires to parents they thought had done a particularly good job of encouraging and supporting their young instrumentalists or singers. I received questionnaires from 130 parents and conducted in-depth phone interviews with dozens of them. Music experts recommended other parents to interview, including some whose children participate in new El Sistema programs that provide free music instruction in low-income communities. Several parents of professional musicians kindly agreed to be interviewed, as did fifty-two music

Bassist Christian McBride working with students at a Newark middle school in a program sponsored by Jazz House Kids, founded by his wife, singer Melissa Walker.

SPOTLIGHT ON: CHRISTIAN MCBRIDE, BASS

Set them up: "My father was a bass guitar player. That was my initial inspiration for playing bass, but my mom was the navigator of the ship," says jazz musician Christian McBride. He notes that his parents "split up when I was young." His mom handled most arrangements for his music education. "My mother recognized the passion I had for music and put me in situations where I would be around the best musicians possible, the most inspirational people, so she wouldn't have to tell me to practice. If anything, she was about balance. She'd say, 'Would you do your homework, or something beside have that bass in your hand all day?' If kids love what they're doing, you don't have to push them. It's a parent's job to help them find what they love. Set them up, as in basketball. Set up your shooter for the best possible position. You can't make him shoot, but you can set him up."

educators and other music experts. Also participating are a dozen individuals who, like my younger son, studied music as youngsters but chose not to become professional musicians.

In addition, I reached out to professional musicians to learn about the helpful (and *not* so helpful) things their parents did. I was overjoyed when more than forty musicians agreed to participate. These pros include Grammy winners and nominees, three recipients of the MacArthur Foundation's "genius" award—conductor Marin Alsop, cellist Alisa Weilerstein, and saxophonist Miguel Zenón—and one Pulitzer Prize winner, Wynton Marsalis, a trumpeter and composer.

Among the classical musicians on the advice team are pianists Emanuel Ax, Jonathan Biss, Gloria Cheng, and Erika Nickrenz; violinists Adrian Anantawan, Joshua Bell, Sarah Chang, Robert Gupta, Jennifer Koh, Anne Akiko Meyers, and Dana Myers; flutist Paula Robison; clarinetists Anthony McGill and Richard Stoltzman; oboists Toyin Spellman-Diaz and Liang Wang; trumpeter Mark Inouye; double bass player David Grossman; and several others. Opera singers Stephanie Blythe and Lawrence Brownlee contribute suggestions, as does Broadway star Kelli O'Hara. Three musicians who perform with new-music ensembles offer advice. So do several jazz musicians: Joining Miguel Zenón and Wynton Marsalis, are jazz bassist Christian McBride, drummer Ali Jackson, and pianist Ellis Marsalis. (For more on the advisors, see About the Advice Panel at the end of the book.)

Profile of the Advice Panel

This way of assembling a research panel yields anecdotal information but not statistical data. However, because the goal of the book is to offer diverse strategies that others have found effective, anecdote-based research seems a useful approach. This method skews the parent mix toward those who have had a positive experience, but not totally. In quite a few of our advisors' families, not all the children were equally enthusiastic about music. Some youngsters gave music a try and quit—while others had no interest in music at all. In addition, there was no attempt to focus on families whose children could be labeled as prodigies, although a few of the young musicians described in the book fit that description. Instead, the youngsters cover a wide range of musical interests, abilities, aspirations, and accomplishments.

The parents on our advisory team are in varying stages of parenting. Many have youngsters still in school—others have sons and daughters in college or beyond. The team's music-parenting styles span a wide range, from those who exercise tight control to those who employ a laissez-faire approach. Over the course of raising their musical youngsters, several parents at either end of the spectrum—along with many in the middle—modified their approach. Some tightened up, while others loosened up. This book takes no sides. The goal is to air opinions on different approaches.

Music is a family tradition for many of the parents. More than half were involved in music as youngsters. About a quarter of those who aren't professional musicians continue to play an instrument or sing in choirs. Most agree to be quoted by name, but a few prefer to remain anonymous, especially when discussing sensitive issues. As one parent explained: "One of the best tips I ever received as a new music parent was that the music world is very small and to always be careful what you say and never burn bridges."

A Different Kind of Advice Book

This isn't a book of charts on the right way to approach a problem, the best products to buy, or the top-ten schools to attend. Although there are a few lists here and there, most of the text in *The Music Parents' Survival Guide* consists of descriptions of personal experiences and helpful suggestions from parents, musicians, and educators—an array of possibilities for the book's readers to mull over as they chart their own course.

Some scholarly works have also emphasized personal accounts from music parents, such as Andrew Solomon's 950-page opus *Far from the Tree,* which presents the experiences of hundreds of families with children who could be termed "exceptional," mainly because of physical or psychological issues. However, one of the chapters in the Solomon book is devoted to musical prodigies and features commentaries from dozens of prodigies and their parents. Parental accounts are also included in *Developing Talent in Young People,* published in 1985, which presents a landmark study on the role that parents play in the development of high-performing youngsters in a range of fields: music, as well as visual arts, sports, and science. The late Benjamin S. Bloom, a distinguished researcher and professor of education at the University of Chicago and Northwestern University, served as that book's editor and research leader. His team conducted a longitudinal study of twenty-one top musicians and ninety-nine other world-class achievers. Professor Bloom describes the important role played by the parents of all these high-performers: "No one reached the limits of learning in a talent field on his or her own. Families and teachers were crucial at every step along the way to excellence." He explains that it took "a long and intensive process of encouragement, nurturance, education, and training" for the individuals profiled in his book to "attain extreme levels of capability." (Both books are listed in the Bibliography.)

Professor Bloom's conclusions are seconded by many of the educators and other experts who share their observations in *The Music Parents' Survival Guide.* According to one of our educator advisors, "When parents are willing to make a commitment, willing to go to the child's lessons, to help with practice, to pay for lessons, that's a huge support system." This comment comes from Mark Churchill, former dean of the Preparatory School of New England Conservatory (NEC).

Dr. Gene Beresin, a child psychiatrist at Harvard Medical School (and a music dad himself), notes, "We would not have our star performers in music, art, literature, and athletics if they didn't have an incredible amount of support from their parents."

Our book differs markedly from these two scholarly books, however. Unlike the Solomon book, our book covers a much wider cross-section of musical youngsters. Our book also presents a different type of advice than the Bloom book, which has a broad and formal focus but doesn't include the kind of practical, specific, hands-on suggestions offered by our parent advisors—tips that can help with the day-to-day problems parents may face.

The parent-to-parent sharing in our book is similar to what might occur during informal conversations with fellow music parents sitting in a music school lobby, as they wait for their kids' rehearsals or lessons to end. However, during actual music school conversations, there may be a certain hesitancy to really open up, as one of our parent advisors notes. "Sometimes parents don't always want to share that their child is not doing well, especially if there's a competitive atmosphere at the school," says Janice Fagan, whose daughter took piano lessons every Saturday for

Violinist Sarah Chang

many years at a music school in New York City. But Ms. Fagan and our other parent advisors showed a remarkable degree of openness in the questionnaires they completed and in the telephone interviews they participated in as members of the research panel for *The Music Parents' Survival Guide*. They were willing to acknowledge mistakes made, problems encountered, and lessons learned. This openness may result in part from the non-face-to-face nature of their advice giving. Most of our team members seem genuinely interested in being as helpful as possible to parents struggling to do their best by their musical youngsters.

Another advantage our book has over music school lobby encounters: Our advice panel includes many more parents than can possibly fit in a school lobby, offering a wider variety of ideas than music school chats can produce.

Of course, the suggestions from our advisors won't fit every family nor solve every problem a musical family encounters. Equally certain, the book's readers will have many other, tried-and-true strategies of their own. Perhaps this book will spark discussions on music parenting at music schools around the country, allowing parent-to-parent sharing to continue long after the last chapter of this book has been read.

But before diving into the anecdotes, reflections, and suggestions that our team has to offer, the next chapter explores two fundamental questions that can help parents set a framework for their music-parenting experience—why parents might want to involve their kids in music and what they and their kids are likely to gain from the experience.

SPOTLIGHT ON: SARAH CHANG, VIOLIN

Support Team: "My dad was involved with the music side of everything. Mom was more of a mom, bugging me about taking my vitamins, eating my vegetables, fussing about the dresses I wore in concerts," says Sarah Chang, who made her professional debut at age eight. Her father, a violinist, offered musical advice when asked, but her mother, a pianist, "backed off when it came to anything music related. Mom understood that I had enough music teachers in my life. The best thing she did was leave the musical part to everyone else and be a mom. She was into the dresses and the visual side of a performance. She worried when I was on tour. A lot of the time, she was on tour with me. She was always encouraging, my number-one supporter."

THE BOOK'S "PROGRAM NOTES"

Just as reading program notes before a concert can help listeners gain a better understanding of a piece of music, the following description of this book's structure can help readers gain more from what it has to offer.

- **Chapter topics:** Each of the following eleven chapters focuses on a different general area of concern for music parents.
- **Introductory anecdotes:** The parental exchange of experiences starts at the top of every chapter, with an extended introductory anecdote or vignette from a parent or a professional musician that provides an engaging window into the topic the chapter explores.
- **Unfolding:** The stories of some families or musicians will unfold gradually over the course of the book, with readers learning in early chapters how a child got started in

music but not finding out until later how the youngster dealt with practice problems or carved out a career.

- **Repetition:** As in a musical composition, there is a certain amount of repetition because some suggestions relate to more than one area of concern. Moreover, some readers won't read this book cover to cover but will dip in here and there, depending on their interests.
- **Sidebars:** Each chapter has sidebars containing anecdotes on the topic at hand. In most chapters, the sidebars feature professional musicians. In chapters 2 and 12, the sidebars feature individuals who studied music as children but chose to pursue other careers.
- **Resources:** In addition to the Bibliography at the end of the book, a Resources section provides help for one of a music parent's main jobs—becoming an instant expert on topics about which the parent previously knew little.
- **Narrator:** Although I experienced many of the problems discussed in this book with my two sons, I don't comment further on our family's experiences in the body of the book. I want to keep the focus on the ensemble of advisors and limit my role to that of an objective narrator. But because personal experiences can influence even the most well-meaning effort to be objective, the Author's Note section at end of the book presents an outline of the routes my sons have taken.

Toyin Spellman-Diaz (right) performing during high school at the Interlochen Summer Arts Camp, which she attended on a scholarship. Below is a more recent photo of this professional oboist, now a member of the Imani Winds quintet.

2 Music Parenting—The Whys and Worth of It

LET'S START OFF BY HEARING HOW two veteran music parents describe music's impact on their family. "When I look back on it now, I wonder how in the world did I do it?" says Karen Spellman. She shepherded—and chauffeured—two daughters through music lessons, youth orchestra rehearsals, performances, and more. "For parents who are thinking about helping their children get into music in a serious way, be prepared to put in hours after school, in the evenings, and on weekends," she warns. Her older daughter, Toyin Spellman-Diaz, is now a professional oboist with the Imani Winds woodwind quintet. Her younger daughter, Rev. Kaji Spellman, took a break from music during high school, but came back to it in her late twenties through choral singing and now makes music a central part of her ministry.

"My husband and I played different roles as music parents," explains Ms. Spellman. Her husband, A. B. Spellman, worked at the National Endowment for the Arts in Washington, DC, and took on much of the research role, tapping into his arts contacts to find teachers, music camps, scholarships, and so on. "I handled more of the support role as the chauffeur and the gofer," says Ms. Spellman. "I spent so much time in my car taking the children to their lessons and practices. I sat through their rehearsals and went to all their competitions. The car would be filled with anything I might need for any three-hour period: books, telephone, changes of clothes, food, drinks. I was a rolling supply center for the children's musical careers. Then there were the reminders: 'Did you practice? Where did you leave your reeds?' There were reeds all over the house, and reed strings hanging from all the furniture. Oboe is a double-reed instrument and Toyin had to carve tiny reeds out of bamboo and tie two of them together with string."

Family activity centered on the DC Youth Orchestra Program, where the parents began volunteering shortly after Toyin joined at age nine. At first Toyin played flute with this youth orchestra but later switched to oboe. The Spellmans' younger daughter, Kaji, started violin there a few years after her sister joined. "By the time Kaji left the youth orchestra during high school, my husband and I were pretty wiped out from all the volunteering. But it was absolutely worthwhile," notes Ms. Spellman. "The payoff was when they performed. It was thrilling to hear them. The world of classical music opened up for me. I learned so much about music by being the mother of two musicians. This orchestra provided a stepping stone for so many kids, expanding their contacts within the music community. Had they not been in this youth orchestra, I don't know whether either of our children would have continued in music."

"The orchestra was also important in the development of our daughters as people," observes her husband. "It not only gave them a chance to grow as musicians, but they were with other kids who were 'about something.' They learned professional behavior, how to be on time, know their music, take direction and criticism. That would prepare them for whatever careers they decided to pursue."

"Opened Up a Vast New World"

As the Spellmans discovered, music parenting involves more than making sure kids practice. Not all our parent advisors have engaged in such heavy-duty chauffeuring and volunteering as the Spellmans, but most have shouldered a good chunk of support work. Some have also taken on even wider advocacy and fundraising roles to help keep public school music programs afloat in the era of slashed music-education budgets.

Family budgets can also experience a strain because music can be an expensive hobby. "It was an enormous financial burden," says Annette Radoff. Costs ran especially high for this Philadelphia mother because of her daughter Elena Urioste's choice of instrument: violin. Quality string instruments are pricey. So are private lessons, camp tuition, and youth orchestra fees. When her daughter began performing professionally, there were also travel expenses. In later chapters, our team members share ideas for how to lower costs, but Paul Babcock offers a dose of perspective, noting that outfitting a sports-enthused youngster can be budget busting, too—something he knows as a music dad, a sports dad, and president of the MacPhail Center for Music in Minneapolis.

Despite all the worries, time commitments, and expenses, nearly all the parents on our research team agree with the Spellmans that music parenting is well worth the effort. Many cite the same benefit as Karen and A. B. Spellman—that helping their kids become involved with music enriched the lives of the whole family, parents and kids alike. Here is a sampling of quotes from some of our parent advisors who feel this way:

- "It has totally changed our entire household, opened up a vast new world of music for us. Our lives include so much music every day—the most wonderful experiences imaginable. We listen to classical music on the radio now, attend concerts, and are familiar with so many styles and composers that we weren't before," says Peter Maloney, a New Jersey dad of two young musicians.
- "Our kids bring new music into the house that we haven't heard and end up loving," says Jackie Yarmo, mother of two teens who play piano, drums, and guitar at a School of Rock in New Jersey.
- "It has greatly enhanced my own understanding and appreciation of jazz," says Damian Conrad, father of a trumpeter who excelled in his Oregon high school's jazz band.
- "I like to see them enjoy the beauty of the sound and their sense of accomplishment," says Donald Tam, whose teenagers study piano at the San Francisco Conservatory.
- "It may never pay off monetarily, but my daughter feels that singing is as much a part of her now as her hair or her eyes," says Tamara Dahling, Indiana mother of a singer on the cusp of a vocal career. "I've gained much more respect for musicians. My ear is better, too. I can spot a bad singer a mile away."
- "There are payoffs no matter which way you go," says Richard Meyers, who shares the outlook of many of our advisors who are upbeat about the value of music parenting whether or not their kids have gone on to musical careers. His older daughter is professional violinist Anne Akiko Meyers. His younger daughter took piano lessons for many years but has become "an eye surgeon specializing in treating children's glaucoma, which requires great eye-hand coordination. She feels she could not have done this without the sense of touch and coordination that playing piano gave her."
- "Music should enrich everybody's life," says Thanh Huynh, whose daughters are not pursuing musical careers but were serious piano and violin students in

the preparatory division of Baltimore's Peabody Institute of Music. "I don't think their musical training was wasted. Music shouldn't just be for professionals, leaving the rest of us to stand by and watch. Everybody should have the pleasure of participating in these artistic activities. That makes life more interesting. That's what I wanted for them—to have this training so they can have fun, creative lives. There's a rhythm to life that you learn from music."

WORTH IT REPORT

Kevin Powers: Studying music "taught me lessons that affect what I do every day professionally," says Kevin Powers, a lawyer in a Massachusetts district attorney's office. Those lessons include "the relentless pursuit of improvement" and "the sense of team is more important than your own ego, so get over yourself and respect your peers." He played saxophone in his high school jazz band, which took part in Jazz at Lincoln Center's Essentially Ellington competition. "In terms of work ethic, is there any better preparation for the demanding commitment of law school than the pursuit of excellence in playing the music of Duke Ellington? I practice criminal law. Like jazz, it's a pursuit you can never master. It requires that you be constantly moving forward. As much as you learn, you'll only come to understand how much there is you don't understand. I still play sax from time to time and go hear live jazz. There's nothing like it."

Strengthening Ties to Family and Friends

Many parents note another benefit from their youngsters' involvement with music—the role it plays in forging closer ties within the family, while also opening opportunities for making new friends. The Spellman's younger daughter, Rev. Kaji Spellman, explains that the hours she and her sister spent with their mom in the family car going to lessons, rehearsals, and concerts were a plus. "That was great bonding time," she says. "We'd talk and go get ice cream on the way to lessons. We turned all the crazy commuting into time that we spent loving each other and being a family."

"Music can be a way to understand your child at times when they may otherwise be uncommunicative," observes Ms. Yarmo. "I can tell when my teenager is unhappy by what she plays when she may not want to talk about it." Parents who have musical skills themselves say that being able to play music with their kids has also provided a way to keep lines of communication open. "One of the best parts is that my daughter still likes it when I accompany her," says Melissa Tucker, a pianist whose teenaged daughter plays flute. This Massachusetts mom admits that for a while it was hard figuring out how to offer musical advice in a way that didn't get on her daughter's

A performance by one of the ensembles of the Young People's Chorus of New York City.

nerves, but now they've hit on a good balance. "It's a treat to play music together." Improving sibling ties can be another benefit, according to parents who have been lucky to witness those special moments when sons and daughters put sibling rivalry aside for a while to do a little jamming together.

Also important are friendships outside the family that music makes possible. "It's hard to make a space for yourself growing up. Being in the school band and choral groups gave my kids a way to make deep friendships with other kids," says California cardiologist, Dr. Jeanny Park. Ohio mom Ann Turner agrees, "Most of the friends that both of our children still have at this point in their lives were the musicians that they did things with in high school or college."

"Ours is a big high school, about 2,000 kids. Marching band helped make the school seem smaller for our daughters," says Roger Cash, who headed the marching band parent association at his daughters' Missouri high school. Band members "became our daughters' closest friends." But it wasn't only the kids who made new friends. Mr. Cash notes that he too "made a lot of friends with other families."

Music parenting has even helped a few parents deal with the dreaded empty-nest syndrome. Seeing the fun her daughters had with piano and violin inspired Thanh Huynh to start piano lessons again, including trying a new genre, jazz. "I knew I'd have an empty nest soon. I've been getting a running start preparing for it," she says, hoping to become skilled enough to join the amateur jazz ensemble at the medical center where she works. Missouri mom Cindy Buhse started practicing viola again when her daughter, also a violist, was in middle school. After her daughter left for college, Ms. Buhse inherited her daughter's old viola and joined a community orchestra. "I don't have a lot of time to practice," she says. "I go to orchestra once a week and have a good time. It definitely helps with the empty nest."

Building Life Skills

As Mr. Spellman noted earlier, there are important nonmusical skills that young people absorb from studying music and participating in ensembles. Another music dad observes, "The life skills they are learning—discipline, goal setting, teamwork—will provide a huge benefit to them as they proceed through their lives," says Joseph Rakoski, father of two teen violinists who performed with the Portland (Oregon) Youth Philharmonic but who aren't planning on performing careers. Gail Caiazza, a Massachusetts mother of a flutist who is now in law school, adds, "From studying music, my daughter learned to manage her time, prioritize, and present herself in front of large groups with confidence."

Dominique van de Stadt, an Arizona mother of four musical youngsters, notes, "Music has led them to use their skills to help others, by teaching at a nonprofit that provides free music lessons for disadvantaged children. Their involvement in music also kept them away, in large part, from spending inordinate amounts of time watching TV or playing video games while growing up."

Music teachers report that helping youngsters learn patience, persistence, and a healthy sense of perspective is a rewarding part of their job. For some of our educator advisors, it's as important as teaching études and scales. "My job satisfaction came from the joy in helping kids grow. Music was the means to help them," says Carol Prochazka, former head of the piano department at Peabody's preparatory division. "I realized I

WORTH IT REPORT

Rev. Kaji Spellman: "I was a competitive kid. I wanted to play violin so I could be concertmaster of the DC Youth Orchestra. The concertmaster has her own entrance and everyone applauds. I thought that was the coolest thing. Once I achieved that, I had done what I wanted with violin," explains Rev. Spellman, who quit violin toward the end of high school and worked after college at a financial company. But, she says, "I missed using the part of the brain that music uses." She joined a church choir and changed direction, leaving the world of finance to earn a master of divinity at Yale's Institute of Sacred Music. "I'm not competitive anymore, but I'm still driven. My work ethic comes from the serious rigor of developing the craft of playing violin, the discipline of daily practice."

probably wasn't going to turn out the world's greatest pianist, but I was helping them learn life lessons through music."

Recent education research emphasizes the importance of these character-building life skills. Studies show that students tend to do better if they have internalized what researchers call "grit"—self-discipline, determination, and resilience—which can enable youngsters to not only pursue goals but to also bounce back from disappointments, as described in Paul Tough's book *How Children Succeed* and Madeline Levine's *Teach Your Children Well*. Research has also shown that it is possible to teach youngsters these skills in order to help them have more success. Our parent advisors have noted that "grit" seems to go hand-in-hand with music study, although which comes first—the grit or the mastery of music—is a puzzle we'll leave for researchers to solve.

Music's Impact on the Brain and Learning

Most of our parent advisors gave the same reasons that Thanh Huynh noted earlier in this chapter for why they involved their kids in music: to provide them with a life-long love of music and a way to have fun. But a few parents said they also hoped that music would provide "cognitive benefits" and might even, perhaps, improve performance in academic subjects. One mother was counting on her daughter's music studies to help "make math easier."

Some of our parent advisors report that they have actually noticed positive impacts on their children's performance in other subject areas as a result of their music making. One mother with a learning-disabled son feels that playing cello has helped him concentrate on regular schoolwork. She feels also that his success at music has helped him "deal with the frustrations in academics." Another mom states that her daughter, who has reading difficulties, has used the same kinds of practice strategies that help her "get the flow of music going" to help her also get into the swing of learning vocabulary words.

Parents of youngsters without learning issues have also noticed academic benefits from their children's study of music. "We can see in all our children positive change in their schoolwork. They are more comfortable in mathematics," says one of the mothers whose children take part in YOLA (Youth Orchestra LA), an after-school program sponsored by the Los Angeles Philharmonic and Heart of Los Angeles (HOLA), a Los Angles community center. YOLA offers free ensemble-based classical music instruction and academic support to children in underserved neighborhoods. Another YOLA mom has noticed an improvement in her daughter's reading ability. (More on YOLA in chapter 3.)

Of course, it isn't clear whether the nonmusical gains that these parents observed resulted from something inherent in music. Perhaps the academic improvements come from the increased adult attention that often accompanies music lessons or from the focused study habits and time-management abilities that regular practice instills. The same chicken-or-egg question can also be raised for studies which show that students who participate in music groups during high school tend to have higher math and verbal SAT scores than other students. Whether this is a cause-and-effect situation isn't clear.

However, recent research is beginning to suggest actual causal connections between studying music and academic improvement. New discoveries that neuroscientists and educational researchers are making may help music parents clarify for themselves why they want youngsters to study music and what kinds of benefits they might reasonably expect to occur.

The newly reported links between music and academics are quite different from the so-called Mozart effect hoopla of the late 1990s. Back then, there was a lot of media hype over claims that listening to Mozart could boost IQ scores. Those claims went way beyond the modest findings of the original study, which saw only a temporary gain in spatial reasoning for a small group of college students who listened to ten minutes of Mozart. Subsequent researchers were unable to replicate those results.

However, even though Mozart as an IQ booster has fallen into disfavor, the new field of brain imaging has shown that studying and listening to music "not only benefits music processing but also percolates to other domains, such as speech processing," according to a 2010 article by Northwestern University researcher Nina Kraus. Her article summarizes research by scientists around the world who have studied music's impact on the brain, leading her to conclude, "Music is a resource that tones the brain for auditory fitness." For example, one study cited in the article found that musicians are better able to hear sounds in a noisy "soundscape," suggesting possible benefits for easily distracted youngsters in noisy classrooms. Another article by Northwestern University researchers, published in 2012, notes, "Adults who received formal music instruction as children have more robust brainstem responses to sound than peers who never participated in music lessons."

Researchers are wary of drawing far-reaching conclusions from such studies. As neuroscientist Daniel Levitin warns in his book, *This Is Your Brain on Music*: "Whether these structural changes in the brain translate to enhanced abilities in nonmusical domains has not been proved, but music listening and music therapy have been shown to help people overcome a broad range of psychological and physical problems." His book and Oliver Sacks's *Musicophilia* describe many examples of such therapeutic benefits.

To see whether learning transfer really does occur, education researchers have embarked on a new type of study that measures whether integrating music instruction into a school's regular academic curriculum boosts performance in nonmusic subjects. Spearheading this research is one of our advisors who is both a music dad and a researcher, New England Conservatory (NEC) professor Larry Scripp. He heads up NEC's Music-in-Education (MIE) program and also started the Center for Music-in-Education. Since 1999, he has been exploring this new line of research at the Conservatory Lab School, a charter elementary school he cofounded in Boston. In addition to providing students with free violin instruction, the school integrates music skills into regular academic subjects. Using standardized tests to measure skill levels in music, literacy, and math, Professor Scripp's team has found that gains in musical skills correlate positively with gains in language and math, with greater gains occurring the longer students have been in the school. His team has observed similar results at elementary schools in California and Minnesota. Other researchers have also observed signs of academic gain from music involvement.

This new line of research has led Professor Scripp to conclude, in one of his articles: "Music should be taught both for its own sake and for the sake of learning transfer…across disciplines." When interviewed for this book, he noted, "What we're beginning to sense from research is that music is a language of learning at its core and can be learned by everyone." (See Bibliography for a listing of all the books and articles mentioned.)

Good for All?

The conclusion Professor Scripp draws from his research—that anyone is capable of learning to make music—is given support by the success of two innovative music-education systems that have become popular in recent years and that were used by some of our parent advisors. One is the Suzuki system, developed in the mid-twentieth century by the late Japanese violinist Shin'ichi Suzuki. He believed every child could learn to play a musical instrument if taught using the same techniques that allow children to learn their native language—listening to and imitating sounds, with encouragement from a nurturing parent. Suzuki training is now one of the main ways used in the United States for teaching young children to play string instruments.

Another anyone-can-learn-it method comes from Venezuela, developed by José Antonio Abreu, a pianist, economist, and social reformer. He founded El Sistema ("the system") in 1975 to improve the prospects for Venzuela's poorest children by involving them in performing classical music with other kids, without prescreening for musical aptitude. His goal wasn't to turn them into professional musicians, although some have done so, including Gustavo Dudamel, music director of the

Los Angeles Philharmonic. Rather, Mr. Abreu hoped that through music, young people would master life skills that would let them lift themselves out of poverty. The enormous success of El Sistema in Venezuela has led to the opening of dozens of El Sistema-inspired programs in the United States in underserved areas, including the YOLA after-school program in Los Angeles mentioned earlier in this chapter.

The next chapter has more details on Suzuki and El Sistema programs, but their importance for the current discussion is the support they offer for the idea that music instruction can benefit anyone. "If parents think only kids who are innately 'talented' will profit from music instruction, they might not want to start lessons for their children," explains Professor Scripp.

His NEC colleague Mark Churchill adds, "You can't lose by pursuing rigorous music education with your child." This cello teacher and former dean of NEC's Preparatory School is now also involved with the new El Sistema programs. He believes in encouraging young people to pursue music wholeheartedly in whatever setting is available. "If a child dabbles in music or does music halfway, it's not a bad thing. But they won't get the deep transferable benefits that serious study of music brings. The more intensely you study music, the more lasting benefits you gain in terms of memory, dealing with abstract language, and understanding the balance within oneself between the emotional, intellectual, physical, and, some will add, the spiritual or transcendent."

Of course, because someone *can* learn music doesn't mean they will *want* to. "Parents need to know their kids, give them a variety of opportunities to try, and when they see the one the kid really loves, find a means to continue it," says Dr. Gene Beresin, child psychiatrist, part-time pianist, and music dad whose own kids explored music for a while but then went on to other interests.

Jenny Liu (left), shown here during high school with the St. Louis Symphony Youth Orchestra, went to Princeton, and Haohang Xu (right) went to Yale; neither majored in music.

Professional violinist and educator Isabel Trautwein wishes that signing up kids for music lessons could be seen in the same way as signing them up for softball or soccer. "We know that being on a softball team is good for kids. They make friends, get exercise, and there's usually a cool coach who is a good role model. We don't worry about whether the kids are going to become professional softball players. I wish we would do the same with music. Having a kid make music with other kids is just good," says Ms. Trautwein, a violinist with the Cleveland Orchestra who has started El Sistema-based programs in Cleveland. "If the love for music captures the kid, fine. If not, then it's OK that they try something else." But in the meantime, she notes, they will have had a chance to have "songs and music in their minds. That's a friend for life."

Shifting Goals

Grooming sons and daughters for professional music careers wasn't on most parents' agendas when they started children on music lessons. Parents seem to have realized what Mark Churchill has observed from his years of teaching: "Most kids who study

These two brothers—sons of one of our parent advisors, Jiji Goosby—like playing string instruments and pick-up games of basketball, too. The older brother, Randall, plays violin; his brother, Miles, plays cello. To the right is a photo of Randall at age nine, about two years after he started on violin. There's more about Randall and how he has balanced his interests in music and sports in chapter 9.

music will not and should not become professional musicians." However, goals changed along the way for some parents, as they saw their youngsters become increasingly skilled in music, with a flair for performing and a real zeal for music. Those parents began to realize that a musical career might indeed be in their child's future.

For some, the worry then became "how to encourage them to pursue their dreams but also help them keep their feet firmly planted on the ground, knowing that many of them will never be able to make a living at it," comments Tamara Dahling.

However, for a few parents, the fear was exactly the *opposite*—that their kids might actually *become*

WORTH IT REPORT

Meara E. Baldwin: "Although I do not earn a living with my cello, I perform with community orchestras," says Ms. Baldwin, a social worker. "I use skills garnered as a musician, especially those learned in chamber ensembles, in which not only must you master your part, you must see how it fits into the overall picture, understand when to take leadership, when to step back and listen, and how to support others in their moments to shine. I use these skills in family therapy sessions, figuring out how to let every individual's voice be heard. Many people think there are only two roles in a group: leader or follower. From chamber music, I learned to appreciate the beauty of a complicated counter melody, a theme repeated with variations, an unexpected duet, and a driving bass line. All are metaphors for behavior in a group."

professional musicians, instead of doctors, lawyers, or engineers. This fear gripped the parents of some of the professional musicians on our advice panel. Those parents struggled with accepting the fact that their teenagers were abandoning other careers to focus on music, an issue explored in chapter 10.

For many parents, goals changed in smaller ways several times throughout the years of music parenting. Looking back, the road from first music lesson to college or conservatory may seem to follow a logical progression. But while trudging along music's winding path, the way forward doesn't seem so clear. "When you're going through it, it's such a play-by-play," says Susan Raab, a Pennsylvania mother whose adult son is pursuing a career in musical theater. "The decisions a music parent makes are not big global decisions but rather: 'OK, this came up, what do we do?' You go step by step and don't know where each thing can lead or if it will even lead anywhere. We were fortunate to have had people to turn to who could be mentors for us." The suggestions in this book from Ms. Raab and others may help provide enough guidance so that more music parents can reach the point of saying, like the Spellmans, that it was all worthwhile.

The DC Youth Orchestra in a 2011 performance at the Kennedy Center in Washington, DC. This is the youth orchestra that played such an important role in the lives of the Spellman family.

Professional violinist Joshua Bell at about age five (top left), at age ten on his way to a tennis tournament, and in a recent photo.

3 Starting a Child's Musical Journey

A CHILD'S MUSICAL JOURNEY can begin in many different ways. Often it's the children themselves who get things rolling, when they beam out signals at a very early age that an alert parent notices. Shirley Bell, mother of acclaimed violinist Joshua Bell, recalls a very unusual signal that gave her the idea that her son had a special connection to music. "When Josh was about two and a half, he would pull out the drawers of a dresser we had, with little knobs on the drawers. He would take different-sized rubber bands and stretch them from one knob to another, creating various tensions, and then pluck them to pick out little melodies of tunes he had heard me play on the piano," she explains.

Other observations added to her feeling that there was something special about the second of her three children. "He did everything a little earlier, a little faster, a little differently than most, which is characteristic of a gifted child. Music was valued in our household, but nobody in our family was a professional musician. I played piano. My husband was a choirboy as a child. We always had music on in the house. There was no question that all my children would be exposed to music in one way or the other, but I never anticipated that it would be a career."

When Josh was about four, she signed him up for a once-a-week eurhythmics class that was held at a friend's house in their hometown of Bloomington, Indiana. As is typical of these early childhood music-and-movement classes, the teacher let Josh and the other children explore moving to the rhythm of music and play little percussion instruments. "She told me that Josh stood out among all the kids in the class and that I should consider having him learn to play an instrument," Ms. Bell recalls. "It never would have occurred to me to start a child on an instrument at four years old. I'm grateful to her to this day for making this recommendation. It was nice to get that feedback from her. Parents need to hear that kind of confirmation, even later on after lessons start, that there's something there that's worth all the effort that goes into making a musician."

With that comment from her friend, Shirley Bell took on what would become a gradually increasing role for her, as it is for most music parents—that of music-opportunities researcher. Her first task was to discover what kind of an instrument a four-year-old in Bloomington could be taught to play. She asked around and found that a good option was violin. "A lot of young kids in town were taking violin lessons, using the Suzuki method. The violins they played were small. Josh was small. It seemed like a good fit. There were a few local teachers. I chose one who was highly recommended, a kindly woman who connected well with Josh and from whom he developed a love of music. She wasn't a certified Suzuki teacher but incorporated some of the Suzuki method into what she did. He began lessons with her the month before he turned five. He took to it easily. She was a little overwhelmed because he learned the Suzuki tunes so fast, was loving it, and sounding good, not a scratchy violin sound but a sound that was pleasant. That was the beginning."

Picking Up on the Clues

Others of our parent advisors may have also been planning to involve their kids in music at some point but were taken by surprise, as Shirley Bell was, when an especially intense fascination with music surfaced very early. The two activities that Ms. Bell chose for her son are among the main instructional possibilities for very young children: music-and-movement classes and Suzuki training. Both will be described in more detail later in this chapter, but first here are a few more examples of the kinds of clues our advisors spotted.

Several parents were amazed to see their toddlers pick out tunes on the family piano. Yoko Segerstrom was even more astonished by how determined her son, Eric, was to reach the piano when he was only a year old. "Before he could even walk, he would crawl backwards down the stairs, and make a beeline to our piano. He didn't bang the piano like some babies do, but his face was full of joy as he played little tunes," she recalls. She was already a music mom, having enrolled Eric's older sister in

Suzuki violin lessons, but she felt that she needed to do something to support Eric's keen interest in music before he would be old enough for Suzuki lessons. So she enrolled him in a music-enrichment class for toddlers at age two. "The keyboard was the main thing he liked in that class. That led to his first piano lesson when he was five," she says. By the time she was interviewed for this book, Eric had mastered several other instruments and was at the Juilliard School, studying to be a composer.

A kitchen-table, jelly-jar concert caught the eye and ear of Philadelphia mom Annette Ramke. "My daughter Pearl would line up jelly jars on the kitchen table when she was about four and start 'playing' them, hitting them, listening for different sounds. She also sang all the time," notes Ms. Ramke. She followed up on this interest by enrolling her daughter in a preschool music class, which let Pearl tap away on real percussion instruments and also gave the parents a chance to adjust to the idea that percussion instruments—despite their expense, size, and noisiness—were the ones their daughter loved. When her mom joined this book's advice givers, Pearl was a teen percussionist who had also started composing.

Singing and dancing enthusiastically to music—on the radio, stereo, or in live performances—captured the attention of quite a few soon-to-be music parents, including Theresa Chong, the visual artist who proposed the idea for this book. When Ms. Chong's sister, a professional violinist, would visit and play her violin for the family, Ms. Chong's preschool-age son, Chase, would run around to the music, mimicking his aunt's every move, having a great time. His mom decided this was a child who would love to play a real instrument. She had played cello as a child and thought that might be a good choice because she could help him with the basics. She found a Suzuki cello teacher and began him on lessons at age four. All went well at first until her efforts to help him ran into some snags, which will be discussed in chapter 8.

Beth Norden's younger daughter, Claire, was always singing, even as a toddler, but it took comments from other parents to prompt Ms. Norden to do something about it. "When Claire was six, we were in the waiting room at my older daughter's piano lessons," recalls Ms. Norden. "There was Claire, so tiny, belting out songs as usual. The other parents said, 'You should let her try out for a play.' I said, 'What! She's only six.' But we kind of fell into it. She went to an open audition, sang a song, and got in a play. Other parents said we should get her singing lessons." After a bit of searching, Ms. Norden found a teacher who taught young children, and Claire started private singing lessons during elementary school.

Juli Elliot's daughter also "sang from day one," but this upstate New York mother, a singer herself, approached singing lessons differently. She encouraged her daughter to sing in a church choir and school choruses but didn't have her begin singing lessons until high school. The different timetables for these two families reflect a split in the music-education world about when and how to train young singers, a debate that will be discussed in chapter 6. Starting ages for instruments will be explored later in this chapter and also in chapter 4.

Kids Make the Call

Some parents didn't have to search for clues. Their children announced their musical preferences loud and clear at a very young age. Annette Radoff's daughter, Elena Urioste, now a professional violinist, made her request at age two. "Elena saw violinists Isaac Stern and Itzhak Perlman on *Sesame Street* when she was two and announced that she was going to play violin," says Ms. Radoff. "My husband and I don't come from musical families. We were unaware that children could start at such an early age. Elena continued to nag us for violin lessons for the next three years. In kindergarten, violin was offered in her public school and she began to take lessons there." *Sesame Street* also performed its magic on flutist and Texas native Alice Jones. As her mother, the late Sue Jones, explained during her interview for this book:

"When Alice was six, she saw a girl play flute on *Sesame Street* and asked if she could do that. Her father and I weren't musicians and we discouraged her for a year or so. But Alice was insistent. So we started lessons, and I fully expected that within six months it would go by the wayside, but it didn't. She surprised me and made me feel guilty that I had put her off for so long."

Movies won over some youngsters, including Dominique van de Stadt's three-year-old son Stefan, who was "totally awed by the guitar bit in the movie *Back to the Future*. He stood up and said, 'I want to do that!' We explained that to get there he had to go through classical guitar first. Being three, he was cool with that and started a Suzuki guitar program

> **SPOTLIGHT ON: ALISA WEILERSTEIN, CELLO**
>
> **Cereal-box cello:** Cellist Alisa Weilerstein loved listening to her violinist father and pianist mother practice. "When I was about two and a half, both my parents were away, and I came down with chicken pox the night before my mother left," says Ms. Weilerstein. Her grandmother, who came to take care of Alisa, cheered her up by using cereal boxes to make instruments for a pretend string quartet. "The cello was a Rice Krispies box with an old green toothbrush as the endpin. I fell in love with it and shunned the others," says Ms. Weilerstein. "When my parents returned and would rehearse, they would put out a stool so I could participate with my cereal-box cello. I desperately tried to make a sound. About a year later, I said, 'Mommy, I want a cello and a cello teacher.'" They put her off for a while, but gave in when she was four.

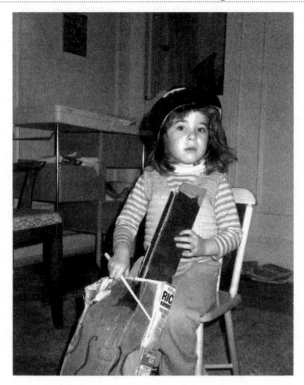

Cellist Alisa Weilerstein, age three, pretending to make music with a cereal-box cello made by her grandmother.

when he was four," explains this Arizona mother. A Dr. Seuss alphabet book created a young violinist. "The page for *V* in the book always made my daughter laugh," recalls Marylander Dominique Kaul-Boiter. That page says: "Vera Violet Vinn is very very very awful on her violin." This mother had planned to start her daughter on piano. But her daughter, captivated by Vera, insisted on violin.

Watching other kids make music ignited an interest in some children. "When my son was four years old, he fell in love with a nine-year-old girl—and her violin. He asked so many times to play violin that I asked a friend who was a music therapist where he could take lessons. She recommended a local music school," recalls Judy Merritt. Her son, now a professional bassist, started Suzuki violin at age four at that Pittsburgh music school, switching to bass as a teen.

The "Just Because" Approach

Quite a few of our parent advisors didn't wait until they noticed signs of special musical ability or interest. They seem to agree with many of today's education researchers that not only does music making provide many benefits, but with age-appropriate instruction, anyone can learn to do it. These parents enrolled their sons and daughters in musical activities just because it was a good thing to do.

"You present something to a kid and if it's fun, she'll do it," says Thanh Huynh of her decision to sign up her daughters for preschool music-and-movement classes in Baltimore when they were two years old. Another Maryland mother, Jennifer Ward, gave her kids an early start on piano because, "We homeschool our kids and include basic piano skills as part of their school work, after they have a good start on reading. Whenever they express interest in trying another instrument beside piano, we let them do that." Another mother says she started her daughter on piano at age four so she could "become used to the discipline before she was old enough to object."

Mei Carpenter had a different "just because" reason. "When my first child was three years old, I was looking for things to do with her and saw an ad for music lessons. I have no musical background, but they said I could observe a lesson and I saw this little kid having a great time in Suzuki violin. That's how the whole family got started," explains this Ohio mother, who enrolled her next two children in Suzuki programs, too. All three kept on with music through high school, and two went on after high school to study at conservatories.

Other parents decided to immerse their kids in music to help fill a gap the parents felt in their own lives. "I played piano as a child but lost interest and quit. I greatly regret it. I wanted my kids to choose instruments to play that they can enjoy later in their lives," says Tennessee mother Jiji Goosby. Her three teens started lessons between ages four and seven. Each has settled on a different instrument: violin, flute, and cello.

The Age Story

Not all of our parent advisors opted for an early start in music for their children. Among parents who filled out questionnaires for our research team, about two-thirds had youngsters who began some kind of formal music program between the ages of three and seven—either a group class of some kind or actual instrumental or voice lessons. The sons and daughters of the rest of the parents began music lessons or classes between the ages of eight and twelve.

Later in this chapter, there is information on the three major educational programs that are available for the early childhood years. But because exploring one of those options—Suzuki instrumental instruction—involves being aware of the ages at which children are able to start various instruments, we'll begin by discussing age guidelines. Although there is no firm agreement among music educators as to the best starting ages for various instruments, it is possible to give rough age ranges, as is done in the next section of this chapter. These age ranges can help new music parents gain a general idea about timing. Then, in the following chapter—chapter 4—there is a discussion on how to help children decide which instruments seem right for them.

As for singing, because the debate over when to start singing lessons involves fundamental differences of opinion over instructional approach, we devote a separate chapter—chapter 6—to singing, from when to start to what to study.

Professional violin soloist Anne Akiko Meyers began violin at age four with a teacher who used the Suzuki method.

Age Guidelines for Starting Instruments

A good age to begin playing any instrument depends on when a child is physically big enough to handle the instrument—as well as emotionally and cognitively ready to receive instruction.

However, even when children aren't physically big enough to handle a particular instrument, sometimes ways can be found to let them start on instruments they are determined to play. The daughter of one of our educator advisors fell in love with trombone at age ten, but her arms were too short to reach the end of a trombone's slide. That meant her fingers couldn't reach the spit valve located at the very tip of the slide and click it open to let moisture drip out of the horn. She started trombone lessons anyway. "To empty the spit valve, she would take off her shoe and use a toe to push open the valve," says her mother, Sandra Shapiro, dean of the preparatory division of the Cleveland Institute of Music. The trombone teacher was amazed at this youngster's enthusiasm and also at how well she has done on trombone, which she has continued to play as a teenager.

Below are general age guidelines for the major types of instruments. But as that trombone anecdote demonstrates, these ranges should be viewed as suggestions only. They are based on conversations with music educators on our advice panel and also from the age listings posted on the websites of several music schools around the country.

- **Strings:** A very early start is possible for string instruments because they come in a graded series of small sizes appropriate for preschoolers and children in early elementary school grades. There are tiny violins and cellos that are one-sixteenth the size of a regular instrument, as well as ones that are one-eighth size, one-fourth, and so on. String-instrument instruction for preschoolers would most likely be Suzuki in nature. Many music schools offer Suzuki violin and viola programs for children as young as three or four, with Suzuki cello instruction often starting as young as age four. Suzuki guitar lessons might be offered a year or so later, and double bass several years after that. An early start on strings is not an absolute requirement for doing well, although many educators feel it's best to start before the early teens while the body is growing and can adapt more easily to the arm and hand positions needed to play a string instrument. Some pros on our panel started way past their preschool years. Lauren Chipman, a classical and rock violist, began with group violin lessons in fourth grade. So did Caleb Burhans, now a violinist, violist, and a composer.

- **Woodwinds and brass:** A preschool start generally isn't possible for brass instruments (such as trumpet, trombone, French horn, and tuba) or most woodwinds (clarinet, saxophone, oboe, bassoon) because they don't come in pint-sized versions. Flutes are an exception among woodwinds; small-sized flutes are available, which are used in Suzuki flute programs that some music schools offer for young children. With most brass and woodwinds, youngsters need to be big enough and have enough muscle strength, particularly in their mouths, to handle adult-size instruments. Some schools and teachers let children start as young as eight or nine on the easier to handle brass and winds—trumpet, flute, clarinet, and saxophone—but other educators prefer waiting until fourth or fifth grade. Recorder is often offered as a prelude instrument for young children who may move on later to other woodwinds or brass. A late elementary school or middle school start time is often advised for oboe, a tricky instrument to learn to play, and for the large brass and woodwind instruments, such as French horn, tuba, bassoon, baritone sax, and trombone. Often youngsters who play these larger instruments started out on other instruments. By the time Toyin Spellman-Diaz began oboe as a young teen, she had experience playing two other instruments: piano, which she started at age five, and flute, which she began at age nine.

- **Piano:** The starting age for piano depends partly on the nature of the instruction. Some music schools offer Suzuki piano or other group piano classes for children as young as five. Teachers who use a more traditional method often prefer that a child knows how to read—books not music—before starting lessons. This is because a traditional approach usually involves teaching students to read music right from the start, whereas Suzuki instruction doesn't teach music reading at first but has beginners play by ear. Understanding how to read one set of symbols—letters—can make it easier to learn to read another—musical notes. "Being able to read real children's books, not just baby stuff, is also a sign that they have the patience to sit through a lesson and comprehend what I'm teaching," explains Hiroko Dutton, a Connecticut piano teacher.
- **Percussion:** Many schools begin percussion instruction during the elementary school years, but this can differ from teacher to teacher.
- **Harp:** Age levels vary from school to school. For example, Peabody Preparatory offers lessons on harp for children as young as age five, whereas the Cleveland Institute's preparatory division suggests that youngsters have two years of piano lessons before starting harp.

Music-and-Movement Classes

The two main types of programs for preschoolers are the ones Shirley Bell picked for her son: movement-and-music-classes and Suzuki training. There's another option for certain low-income families: the El Sistema programs that are offered in several communities and may include prekindergarten activities. This section and the next two give a rundown on each of these possibilities. (The Resources section has links to websites that provide more information.)

Music-and-movement classes offer a way to let youngsters explore music with other children before beginning formal instrumental or vocal instruction. There are a variety of such classes. Most have children do what's called eurhythmics—being physically engaged with music by clapping rhythms, dancing, singing, and playing drums or other rhythm instruments.

These classes are often named for the famous music educators on whose ideas they are based, although some music schools develop their own versions, combining elements from several of the established methods, such as the classes that Lydia Zieglar's son took as a preschooler at Peabody. He loved the classes. She did, too: "They gave me activities I could repeat at home with him." Thanh Huynh's daughters also attended Peabody's preschool program, noting, "It was a real social event.

The Marsalis brothers—Branford (left) and Wynton—playing toy versions of instruments that became the focus of their careers, saxophone and trumpet.

Parents and children sat in a circle on the floor doing little activities and songs with hand motions that we had practiced at home with a cassette tape. We learned that music is a shared experience."

Below are some of the main types of music-and-movement classes that are offered for preschoolers—and sometimes also for older students:

- Dalcroze classes combine eurhythmics, ear training, and improvisation, using a method developed by French educator Émile Jaques-Dalcroze.
- Kodály classes use a singing-focused technique developed by Hungarian composer Zoltan Kodály.
- Orff classes use a percussion-centered method developed by German composer Carl Orff.
- Kindermusik and Music Together use an amalgam of various methodologies.

Suzuki Instruction

Suzuki instruction offers another way to give young children an early start in music. This method makes significant time demands on a child's parent. Its founder, Shin'ichi Suzuki, modeled his techniques on the way parents teach children their native language, and so a parent is an important partner in the instruction, at least in the early years. Parents are expected to attend the child's private lesson and group class each week, to serve as at-home coaches, and are encouraged to have some hands-on training with the child's instrument. Suzuki teachers don't have students learn to read music at first but have them play by ear, imitating what the teacher plays or what they hear on recordings that the program provides.

Suzuki instruction is available mainly for string instruments, piano, flute, or guitar. For each instrument, there is a graded series of books and accompanying recordings of the pieces to be mastered. One of the first pieces most students play is Shin'ichi Suzuki's variations on "Twinkle, Twinkle, Little Star." Professional violinists on our advice panel who began with Suzuki instruction include Joshua Bell, Jennifer Koh, Anne Akiko Meyers, Elena Urioste, and Robert Gupta. Alisa Weilerstein didn't have Suzuki training, but she explains, "I actually learned all of the Suzuki repertoire for cello through book 7."

Many Suzuki parents on our advice team are enthusiastic about Suzuki instruction. Some of their sons and daughters continued with a Suzuki teacher through high school. Others moved on after a few years to teachers who used a more traditional approach, either because the children figured out on their own how to read music or because they learned the Suzuki repertoire faster than the program envisioned.

Parents generally stopped sitting in on lessons and became less involved with practicing during the preteen and teen years, although some independent-minded youngsters balked at parental hovering even earlier. "Some kids thrive on Suzuki and love the parent support, but some cannot stand it," notes psychiatrist Dr. Gene Beresin. "Not every parent can do the Suzuki method in a constructive way, so that it isn't grating on the child. But the Suzuki method is about more than just the parents being there. It's about learning the form, the technique, and the connection to the instrument at an early age. There are no magic bullets in this world, no one best method. You try one method and then you may need to change gears."

El Sistema Programs

Free after-school programs inspired by Venezuela's El Sistema music-education network (described in the previous chapter) are cropping up in some low-income US neighborhoods. A few offer instruction for preschoolers, such as OrchKids, the first US program, set up in Baltimore in 2008 under the guidance of Marin Alsop, the conductor of the Baltimore Symphony Orchestra. A key feature of El Sistema instruction involves having children play in ensembles. By 2013, OrchKids was offering free music instruction—and free instruments—four afternoons a week for more than 600 students at several elementary schools. Pre-K and kindergarten children start by playing record-ers and performing in a "bucket band," tapping out rhythms on plastic buckets. After about a year, they choose an orchestral instrument and begin playing together in a student orchestra, while also singing in a choir. "We do a lot of cross-genre music. We play 'Twinkle' variations, but we'll add a beat box to change it up. Our concerts have Beyoncé songs, and also Bach, Mozart, Bob Dylan, the Beatles, and Jay Z," says Dan Trahey, the tuba player who helped start OrchKids and serves as its artistic director.

"My kids would always dance around the house to music but I never thought they'd play an instrument at such a young age," says Lynette Fields, whose children started in OrchKids during first and second grades. By fourth grade, they earned scholarships to study on Saturdays at Peabody Preparatory, in addition to their OrchKids music making. Rodney Brewington, another OrchKids parent, likes the program because "it teaches them discipline and lets them do something construc-tive to help with their future." The free tuition, of course, is another attraction. "This is a wonderful opportunity for us because we don't have the ability to pay for music lessons," says the mother of a child who participates in YOLA, the free El Sistema after-school program in Los Angeles.

Mark Churchill, executive director of El Sistema USA, which encourages the crea-tion of more such programs around the country, notes that the focus on ensemble play-ing in El Sistema is similar "to what happens in every good school band and orchestra. El Sistema isn't replacing traditional instruction. It's simply an intensive after-school program that demonstrates and shines a light on the effectiveness of music in kids' lives."

Music-Friendly Households

Whether parents enroll children in formal programs at a young age or opt for a later start, many make music a big part of family activities. This serves to spark an interest in music in young children and also keep that enthusiasm alive after formal instruction begins. Here are ways our advisors have made music part of family life.

Ellis Marsalis, a jazz pianist, educator, and father of a quartet's worth of jazz pros (including one of our other advisors, Wynton Marsalis) points out a cost-free way to have family-oriented musical outings. "You can expose your kids to great music free of charge. You don't have to pay a nickel. If you're near a university that has a good music program or near a conservatory, find out when the student recitals are. There are also faculty recitals and orchestra concerts. Some of the better schools have pretty good jazz bands—a whole slew of free concerts. What I say to any parent that wants to know the best approach to get kids interested in music: There's nothing better than exposure," explains Mr. Marsalis.

Anya Steger, a suburban New York mom of two string musicians, found lots of free concerts to attend with her daughters, including "concerts in the public library and in the park, or choir concerts at church. We also go to youth orchestra concerts. Seeing kids play music who are just a little older than our daughters is a huge inspiration, showing that you don't have to be your parents' age to make music." Parents who took very young children to more formal concerts—such as young people's concerts offered by orchestras—recommend bringing along things to keep young concertgoers engaged if their attention should wander. "When I took my son to concerts when he was very little, I'd bring items to occupy him if he lost interest, books to look at, lots of paper for doodling," says Lydia Zieglar.

Yakko Meyers made music a part of her everyday relationship with her daughter Anne even before she was born. "I listened to a lot of music when I was pregnant. After Anne was born, every time I fed her when she was a baby, I let her listen to David Oistrakh play a violin concerto," says this mother of professional violinist Anne Akiko Meyers. Melissa Tucker also started early. When her daughter was an infant, "I would dance her around to a James Galway flute recording. It's interesting that she has become enthusiastic about playing the flute," notes Ms. Tucker, a pianist and Dalcroze instructor in Massachusetts. An extremely early experience with music may also have left an imprint on April Hansen's daughter. "My daughter spent weeks in the hospital after she was born. I sang to her every morning when I arrived to visit her and every night before I left," recalls Ms. Hansen. When her daughter reached her teens, she was singing up a storm at the School of Rock in Omaha.

"Playing music was the best way to stop my older son from fussing as an infant. Later, we sang together, listened to music all the time, and spent many hours dancing in the living room," says Martha Woodard, Massachusetts mother of a violinist and a

SPOTLIGHT ON: DAVID GROSSMAN, BASS

Sing-alongs: "Music was woven into the fabric of our family," says the New York Philharmonic's David Grossman. His mother, a pianist, and his father, a photo-journalist, often hosted recitals at their home, not something most families can arrange, but many can try another Grossman family tradition: sing-alongs. "On car trips, we would sing canons [rounds] like 'Dona Nobis Pacem.' My sister was amazing at finding the counter melody, singing in harmony. That probably influenced her choosing viola, which plays the inner harmony lines in a piece." His experience singing melodic lines may explain his reaction at age twelve when he started double bass and played in his first concert with his music school's orchestra. "I couldn't play all the notes on bass yet, but hearing the counterpoint in that Bach concerto, I felt I was in the midst of something great. That clinched it for me."

drummer. Family singing and dancing filled many other panelists' homes, too. "My husband would play piano, and our kids and their friends would dance and move to the music and make up stories to go with it. It was exuberant and hilarious," says New Yorker Jocelyn Stewart.

Judy Merritt notes that her Pittsburgh home was "filled with art materials that the kids used to make their own toy music-makers—shakers, rattles, and kazoos. We would also record silly songs on a cassette recorder." Kitchens offered possibilities, with pots and pans providing sturdy instruments for spur-of-the-moment marching bands. Sandra Johnson, a Chicago mom who notes that her pianist son "was beating out rhythms ever since he could hold a spoon," adds that she "bought toy instruments for him. We'd sit together, sing, and pretend to play the instruments."

Toy instruments captured the interest of Ellis Marsalis's sons, as can be seen in the photo of his two oldest sons, Wynton and Branford, having fun as preschoolers. The Marsalis parents also bought a toy drum set for their youngest son, Jason, when he was three years old because he "always had an interest in drums." By then Wynton and Branford—more than fifteen years older than Jason—were performing as jazz musicians. The Marsalis parents played a game with Jason, pretending that he too was a famous musician. "We would introduce him, saying 'Ladies and gentlemen, introducing the fabulous Jason,'" recalls Ellis Marsalis. Their preschooler would then walk into the room and bang away at his toy drums to wild parental applause. Before long, he started Suzuki violin, switched later to percussion, and has, indeed, become a professional jazz drummer.

Computer music programs fascinated some kids. At age four, Bradley Detrick's son figured out how to use a trial copy of music-writing software that was lying around the house before Mr. Detrick had learned to use it. "I had to take a course to figure out what he was doing," says this New York composer whose son has been writing music ever since.

These fun activities can help young children begin to learn about sound, rhythm, and music making. So can talking about music, as Jennifer Stefanovic did with her three youngsters, who study violin and cello at Peabody Preparatory. "We provided a lot of music-making opportunities, but we also talked about trying to make happy or sad-sounding tunes," she says. Chicago mom Jennifer Ingerson adds, "We talk about what we like about the music, what we notice in it." Such musical discussions can let youngsters develop a critical ear and become active, questioning learners, which will help them later in learning about music or anything else.

More Than Music

Our panelists' homes aren't music-only households. Many of their sons and daughters pursued sports and other activities in addition to music. Sports were important to Shirley Bell's son, Josh, who placed fourth in a national junior tennis tournament at age ten. He also played pick-up basketball with friends, liked to ski, and played video games as a teen on a computer he bought with prize money that he had won in a violin competition.

Violinist Sarah Chang also had other interests. "At the beginning, I wasn't just playing violin," she says. "I had horseback riding lessons, gymnastics, ballet, a whole list of things." But when her professional performing career began at age eight, some activities slipped away. "Ballet went and swimming went, but I loved gymnastics. I kept up with gymnastics as long as I could, until I was in my early teens and started injuring myself too much." For kids who manage to do music while also playing on a sports team, their parents often have to take on another music-parenting role: negotiating scheduling conflicts between coaches and music teachers (discussed in chapter 9).

"I am convinced that the secret to raising great kids is to let them find something they are passionate about and then help them pursue it," says Buzz Ballenger, a California dad whose daughter explored soccer, sailing, and dance in addition to singing. Dr. Gene Beresin agrees, "You want to give them opportunities to do a variety of things and see what they're good at, what they like, but kids need to find their own passions. Some parents want their kids to excel at everything—be an 'A' student, play the violin and piano, be the star of the lacrosse team, do community service. They'll never have a moment to themselves. Some kids can do all this, but others fall apart. There needs to be a balance between work (skill building), downtime, and building relationships. If you don't have all three in your life, you may be the greatest pianist in the world, but you could be completely miserable. We all want our kids to be great at something, but they can't be great at everything. The question is what that something is, how it is chosen, how it is balanced, and how the kid takes ownership of it."

SPOTLIGHT ON: JENNIFER KOH, VIOLIN

Imagining it: "My parents were shocked when I became a musician," says Jennifer Koh, whose parents aren't musicians. "They joke that they 'play the stereo.' My mother's family were refugees from North Korea. My parents wanted to offer me everything they didn't have as kids—violin lessons, ice skating, gymnastics, ballet, swim team—so I could choose what I enjoyed. Most fell by the wayside, but music and swimming stuck. I loved swim team, was in the Junior Olympics, but stopped about age ten. I loved music more." The symphony and opera performances that her parents took her to from an early age helped nurture that love. "There's a steep learning curve with a string instrument. In the beginning it sounds scratchy. Going to concerts lets you imagine the sound you'd like to make. To develop that ability, you have to have in your mind the sound you want to create."

Lena Couillard in third grade (top), and at
age fourteen, when she performed as a soloist
with a student orchestra at the Interlochen
Summer Arts Camp.

4   Helping Kids Choose an Instrument

AS A LEAD-IN TO THIS CHAPTER'S TOPIC—instrument choosing—one of our parent advisors offers a warning based on her family's experiences. "My husband and I began our son and daughter on piano because we thought piano is a good starting instrument," says France Couillard. Her two children had different reactions to those lessons. "With my son, it was a constant battle, bribing him to practice, even for fifteen minutes. We kept him on piano for a year and a half, but he showed no interest and made no improvement. He tried flute at school for half a year. That wasn't going anywhere either. He's a gymnast. We let him drop music to give him more time for gymnastics. We didn't want to force it so he'd never like music."

His older sister, Lena, who started piano at age six, was more willing to practice piano if her parents reminded her, but she wasn't especially enthusiastic. Then everything changed: Lena discovered double bass.

"Practicing double bass has never been a battle. I don't even have to remind her to practice. Sometimes I have to ask her to *stop* practicing," explains Ms. Couillard. "Piano was *our* idea. Lena picked double bass." That made all the difference.

Lena fell in love with bass during second grade when the local middle school orchestra visited her Pennsylvania elementary school to showcase different instruments. "Lena came home and said she wanted to play double bass. I was surprised," explains Ms. Couillard, "My husband made a bargain with her: If you keep up with both instruments for a year—piano and bass—then you can make a decision. The school let us borrow a bass, smaller than half size, so we didn't have to buy a bass right away. Bass was absolutely natural for her. She had a good ear and could play it right away, no squeaks. The teacher couldn't believe it. After a year, she wanted to let go of piano and have private lessons on bass." The Couillards agreed to stop the piano lessons and found a private teacher who helped Lena learn more about playing this largest of all string instruments.

Lena has continued to love bass and at age fourteen won a high school concerto competition during her first summer at the Interlochen Summer Arts Camp in Michigan, which she attended on a full scholarship. Ms. Couillard's advice to other parents: "Listen to what your child wants to play, not what you want the child to play. It has to come from them."

Picking and Switching

Many parents on our advice team had experiences similar to the Couillards'. They started children on one instrument only to find a few years later that their young-sters wanted to play a different one or focus on singing instead. For Randall Non-emaker, another Pennsylvanian, his older daughter's switch went in the opposite direction from Lena Couillard's. His daughter quit a string instrument to play piano. "She had asked to play violin when she was six. Later she became fascinated by piano, taught herself how to play using a small electric piano, and then began formal piano lessons in seventh grade," says Mr. Nonemaker. "I never had to en-courage her to practice piano. When she wanted to stop violin, I let her. You cannot make someone do something they don't want to do." Soon she also developed an interest in composing and majored in composition in college.

Of course, some kids wind up loving the first instruments their parents chose for them, as happened with violinist Joshua Bell. Other youngsters also do well with an instrument that they wind up with by chance, not because of any burning desire to play it. Jazz artist Miguel Zenón wanted to play piano as a child, but took up saxo-phone during sixth grade because that was the only way he could keep having free music lessons at an after-school program in his working-class neighborhood in Puerto Rico. "The teacher taught us how to read music and about music theory, but he wouldn't let you pick an instrument until he thought you were ready. Then he would let you pick an instrument to play in the neighborhood marching band," notes Mr. Zenón. "You can't play piano in a marching band. I had to pick another instrument. Someone in my family happened to have a saxophone and that's how I started. It became my vehicle." A very good vehicle as it turned out. Mr. Zenón never actually got to play in that marching band, because when it was time to do so, he had been admitted to a public performing arts school in San Juan.

For youngsters who don't bond with their first instrument, parents may wonder: Was it a waste of time and money to have had lessons on the first instrument? Absolutely not, say parents who found themselves in that situation. Those early lessons help smooth the way for future musical activities. By the time the Couillards' daughter began playing her big string bass, she already knew a lot about music making, including how to read music. Later, when she became interested in composing, her early piano training proved its value once again, because having good keyboard skills helps in writing music.

Viewing early instrument lessons as trial runs might lessen parental shock if switching should occur. After all, it's a rather narrow slice of the musical instrument world that very young children can study formally—mainly strings and piano—with guitar, recorder, or flute possible if lessons for young kids are offered locally on those instruments. If youngsters wind up liking the first instrument, great. If not, they can pick up musical know-how and be ready to make another choice later when a wider array of instruments beckons from third grade through middle school and beyond: most woodwinds, brass, percussion, and harp. The "cool" factor of a slide trombone turned Mary Heafy's daughter from a violinist to a trombonist when her Massachusetts school offered fifth graders a chance to play a band instrument. (See chapter 3 for general age ranges for starting to play various kinds of instruments.)

Teachers can play a role in instrument switches. "I'm on the lookout for kids in third and fourth grade who may be having trouble with their first instrument and may be interested in switching to another," explains Jenny Undercofler, director of the New Music School, a music-oriented New York City public school. In some cases, an instrument choice occurs in order to fill a gap in a school's band or orchestra. That's how Christian McBride began on double bass during junior high instead of trombone, which he had been hoping to play. At the start of the year at his Philadelphia junior high, teachers let students try different instruments to decide who would play what. Mr. McBride tried trombone but couldn't make a sound, not realizing you have to buzz your lips to play a brass instrument. The teacher steered him to double bass, partly because the teacher knew this eleven-year-old had been playing electric bass at home, but also because the school needed a double bass player in its orchestra.

At first, this would-be trombonist wasn't thrilled about the switch, but later he acknowledged that "it was one of the best things anyone did for me. Being eleven, your naiveté helps. I looked at the big acoustic string bass and thought most likely it's just an oversized electric bass that I'd just play vertically. I picked it up and tried. Other than having to adjust to playing an instrument twice the size of an electric bass, the fingers go in the same places. If I had tried to start string bass five years later when I knew more about proper technique, I might not have had such a gung-ho attitude. At eleven, I just went for it."

No matter why youngsters start playing an instrument, they shouldn't switch too soon. "At the beginning every instrument is hard," says Dr. Yeou-Cheng Ma, violinist, music mom, pediatrician, and director of New York's Children's Orchestra Society. "Kids should try an instrument for six months before deciding to drop it. After six months, there should be an evaluation as to whether the child is progressing to everyone's satisfaction—the parent, teacher, and the kid, too."

The "Petting Zoo" Approach

Although random and top-down choices can work, the Couillard family's experience shows that giving children a chance to see, hear, and touch a variety of instruments can help them make a long-lasting choice. Often, sound is the attraction. Research shows that people differ in the kinds of sounds they prefer. Suzanne Smithline explains that it was sound that made her daughter switch from alto saxophone to the much larger and harder-to-lug-around baritone sax. "She loves that low sound. When she had an opportunity to play bari sax, she jumped at the chance," says this New York mom of a budding young jazz musician. In addition to high versus low, people react differently to the quality or timbre of an instrument's sound, such as the bright, sparkling sound of a flute, violin, and trumpet or the smoky tones of a viola, saxophone, and French horn.

Firsthand instrument demonstrations, such as the ones that

> SPOTLIGHT ON: PAYTON MACDONALD, PERCUSSION AND COMPOSITION
>
> **Ditching:** "I liked music but wasn't crazy about the electric organ my mother had me play when I was eight," says Payton MacDonald. His parents aren't musicians but had an organ in their Idaho home. It wasn't a hit with Payton, but it led him to the instruments that would be. "When I was nine, I had trouble with the rhythm of a piece. The teacher suggested getting drum sticks and a drum pad to practice the rhythm. I ditched organ and switched to drums." He took rock drumming lessons from "a farmer by day, a rock drummer by night" until a classical percussionist came to town and introduced him to more percussion choices—marimba, xylophone, timpani. Soon he was the percussionist in school ensembles, local orchestras, and jazz combos. "My parents were baffled, but supportive. But when I began to talk about becoming a musician, my dad was pretty resistant." (More on his dad's concerns in chapters 10 and 11.)

elementary and middle schools organize, can help kids find their favorites. Many schools hold instrument show-and-tells during the early grades for strings, and from third grade on up for brass, woodwinds, and percussion. "We demonstrate the instruments and let students try different ones, sterilizing mouthpieces between tries for brass and woodwinds, so they get a sense of the sound and how the instrument feels. The instrument they like to hear is the one they'll like to play," says Nanette Jordan, elementary school band director and Connecticut mother of two accomplished musicians. She adds that some schools give students a listening test to help determine the kind of sound that appeals to them.

Another way to give kids firsthand experiences with a variety of instrument is to let them take part in the petting-zoo-type events that music schools, orchestras, and other organizations offer. When Melissa Tucker's daughter was seven, she attended such a demonstration at a music school. "She made a dynamic connection with the flute and with the young woman demonstrating the flute. We saw the spark and pursued lessons with that young woman," says this Massachusetts mother, who had started her daughter on piano the year before. Her daughter enjoyed piano and stayed with it even after starting flute lessons, but she liked flute more.

Parents could organize their own instrument explorations by listening with their children to recordings that highlight the sounds of individual instruments. Some possibilities include Prokofiev's "Peter and the Wolf," Benjamin Britten's "Young People's Guide to the Orchestra," or rock and jazz recordings that feature solos by

different instrumentalists. Following up by attending live performances will let youngsters connect the sound of an instrument to its looks and help them see that not all instruments play in all types of ensembles, although genre boundaries are breaking down.

An up-close exposure to drums captured the interest of Keith Fertwagner at age eleven when he heard a drummer perform at his church. This future music director of the School of Rock in Omaha was already a rock fan and had a brief fling with guitar at age six that hadn't turned out well. Having seen videos of The Who smashing guitars, he

Payton MacDonald

smashed up a new guitar his parents had just given him. "I didn't realize it couldn't be put back together, that you had to buy another," he says. He lost interest in guitar for a while but seeing that drummer at church started him playing drums, and then at age sixteen he reconnected with guitar.

Conductor Marin Alsop feels the ideal approach to choosing an instrument is to give children "an intensive introduction over several weeks to a variety of instruments and let them decide for themselves, because there is the perfect instrument for every child." This approach is used in the free OrchKids after-school programs she helped set up in Baltimore. Perhaps persuasive parents can talk their local schools into organizing similar long-term, instrument-immersion experiences.

Piano Power

Many parents choose piano as a child's first instrument, as the Couillards did, partly because it doesn't require much training to make a sound. "When you press down a key, there it is. Whereas on a violin, you have to learn how to produce the sound," explains violinist Sarah Chang, who began piano at age three, a year before starting violin. Her mom, a pianist, taught her to pick out melodies with one finger.

Piano skills can help any musician. The arrangement of notes on the keyboard mirrors how those notes are written on a musical score. Familiarity with a piano keyboard can make it easier to learn to read music and see the relationships between notes, a big help in learning music theory, which explains the basic structure of music.

"Piano is the ideal base for learning any instrument," says Ruth Cahn, head of the percussion department at Eastman's Community Music School. "If students have had some piano before they start percussion lessons, they can move so much faster because they already have an understanding of music. I don't have to spend a lot of time on basic stuff."

"I studied a little piano with my mother, a pianist, and then I took piano as a secondary instrument when I was taking cello lessons at the Cleveland Institute of Music," says cellist Alisa Weilerstein. "I don't play piano very well, but piano is absolutely important for other musicians for being able to read scores, listen to harmony, and gain perspective on how your instrument relates to other instruments."

Opera singer Lawrence Brownlee points out another advantage of piano. "I play piano well enough to help me learn my parts," says this tenor. "A lot of the time when I'm on the road performing, I have to work by myself in preparing music for a concert. It's vital that I have piano and music-reading tools to help me learn the music myself, so that I don't have to rely on someone else to help me learn it."

Another practical benefit of playing piano is the boost it can give singers and other instrumentalists with the teaching that most of them wind up doing. "Playing piano lets me accompany my students," says singer Jamie Jordan, who has a roster of private students. Piano skills can also help students who want to attend a conservatory for college where, regardless of musical specialty, they have to pass the dreaded piano-competency test.

Some children like the solitary nature of piano work, but it may seem like a lonely instrument to others, who may feel frustrated tapping away at a keyboard by themselves and not being able to join the school band or orchestra as beginners on other instruments can. It may take several years of study before a young pianist is skilled enough to win a spot in an ensemble. "That kind of camaraderie is often not part of a piano student's world," says professional pianist Jonathan Biss. That's why his parents started him playing chamber music early on, first by having him play with them—they're both professional string players—and later with other young people. During high school he organized a chamber music trio with students at Indiana University, where he was taking piano lessons.

To deal with the lonely-instrument issue, music schools often offer group piano classes for beginners. Group playing is a key part of Suzuki piano programs, but traditional teachers sometimes organize periodic group classes for their students, or

Ella Cho and Ian Maloney playing a duet at age six after each had been studying piano for about a year with the same teacher at the JCC Thurnauer School of Music.

may pair them up to play duets. In addition, many music schools offer chamber music programs that let youngsters—pianists included—play together in trios, quartets, or other small ensembles. Chamber music became a key part of pianist Erika Nickrenz's life at age nine, when she began playing in small groups with other students at the New York music school she attended. Now, as the pianist for the Eroica Trio, chamber music is the focus of her professional life. Chamber music helps kids learn to listen closely to each other because these small groups usually perform without a conductor. Teachers can guide them in rehearsals, but in a performance, ensemble members have to keep eyes and ears open to what the others are doing.

There is another drawback to pianos: They are expensive to buy and keep in tune. Some parents have found good deals on used pianos. Others started their children on less-expensive electronic keyboards. Although some music schools require students to have a real piano to practice on, independent teachers might be willing to be more flexible about this.

The Singing Advantage

Just as playing piano helps a singer, singing can help an instrumentalist. Music schools often encourage children who play instruments to sing in the chorus, too. "Chorus is so important," says Dorothy Kaplan Roffman, violin teacher and director of the JCC Thurnauer School of Music, a New Jersey community music school. "Singing is the most natural way to make music. It helps you learn phrasing and breathing, things you can apply to any instrument."

Miguel Zenón joined his elementary school's choir two years before he discovered saxophone. Caleb Burhans, a composer and performer in new-music ensembles, joined the Houston Boys Choir when he was nine, a year before his family moved to Wisconsin, where he started violin in elementary school. He kept singing in choirs through college and still sings professionally. Several of our advisors' children sang in choirs or choruses all through high school even though they were primarily instrumentalists, including Sarah Odhner's French horn–playing son. "He would always get into all-state choir *and* all-state orchestra and then have to decide which one to perform with," says this Pennsylvania mom.

Singing has another practical benefit for instrumentalists who hope to apply to conservatories, which usually require students to take a sight-singing test. This involves singing a tune they've never seen before just by reading the music. Singing experience can help in preparing for such a test. (More on singing in chapter 6.)

Sibling Issues

Several panelists report that sibling considerations played a part in instrument choices. One of Dominique van de Stadt's sons chose cello because it was different—and bigger—than his older sister's violin. Jiji Goosby, who started all three of her children on violin, let the two younger ones drop violin when it was clear that they were bothered by feeling competitive with their older brother, Randall, who excelled at violin from the moment he started at age seven. When Ms. Goosby noticed that these sibling issues were causing difficulties, she told her daughter, "'You don't have to play violin. You could try horn, or woodwinds, or any other instrument you want.' She said she wanted to try flute. She did and loves it. My youngest child always compares himself to Randall and doesn't understand that Randall is four years older and so of course he plays violin better. I let my younger son drop violin and not take any lessons for a while. When he turned eight, he said, 'I don't need anything for my birthday but a cello and a cello teacher.' He started cello and is doing well."

According to child psychiatrist Dr. Gene Beresin, it can be helpful to "encourage the second child to learn something the older child doesn't do. Maybe the second child doesn't want to play an instrument at all. It may be the parent's agenda to have a family of musicians, but one child may have strengths in another area."

However, siblings playing the same instrument can sometimes work out, as it did for the Biss brothers. Jonathan Biss and his older brother both play piano. His brother hasn't gone on to a piano career but still plays in his spare time. Dana Myers was concerned when her younger son decided to play cello, like his older brother. "I wanted to make sure he was doing it for himself. I came to see that he really does love cello," says Ms. Myers, a St. Louis Symphony Orchestra violinist. "Every once in a while he would compare himself to his brother. I'd say to him, 'You're a different person, everyone is not the same.'" The brothers didn't play duets often as kids "because accusations would fly," which other parents have also noticed, whether their kids play the same instrument or not. Both sons, now grown, have become professional cellists and recently played cello together at a fundraiser. "It was so special. I hope we can do that again," says Ms. Myers.

Multitaskers

Instead of switching instruments, some youngsters simply add on new ones. Peter Maloney and Felicia Zekauskas' son Ian, shown playing a piano duet earlier in this chapter, began cello at age three, added piano at age five and trumpet at age eight.

Diane Cornelius's son started on violin in fourth grade when his Oregon elementary school offered strings. He added clarinet in sixth grade when his middle school let students choose a band instrument. "Orchestra met before school and band during school. So for a while he did both," says Ms. Cornelius. By middle school he lost interest in clarinet but became intrigued by the bassoon the school music teacher let him borrow. "He realized that if he was going to get really good at violin he'd have to practice more than he was willing to. So he quit violin and took up guitar. These were easy transitions—from violin to guitar and from clarinet to bassoon." During high school, he played bassoon in the Portland Youth Philharmonic, while also playing electric guitar in his high school jazz band and in a funk band he formed with friends.

Yoko Segerstrom's son kept piling on instruments, too: piano, violin, French horn, percussion, and bass. "In eighth grade, the French horn teacher and his youth orchestra conductor told him he better concentrate on one thing or he won't be really good at any of them. So he concentrated on percussion," says his mother, although he couldn't resist adding on guitar. Then he discovered his main interest—composition. "In retrospect, it was probably good for him being a composer that he was interested in so many instruments," she says.

Other Issues to Keep in Mind

- **Practice space:** Before finalizing the choice of instrument, parents should be sure they have a space where the child can practice without a lot of distractions and without waking up the neighborhood. "That can be a problem if your child wants to play a brass instrument or percussion and you live in an apartment. The neighbors may not like the sound, although there are special practice mutes you can get for brass instruments to make them less loud," says band instructor Nanette Jordan. With percussion, students can start with a drum pad or practice on the instruments at school. "When we lived in an apartment, our daughter started by using a drum pad and a small xylophone. These aren't too loud, but we always tried to have practice time during the day, when we assumed most neighbors were at work," says Annette Ramke, Pennsylvania mother of a teen percussionist. "When we got the marimba, it was in our dining room, so close to our table that it was hard to walk around it. So we moved. Now we have a room just for her instruments. We're still close to our neighbor—it's a twin house—and we still aim to do music when our neighbor is not home."
- **Braces:** "Our son decided on a woodwind instead of a brass instrument after watching how hard it was for his older sister to play French horn while wearing

braces on her teeth, knowing that he needed more dental work than she did and would be in braces much longer," says Ann Turner. He started on saxophone and then switched to bassoon. However, braces shouldn't keep kids from playing instruments they really like. There are bumper guards brass players can clip onto braces so it's less painful to press the mouthpiece against their lips. Brace-wearing students note that after a while, you adjust. As one horn player explains, "Braces aren't forever."

Reverse popularity: Playing an instrument that few kids play—such as viola, bassoon, oboe, baritone sax, tuba, double bass, marimba—may open up more opportunities in terms of joining an ensemble, playing solos, being "first chair," or making all-state. "So many kids want to play drums, but you can have only so many drummers in the school band," notes teacher Nanette Jordan. But drummers who also play marimba may have an easier time finding a spot in the percussion section. Oboist Toyin Spellman-Diaz switched from flute to oboe as a young teen because "I wanted to be the best at my instrument and there were too many good flute players in the DC Youth Orchestra, but not many good oboe players. So I thought, 'Why not switch?' Plus my uncle had an oboe which he gave me. It was an easy switch. The fingerings were close enough to flute. I was in love with music and wanted to play music really badly. At first, oboe was just a vehicle. After a while, I fell in love with oboe, especially after I started playing English horn, too." English horn is similar to an oboe, only bigger, with a lower-register sound.

- **Size:** Lauren Chipman started on violin but switched to viola. "It seemed to fit me better," she says. "I teach violin and viola now, and you can see with some students that a viola would fit them better, that they could make a really good sound on it." Viola is a little larger and heavier than a violin, with a lower, more mellow sound.
- **Price:** There are big price differences among different types of instruments, even for rentals. Most parents start by renting their child's first instrument. If a child decides to stick with an instrument after that initial rental, parents often buy a student-level instrument. When a youngster becomes skilled enough to need a professional-level model, prices rise markedly, especially for strings, with professional-level string instruments costing many times more than woodwinds and brass.
- **Multiple models:** One model of an instrument may not be enough for serious brass and woodwind students. "I thought we only had to buy one trumpet," says Dr. Jeanny Park. But as her son became more proficient on trumpet, she discovered, "There are so many trumpets to get!" There's the basic B-flat trumpet for regular playing, a C trumpet for orchestral playing,

and a piccolo trumpet for especially high pieces. Advanced flute students will want to have a piccolo flute as well as a regular flute. Becoming adept at playing these other models may open up performance opportunities. An orchestra may already have enough clarinets but might make room for a clarinetist who can double on bass clarinet. In jazz bands, saxophonists may be more in demand if they can handle a few of the choices: soprano, alto, tenor, and baritone sax.

SPOTLIGHT ON: LIANG WANG, OBOE

Free to be me: "I'm grateful to my parents that they allowed me to be what I wanted to be," says Liang Wang, who grew up in China and is now principal oboist of the New York Philharmonic. "A lot of parents want their kid to fit into what they think the kid should do. Oboe was an unusual choice. There aren't many Chinese oboe players. Piano and violin are strong in China, but I didn't play piano or violin at all. I loved oboe. My uncle was an oboe player. I loved the sound. I begged my uncle to teach me. My grandmother says, 'Don't do it. It will give you a headache.' But I enjoyed it. My mother made sure I practiced. My uncle was self-taught. He was my teacher until I went to Beijing Conservatory. Other parents might think you should be a lawyer or doctor. My mother was an amateur singer and had a love of music. She wanted me to pursue my dream."

Instrument Shopping

"Teachers are the first people to go to for recommendations," says Dominique van de Stadt, an Arizona mother who has done a lot of instrument shopping for her four kids. "Unless a parent is a musician or otherwise knowledgeable, it is difficult to know what is a good instrument and whether the price is appropriate. We had teachers who have gone out of their way to help us find excellent age- and ability-appropriate instruments at the best possible prices." A novice may also not realize that instruments made by different manufacturers vary in ease of use. "If the instrument sounds good and is very playable, the child will be more motivated, make progress more quickly, and enjoy the whole process more," she explains.

Teachers can suggest good stores or other retail options. Some parents report that a teacher actually went shopping with them. However, a few parents note that it's good to make sure a teacher doesn't receive a commission for steering buyers to a certain store or brand, although none of those parents had that happen to them.

Whether buying or renting, negotiate with the store for the option to return or exchange an instrument—even a rental—if it doesn't pass inspection when tried by the child's teacher. "There are music stores I would never send a parent to because I know they don't take good care of their instruments," says violin teacher Dorothy Kaplan Roffman. "With a violin, if it isn't set up correctly, it's harder to play. We have a local store that does a good job. They know that if it's not right, we'll just bring it back."

Good rental agreements usually include a "rent-to-buy" option, so that a portion of the rental fee can be applied to the cost of buying an instrument at the end of the rental. Stores should also provide instrument-care instructions, although often their instruction sheets are rather minimal—another area where teachers can help. Rental contracts for small-sized string instruments should allow an exchange to a larger size as the child grows. Some parents recommend waiting to buy a string instrument until a child needs a full-sized version. Others found it cost-effective to buy a small violin or cello as long as the store let them do trade-ins. Yoko Segerstrom did the size step-ups for her children's violins by mail order with an out-of-state store, a service several stores offer.

Some parents found it helpful to solicit suggestions from more than one teacher. Cindy Buhse discovered that her daughter's first teacher didn't know where the best deals could be found in their hometown, St. Louis. "When we bought our daughter's first viola, she had been studying with only one teacher. We went to the local store he recommended and bought a small viola that was good but very expensive," says Ms. Buhse. "A few years later, she wanted a viola with a bigger sound. By then she had studied with several teachers and discovered that they used different shops. We did more shopping that time, looked at all the shops in St. Louis, and found a viola that sounded good and was less expensive. She took that viola to college. I kept the older, more expensive one. By then I had started playing viola again. So it worked out in the end."

With used instruments inherited from a relative or friend, check with a teacher or other expert to make sure they are worth refurbishing. That's what Gail Caiazza did when her ten-year-old daughter started flute with an instrument that came from a friend. "We had it cleaned and evaluated," says this Massachusetts mother. "She used it for about a year and a half and then used it again later for marching band in high school. We worked with her private teacher to find her first open-hole flute. The teacher recommended a few models and we used an online store. You give them a credit card number for a deposit and they send you a few flutes for ten days to try out. The teacher helped us decide which one to choose. The ones you don't want, you ship back." For her daughter's professional-level flute that she took to college, they shopped at several stores so her daughter could try different flutes. By then, her daughter was knowledgeable enough to know what she needed.

Finding Financial Help

Some music schools provide instruments for free to students whose families can't afford them. Teachers can help as well. The Couillards, in addition to being able initially to borrow a double bass for two years from the elementary school, had good luck later on with a private teacher who lent their daughter an excellent instrument for a special performance and then sold it to them at a reasonable price. The Ramkes have a marimba on loan from a friend of their daughter's teacher.

Pennsylvania high school band director Matthew Ceresini notes that while many of his students have their own instruments, the school provides the big, expensive ones, such as tubas or bassoons, as well as those used only for marching band. At another high school where he taught previously, the parents' band-boosters organization ran a fundraising effort to keep the music program solvent. If students helped with the fundraising, they could use a percentage of the amount they raised to help with the cost of their lessons or instruments.

The El Sistema instructional programs provide instruments for free to all their students. So do the education programs that some music organizations sponsor. "There are foundations and organizations out there that will support young musicians. You have to ask around," says Ms. Goosby, who has made good use of this strategy to find support for the emerging violin career of her teenaged son Randall.

High-End Loaners

"Wealthy parents can afford good violins and bows, and the sound is different. Don't believe the myth of being able to sound great on any violin, even the cheapest. At piano competitions, everybody plays on the same piano, but at violin competitions, musicians come with their own instruments," notes Dominique Kaul-Boiter, Maryland mother of a teen violinist. "My daughter is very musical, practices a lot, wants to succeed, but has been limited by the quality of her instrument because a really excellent instrument is out of reach cost-wise."

Other parents have raised the same concern. Dominique van de Stadt notes that with her oldest child, Milena Pajaro-van de Stadt, now a professional violist, "I had no idea that a good student instrument bought when she was ten was not good enough until she entered her first national competition when she was fourteen. A juror at that competition pointed out to me that her instrument was akin to driving a Mack truck versus a BMW."

Some families deal with the high cost of instruments and everything else that goes into a child's musical pursuit by engaging in serious belt-tightening—cutting back on extra expenses, putting off home repairs, downsizing vacations, seeking financial help from relatives, and even taking out second mortgages. However, belt-tightening won't suffice if the goal is to have superior string instruments whose prices soar into the tens of thousands.

"Most high school students are not playing at such a high level" to need a top-level string instrument, observes Rebecca Henry, head of the string department of Peabody's preparatory division. "I've had a lot of students play in different kinds of competitions. For most of them I don't think it was the instrument that made the call. But it is true that even in high school competitions for a local orchestra or youth symphony, kids who play at a high level often play on very nice instruments. Either the families can afford the instrument or it is not uncommon for students to borrow a fine instrument from a music shop for a competition. When you play at a high level, those pipelines often come your way."

Ms. van de Stadt's daughter Milena found a spot on that loaner pipeline thanks to the Sphinx organization that sponsored the competition at which they learned the importance of having a better instrument. Sphinx holds competitions for African American and Latino string musicians and arranges for some contestants to receive better instruments on loan. Joshua Bell received his first quality loaner at age ten, having already begun to be noticed as an up-and-comer. A violin collector contacted his family and "lent us a wonderful three-quarter-size violin that we gave back when Josh outgrew it," says his mother, Shirley Bell. "Different people lent violins to Josh at different times. He didn't buy his first Stradivarius until he was nineteen."

Annette Radoff's daughter, Elena Urioste, obtained her first loaner by chance. She had done well with a "modestly priced instrument" that she played all through high school and in the audition that won her admission to the Curtis Institute of Music in Philadelphia. However, an influential musician heard her play a concerto near the end of high school and "decided that Elena needed a better instrument," says Ms. Radoff. A wealthy donor contacted the family and loaned Elena an extremely good violin. Five years later, that donor exchanged the first loaner for an even better violin.

Youth orchestras may make arrangements with local music stores to loan quality instruments to students who play solos with the orchestra. A few foundations lend out superior string instruments and allow top students to apply for one. Among these are the Virtu Foundation, Anne-Sophie Mutter Foundation, and Rachel Elizabeth Barton Foundation. The competition is stiff, but one of Sarah Odhner's sons received a violin on loan from the Virtu Foundation. The Stradivari Society of Chicago doesn't accept applications but loans instruments on the recommendation of famous musicians and teachers. (See Resources for links to these groups.)

Jiji Goosby's son Randall received a violin on loan from the Stradivari Society at the recommendation of a violinist Randall met at age twelve while attending

Music in the Mountains summer camp in Colorado. Ms. Goosby persuaded that violinist, who lives in New York, to give Randall extra lessons after camp ended. "We began to fly once a month from our home in Tennessee to meet with that teacher in New York," says Ms. Goosby. "We didn't get any financial help with the travel. I was probably not in my right mind to do this, but I felt this was something I had to do when I saw how much Randall improved from working with that teacher." Randall went back to that camp the next summer and won a competition, which gave the teacher a concrete achievement to cite in making a request to the Stradivari Society. "Because he's young, he didn't get a Stradivarius, but he got a very nice violin," says Ms. Goosby. He used it when he won the junior level Sphinx competition at age thirteen.

Other parents approach music stores directly. "During high school and also before that, my parents got the names of music shops and local instrument dealers and would negotiate with them to borrow good instruments for a week or two for special performances," explains violinist Jennifer Koh. Short-terms loaners have their drawbacks. "Even though the instrument I borrowed was better than the scratch box I usually played, it wasn't like being able to grow with the instrument. You'll never get to know an instrument in one or two weeks." After winning the Tchaikovsky competition at age seventeen with a loaner, she obtained a long-term loan of an excellent violin that she could really get to know. She played it for about fourteen years until its owner asked for it back. "Then I raised funds for six years to buy a Strad," she says.

"A combination of resourcefulness and bull-headedness," is how violinist Robert Gupta describes his parents' strategy for arranging long-term loaners, starting when he was nine years old. They obtained quality violins on loan from music shops and even from a professional violinist. This bargaining was a necessity, he says, because his parents "went into huge amounts of debt" to support his musical studies. Perhaps the success that these violin parents have had in their instrument negotiations might embolden other music parents to try a bit of bargaining with shop owners for non-string instruments, too.

Shopping Tips

- **Set price limits:** "Don't look at anything out of your price range because you *will* want it! I was cautious about investing in an expensive instrument too soon. It might make my son feel obligated to pursue violin, and set up a guilt complex, leaving him no emotional way out if he chose to pursue another interest in life."—Sarah Odhner, Pennsylvania

- **Festivals:** "My daughter's teacher encouraged us to go to flute festivals. My daughter got to see a lot of great flute players, take master classes, and try out flutes from all the vendors. She bought her best flute from a vendor at one festival. Her teacher was at the festival and tried out the flute."—Cindi Russell, Kentucky

- **Research online:** "Check websites of different instrument companies and online stores to learn more about the instruments and to compare price versus buying locally. We found a better deal at an online store, but the local shop would still service the instrument."—Roger Cash, Missouri

- **Kid input:** "We told our son he was paying for part of his saxophone when we bought his second one, although we actually kept the money he gave us and put it in his college fund. We drove all over and had him try lots of saxophones. Until he found one he loved, I wasn't budging."—Sue Woods, Missouri

It pays to shop around when renting or buying musical instruments, by checking prices and services at stores and online retailers.

- **Networking:** "We became friendly with symphony orchestra members who teach at our children's music school and that's how we found out about a music shop where orchestra members have their instruments repaired. The shop builds instruments and sells them, too."—Judy Merritt, Pennsylvania

Bold Choices

Adrian Anantawan's mother made a bold instrument choice for him when he was ten years old—violin, which might seem an unlikely instrument for a child born without a right hand. But the family managed to find teachers in their hometown of Toronto who were willing to take on the challenge of adapting violin instruction to fit his needs. "This was all my mom's idea," says Mr. Anantawan. "I liked music but didn't have any special desire for any particular instrument. My dad had played violin when he was younger. When my mother brought home the violin she got at an instrument shop, my father played the 'Twinkle' variations. I was immediately hooked by the sound," he says. He went on to excel at violin and along the way received a violin on loan from the Anne-Sophie Mutter Foundation.

Catherine Getchell's mother also made a bold choice by allowing Catherine, blind from birth, to play trumpet during elementary school and stop her lessons on piano, a more traditional choice for visually impaired youngsters. "I wanted to be in the school band after hearing them play at elementary school assemblies," says Catherine Getchell. "I thought that would be the coolest thing. During band tryout day at school, I got to try the trumpet. It felt really natural. I was able to get a decent beginner sound right away." Her mom found a trumpet teacher who, despite misgivings, adapted his teaching techniques for Catherine, who became a terrific trumpeter, winning spots in all-state ensembles and serving as principal trumpet in her college orchestra. As an adult, she has played with community ensembles in her spare time from her job with a vocational rehabilitation agency in Pennsylvania.

Eveylyn Glennie's instrument choice might also seem surprising. This world-famous solo percussionist started percussion at age twelve when she was profoundly deaf as a result of a childhood infection. These successes may reassure parents whose kids want to play instruments that may seem a bit of a stretch for various reasons. A key ingredient in all these positive outcomes was a creative, flexible teacher—essential for helping any music student succeed. In the next chapter, our advisors discuss how to find such teachers.

Professional violinist and music educator Adrian Anantawan warming up before a performance.

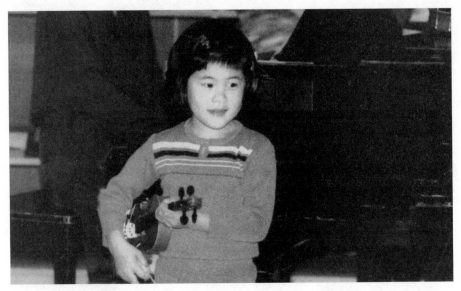

Jennifer Koh at an early Suzuki performance (top), at swim team practice, and in a more recent photo.

5   Finding Teachers

A CHILD'S FIRST MUSIC TEACHER helps set the tone for all that follows, as professional violin soloist Jennifer Koh explains in her reminiscence that starts off this teacher-focused chapter. "I was lucky with my first violin teacher. She played an incredibly important part in my musical development," says Ms. Koh, who began Suzuki violin lessons very young at a music school near her home in a Chicago suburb. "I started violin because that was the only opening the school had at that time. There were waiting lists for cello and piano classes. Those early violin lessons were totally fun. The teacher was wonderful. With Suzuki lessons, it was like playtime with instruments. I remember we started playing on a pretend violin made out of a Cracker Jack box and a stick. I liked that because I got to eat all the Cracker Jacks. My mom sat in on lessons. It seemed very natural.

"After a few years, the teacher told my parents, 'I've taught your daughter everything I know. It's time for her to move on.' She encouraged my parents to take me to a new teacher. They didn't know other teachers. So she drove me and my parents to meet other Suzuki teachers. She checked out the new teachers with us and told us what the best qualities are of this and that one. Finally she recommended that I study with Almita and Roland Vamos."

The Vamoses are a husband-and-wife team who have taught many top string play-ers. Back then, they were an hour's drive from Jenny Koh's home, too long a drive to fit into the schedule of her college professor mother, who was already driving long distances to take Jenny to swim-team practice and swim meets. "So for two years, my first violin teacher drove me to have lessons with the Vamoses. She attended the les-sons with me and made an effort to practice with me, giving me a kind of mini, extra lesson. The Vamoses had a violin performance class every week. I remember listening to older kids play their pieces and feeling that I really wanted to sound like that. I was being steeped in the culture. At around age ten, when my first teacher stopped driving me, my parents said I had to choose between swimming and violin because they couldn't do that much driving." She chose violin and studied with the Vamoses through high school and on into college.

"Having grown up in a completely nonmusical family, with parents who were learning about the music world the same time I was, if I didn't have the teachers I had, I would never have become a musician," says Ms. Koh. It all started with her first teacher, now retired. "I'm still in touch with her. She and her husband have grand-children who live in different states and drive their RV to visit them. When I give a concert near one of their grandchildren, they come hear me perform."

The All-Important First Teacher

Not many first music teachers go to the lengths that Jenny Koh's did to support a promising young student. But many musicians on our advice panel as well as the chil-dren of our parent advisors were as lucky as Ms. Koh in having a first teacher who made music fun, while also providing a solid start on good technique. For some it was a ter-rific teacher at the child's regular school. For others, it was an independent teacher in the neighborhood or at a local music school who had a special knack for working with young children. That's the kind of first teacher who nurtured the pianists profiled in Benjamin Bloom's classic book, *Developing Talent in Young People*. As he notes, most of those first teachers were not necessarily the world's greatest musicians but they were world class in knowing how to relate to kids and get them excited about music making.

"Music should be fun for kids. That is key," notes Marin Alsop, a music mom as well as conductor of the Baltimore Symphony Orchestra. "But because kids will rise to the level of our expectations, we also need to challenge them. Finding the right teacher is critical to a child's learning and success. Follow your instincts about teach-ers. You know your child best, even if you don't know anything about music. You know how your child learns, what he or she finds stimulating and fun. My son has had three very good teachers, but the first one didn't 'get' him, so we switched."

"The beginning is the most important time in a child's musical development, when things need to be set up in the best possible way, including how to think and feel about music," says Dorothy Kaplan Roffman, violin teacher and director of a New Jersey community music school. "All teachers have their particular strengths and interests, but for beginners, it's important to find teachers who are skilled with the early years. There has to be an element of fun, although that doesn't mean it's not disciplined. Children don't want to learn to play violin so they can hold the violin correctly. They want to make music. The teacher has to convince them that if they hold the violin and the bow correctly, there will be a huge difference in how they sound." She makes games out of learning basic skills and sometimes puts a congratulatory sticker in their assignment book. "Children know when they've done something well," she says, "but a sticker is a little something extra."

Having a Private Teacher—or Not

Some parents start right away with private instruction. Others let youngsters begin with group classes, either at a music school or at the child's elementary or middle school, and wait to sign up youngsters with a private teacher until it's clear they are really interested. Several of our pro advisors began with group lessons in elementary school, including flutist Paula Robison, as well as Anthony McGill, principal clarinetist with the Metropolitan Opera Orchestra. Richard Stoltzman, another eminent clarinetist, began with group lessons on saxophone in fourth grade, adding clarinet after his parents found him a private teacher.

It is possible to be a successful musician without private instruction. Jazz saxophonist Joshua Redman is a prime example. He had group lessons in school and played in school ensembles but didn't have a private teacher. Rock musician Keith Fertwagner was largely self-taught. "I took drum lessons for about a month when I was eleven. Then I mainly taught myself by listening to recordings," he explains. He lasted about a week in his middle school concert band. He quit because "they had me play a snare drum. Everything was charted, sheet music. That wasn't for me. I wanted to play rock and roll." He taught himself to play guitar as a teenager, matching what he heard on recordings and also picking up tips from his father, who plays guitar, and from fellow musicians in the garage bands he played in as teen. "I spent hours practicing every day. Nobody ever had to force me to practice," he says. Now, however, he is passing on his knowledge to youngsters in a more traditional teacher-student format as the music director of the School of Rock in Omaha.

There are drawbacks, however, to the no-private-teacher route, as French horn player Larry Williams discovered. He started trumpet in elementary school but never took lessons. He also never practiced. "Nobody showed me how to play the trumpet. I just showed up in band and kind of figured it out," he says. "I was probably the worst trumpet player in the elementary school band." But it didn't matter because he and his best friend, also in the trumpet section, had fun just being in the band. During middle school, the music director needed students to play French horn. His friend volunteered. So did Larry Williams. The band director, having heard the way he played trumpet, didn't think he could handle a horn, which can be harder to play than trumpet. She had him come after school to try him out on horn, "probably so I wouldn't embarrass myself in front of the other kids," says Mr. Williams. That afternoon was the first time someone gave him private, personalized instruction on how to play a brass instrument. He was able to do everything she showed him. "Nobody had ever corrected some basic things that I had been doing wrong," he says. She let him join the French horn section with his buddy.

"She was a private-teacher kind of band director. Every time she spoke to my friend and me during band, we were getting quality, private-level instruction in terms of technique. We advanced and excelled," he says. If youngsters are lucky to have a school music director with the time and interest to give personal-level instruction during regular school, that can be a big help, especially if their families can't afford a private teacher.

However, during his senior year in high school, Mr. Williams felt he needed more individualized attention than was offered in the music program of his regular school. It was time for a private teacher because he had decided to major in music at college and wanted help preparing for college auditions. He phoned his old middle school band director and asked if she could give him some private lessons. "After about five minutes of her screaming and saying 'I told you so,' she put me through a six-week boot camp of lessons and got me ready for my auditions," he says. He aimed high, auditioning at Oberlin, which didn't accept him, but Penn State did. After two years there, he transferred to Peabody, where he has become head of the brass and woodwinds department for preparatory students.

As Mr. Williams discovered from his experiences as a student and as a teacher, young musicians make faster, surer progress with one-on-one instruction. In the rest of this chapter, our parent and educator advisors share ideas for how to find good private teachers. Their suggestions apply both to instrumental and vocal instructors. Additional issues to consider regarding singing instruction are explored in the next chapter.

The Independent Teacher Option

A basic choice parents and kids need to make involves whether to have an independent teacher or one on the staff of a music school. There are pros and cons to each approach, as noted in this section and the one that follows.

For the first teacher, many parents choose a local, independent instructor, often one who lives nearby. A neighborhood teacher may mean it takes less time to deliver a child to lessons—a help for busy parents. Such a teacher might be willing to give lessons at the child's home.

An independent teacher, whether in the neighborhood or not, also offers the potential for lower fees because the teacher might be more willing to negotiate than a school with posted tuition. "Our daughter took lessons from a top flute teacher who lives around the corner from my mother. Sometimes our daughter was able to babysit for the teacher and trade that to cover the cost of a lesson" says Massachusetts mom Gail Caiazza.

Convenience played a role in Dr. Jeanny Park's decision to go with independent teachers, but she also liked the flexibility of being able to look for the best teacher to fit the particular needs of her son and daughter at various points in their development. Her family lives in a small college town in California, and she started by signing up her kids at age five with one of the town's most popular Suzuki piano teachers. Dr. Park drove them to lessons the first few years on her day off. Later, they got themselves to lessons by biking, or, when old enough, driving. In junior high, when her son also began playing trumpet, finding a trumpet teacher was easy. "The school band teacher was a professional trumpet player and taught my son for the first three or four years," says Dr. Park. "Then he felt it was time for my son to study at the next level and suggested a professional trumpet player who sometimes plays with the San Francisco Symphony. My son also had extra lessons from the principal trumpet players at the San Francisco Symphony and San Francisco Opera." When her daughter became interested in singing, Dr. Park called around to find voice teachers. Many of our other parent advisors also liked using this calling-around strategy.

The Music School Route

Other parents prefer the music school route, partly to avoid having to hunt for teachers. Of more importance, music schools offer extras in addition to lessons, such as courses in music theory and composition, music-and-movement classes, and the chance to perform in ensembles. An early start in ensemble playing lets children have fun making music together, which can keep them interested and even spur them to practice. Of course, students of independent teachers can also play in ensembles, either by performing with their regular school's ensembles or by auditioning for extracurricular youth orchestras, choirs, or jazz groups. In addition, some music schools allow students to join their ensembles without taking lessons at the school.

Tuition at music schools can be steep, but many have scholarship programs. "Don't be afraid or embarrassed to ask for scholarships," says Sarah Koh (not Jenny Koh's mom). This mother has had success obtaining financial aid for her violinist daughter.

There are two basic types of music schools that provide lessons for children:

- **Community music schools:** These offer lessons to all comers, usually without requiring an audition for admission, although there may be an audition for proper placement.
- **Preparatory divisions of conservatories:** A conservatory trains professional-level, college-age musicians but often has a preparatory division that offers instruction for children. Some preparatory divisions have a two-tiered system: one is for all comers; the other, known often as the pre-college program, is for highly skilled, young musicians who must pass an audition first.

Some parents like the sense of community that they feel at a music school. "It wasn't just the private lessons, but the whole experience. Our whole family was there every Saturday," notes Judy Merritt, describing City Music Center of Duquesne University in Pittsburgh where her kids, Ted and Emma, took lessons from preschool through high school. "Ted's father sat in on his Suzuki violin lessons. I sat in on Emma's cello lessons. We'd have lunch together. Ted would have his extra programs, and Emma hers. They'd come together for performances." One of the extras Ted took when he was thirteen was a jazz class that introduced him to the instrument that would become the center of his professional career—double bass.

David McCollough likes the family feel of the small music school, Diller Quaille, that he and his wife chose partly because it is around the corner from their New York City apartment. His teenager has studied cello and piano there since he was very young. "There are more competitive music schools, but this school offers a warm, comfortable environment," says Mr. McCollough. His wife adds, "Our son said that even if he messes up in a performance, the teachers there realize he's a good musician. So that frees him to do his best."

Other parents find that more competitive pre-college-type programs can also provide a supportive environment. Jiji Goosby's violinist son, Randall, started at Juilliard's pre-college program when he was fifteen, even though that meant airborne commuting on weekends from Memphis to New York. "He loves it," says Ms. Goosby. "We couldn't afford to have him fly there every weekend ourselves." Luckily, he has a sponsor who flies him there each week.

Many parents use more than one option. Their young musicians may start with an independent teacher or community music school and end up several years later in a pre-college program. Some families use several options at once—having an

Charis Yoon, age eight, at a recital her music school held at a piano showroom, which helped make it seem like more of an event.

independent teacher while also enrolling youngsters in extras at a music school. Other families use another possibility during their youngsters' high school years—a music-oriented boarding school.

Meet and Greet

Before deciding on a teacher, it's wise to meet with potential candidates to gain a sense of their teaching style. Trial lessons are helpful, too. Topics of discussion for these exploratory meetings can include the expectations a teacher has in terms of the kind of music to be studied, amount of practice time required, performance opportunities, and expectations for parental involvement. It's important also to discuss the teacher's strategies for encouraging tension-free, injury-free playing. (More on this later in this chapter.)

Also worth exploring is how the teacher handles reluctant practicers, including whether there's flexibility in repertoire to rekindle flagging interest. Sports families can ask whether a teacher will adjust lesson times if the sports schedule conflicts. Another topic: competitions. Some kids like them, but others don't. (More on competitions in chapter 10.)

Teachers value these exploratory meetings. "Families that come to our school can't enroll their children until they meet with me," says Ms. Roffman. "I explain to them what it means to learn about music so they have a sense of what is to be expected, that there are requirements. Learning to play an instrument may not be a passion or

In this photo of the Imani Winds woodwind quintet, oboist Toyin Spellman-Diaz is second from left.

SPOTLIGHT ON: TOYIN SPELLMAN-DIAZ, OBOE

A message: When Toyin Spellman-Diaz began private flute lessons at age eleven, her parents looked for a good musician who could deliver a nonmusical message. "They wanted an African American teacher so I could see a classical musician who looked like me," explains Ms. Spellman-Diaz. Her parents realized that few African Americans perform in symphony orchestras. That's why they urged their daughters to play orchestral instruments, "to try to break barriers." Both her flute teachers were black, as was one of her three oboe teachers. Having African American teachers "made an impact and is partly why I play in the Imani Winds," a woodwind quintet of African American musicians.

priority for everybody, but if you really want to do it, you need to do it in the best possible way."

Pre-lesson discussions "set a tone that we're partners in this endeavor," says John McCarthy, a member of the San Francisco Conservatory piano faculty and former head of its preparatory division. "Some parents come in with stars in their eyes and a distorted sense of what the process is, expecting a magic pill or that I can turn their child into the next Lang Lang. I help parents understand that it's a different process from kid to kid, that children have their own personal response to music. I ask the parents to reflect on what kind of a teacher they would like and how they see their roles as parents. I have found that certain parenting and teaching styles are compatible and some aren't. There are parents that I think of as 'sculptor parents,' who are very goal oriented, very involved in directing the student, who are molding the kid, as with a pot of clay. Then there are 'gardener parents,' who are more inclined to allow the unfolding of whatever the child's innate appetites turn out to be. I tend to prefer the gardeners. These aren't original terms with me, but they help me understand the dynamic between child, parents, and myself."

"Some parents look at a teacher almost like a race horse, counting the number of competition winners in the teacher's studio," says Sandra Shapiro, dean of the Cleveland Institute of Music's preparatory program and a music mom herself. "For a beginner, a teacher's competition record shouldn't be a factor. You want a teacher who is going to develop the complete musician, provide a solid foundation, and who has an educational philosophy aligned with the parents' so the parents and teacher can form a team."

Teacher Switching

After a while, a child's first music teacher may suggest, as Jennifer Koh's did, that it's time to move on to a teacher who can provide more advanced training. Having the teacher suggest the change makes the transition easier. It can be more difficult if the parent or the child decides to switch, as Shirley Bell discovered. She had been happy with the first violin teacher her son Josh had been studying with since he was four years old. But when he was eight, Ms. Bell attended a concert that made her wonder whether Josh's teacher was really giving him the best instruction. At that concert, a famous violin teacher from Chicago brought her young students to perform in Bloomington, Indiana, where the Bells lived. "There was an eight-year-old girl playing exactly what Josh was playing, but playing it beautifully, so much better, with perfect positioning," recalls Ms. Bell. "I thought maybe Josh needs to be in a more structured program like these children. Everything was going too fast for him, too easy. Something was amiss in Josh's playing. I met with Mimi Zweig, a new violin teacher who had come to Bloomington and would run a wonderful string program for kids at the university. I had Josh play for her. She said if he's going to study with her, they had to go back to basics, correct things that are wrong in how he's playing. No more performing for a while. I felt I needed to change teachers, to get him past this performing-little-kid thing. It was hard to tell the first teacher."

Indeed, the first teacher was upset. "I didn't have much contact with her for a while," recalls Ms. Bell. "But after Josh became well known, she would come to his concerts. He always credits her as being his first teacher. After he began studying with Mimi Zweig, he started sounding better. She worked on bow strokes, scales, and études. She was a different kind of teacher, not giving all the praise and compliments as the first teacher." The first teacher had been the nurturer—the second focused on improving his technique. At age twelve, he made another teacher change, but this switch was with the approval of Ms. Zweig.

Several of our parent advisors found themselves in the same situation as Shirley Bell. "I made that mistake with my first daughter," says Larry Scripp, a professor at New England Conservatory (NEC). "I never noticed that her piano teacher wasn't demanding enough of her home practice. I thought, 'Oh, he's great and supportive.' But she wasn't learning consistent fingering. I guessed maybe they don't need to learn fingering so early. I found out that wasn't a good idea when we changed to another teacher."

In situations where the first teacher was nurturing but a little weak on technique, most parents report that the next teacher was able to correct things. It's a tradeoff. Perhaps without an encouraging first teacher the child wouldn't have liked music. One way to monitor whether a child is receiving good instruction would be to involve the youngster in a youth ensemble or summer music camp. Teachers and conductors in those other settings may point out if there's a problem with the child's technique.

The need to switch teachers can occur at other times, not just at the beginning. "It's tempting to stay in a comfortable studio, but when the situation is too cozy, things begin to slip," says Karen Rile, a Philadelphia writer with four daughters who studied violin or viola. "It's important for developing musicians to receive multiple influences. If you find, after a few years, that your kids are at the top of their studio, it's time to switch studios. Your kid and the teacher can remain lifelong friends, but it's important for kids to be in a situation where there are other students who function at a level that your kids can aspire to."

"I've been to a lot of music lessons," notes Sarah Odhner, a Pennsylvania mother of six musical kids. "Some teachers are wonderful in the way they articulate what it is they want a child to do. But they all have their bag of tricks. After a while, if they get to the point of saying the same thing, it's time to look for someone else. Either the teacher has become too much of a friend or the kids need something to challenge them. Teachers have different types of teaching at which they excel."

Listen Up

"Listen to your kids," recommends Betsy McCarthy, who took a while to follow this advice herself. Her son's first piano teacher had been wonderful. "They clicked really well. She got him off to a great start for two years. Technically demanding, she also encouraged him to improvise and write music. It was very freeing and fit him exactly." When this teacher quit teaching, Ms. McCarthy looked for a replacement and chose a highly recommended teacher. "My son came home from the first lesson and says, 'She doesn't know what she's doing.' I thought, 'What do you know? You're nine.' So he kept going to lessons. He didn't practice much and was unhappy. After about six months, the teacher had a recital and I was appalled. The kids played terribly. He had been right. We switched to another teacher, also highly recommended, an old-school, classical teacher. He liked her, but they butted heads a lot because he was born to improvise. We realized jazz fit him better than classical."

So he switched again, just before entering Seattle's Roosevelt High School, which has an excellent jazz program. "We asked around and found a jazz teacher who is classically trained," says Ms. McCarthy. "They worked really hard the summer before high school to get him ready to try out for the school's jazz program, which he got into. My son did both classical and jazz with her. He likes classical now because it's not the only thing he does. I've learned to trust my son. He knows exactly what he wants to get out of his lessons." During high school, he began "to collect teachers. He had his main jazz teacher, then another he would see every other week, and a third he saw once in a while." Others parent advisors report that their teens also had a few secondary teachers they would meet with from time to time to help with various aspects of technique.

Switching Etiquette

"We have a policy in our school that we will not accept a student who is studying with another teacher in the school without that teacher's consent," says Ruth Cahn, head of the percussion department at Eastman's Community Music School. For a teacher change that doesn't occur within a music school, she advises, "If it's a private teacher that the child has studied with since age five but now that the child is in middle school, it's time for a change, the parents need to speak with the teacher. They could say, 'Studying with you has been a fabulous life experience for my child, but we think we need to move on.' Tell what you're looking for. Ask the teacher for some suggestions. I tell kids that when they move on, to remember that first teacher. Go back for a lesson now and then, show how you're playing. That can make it easier on a personal level for the student and for the teacher."

"I tried to be kind and grateful for all the good things we'd had from the first teacher," says Sarah Odhner, describing the transition her son Ben made from his first to his second violin teacher. "It was hard, but I felt my responsibility was to advocate for my child and meet his needs. The transition from the second to the third teacher went better." This change came about because of a competition in which Ben did well. He asked to have a lesson with one of the judges, a violinist in a nearby orchestra that Ben's regular teacher wanted to study with herself. So Ben would have a lesson with him once a month and his regular teacher would come, too. After about three months, it was clear that Ben wanted to study with the new teacher full time. The other teacher agreed to let him go. "I think she saw there were things she wanted to fix for Ben and hadn't been able to but that the new teacher could."

Martha Woodard's younger son, a teen drummer, handled a teacher switch on his own. After attending a jazz camp one summer near their Massachusetts home, her son realized he needed to learn more about jazz drumming because he had been studying with a rock drummer. "He was scared about finding a new teacher because he had a good relationship with the old teacher and didn't want to hurt his feelings," says Ms. Woodard. "So we talked it over, and he called up the old drum teacher and he said, 'I think I need to switch teachers, but I want to have another lesson with you.' They talked it over and the drum teacher, who is very professional, said it was fine. My son e-mailed the coach of his local jazz ensemble who came up with the name of a local teacher who could help him with jazz drumming."

The McCulloughs encouraged their son to sort out his difficulties with his cello teacher so that a switch wasn't needed. His high school schedule made it impossible to do all the practicing the teacher expected. "He wanted to talk to his teacher about this but asked if we'd come as backup," says Anne McCullough. "We went with him but he did the talking. He asked her to be more flexible. They worked out an arrangement that when he was pushed for time, he did less cello. When he had more time, he did more. He had one of his best years, probably because he took more ownership of his music and felt that he had more control."

Sitting In on Lessons—or Not

"Our biggest roles as music parents were to encourage and support their interests, not only financially but by taking an interest in what they were doing. When they started lessons, I sat in, not because I knew anything. I'm not a musician, but I enjoyed listening to what they were doing and watching the interaction between teacher and child," says Ann Turner, whose kids were ten and eleven when they started French horn and saxophone.

Sue Jones did something similar—going to her daughter Alice's flute lessons until Alice could drive herself there: "The teacher taught in her living room, and I sat in another part of the house but could hear the lesson. I'm glad I did that because it gave me an appreciation of the progress she was making and the talent she had. I honestly would not have realized that she was so talented if I hadn't been there."

Dr. Jeanny Park sat in on her kids' Suzuki piano lessons because that was part of the Suzuki method, but she also sat in during her son's first trumpet lessons. "I wanted to make sure the teacher was going to work out, to see what the teaching method would be, that my son was happy with it," she says. "After a while, I would sit outside the room at the music store where he took lessons. Even in the hallway, I could hear what was going on."

Non-Suzuki teachers often recommend that parents sit in during the first lessons to lay the basis for good communication between parent and teacher, an essential part of the triangular partnership of teacher-child-parent. "I've always

Jiji Goosby with her son Randall, age sixteen, after a recital at Juilliard Pre-College.

maintained an open door policy in my lessons unless I feel the parent is interfering. For beginners under age twelve, a parent should be there," says Cleveland Institute's Sandra Shapiro. "How long to continue depends on the maturity level of the child and the parent-child relationship. Some parents try to take control and that creates problems because then it's the parent who is teaching the child. The parent should be there as a support." Ruth Cahn adds, "If a parent wants to come to a lesson, they are welcome, but I ask the student if it's OK when the parent is not in earshot."

"When it's time for parents to stop coming, or not come all the time, I do a transition. I'll have them come for the last ten minutes and we talk about what we worked on, what the expectations are for this week, what sheet music to order. After they stop sitting in altogether, I stay in touch with parents behind the scenes, often via e-mail," says Rebecca Henry, head of the string department at Peabody Preparatory. Sandra Shapiro keeps in touch with parents of her older piano students by inviting them "to come to a lesson at the end of each semester so they can see the kinds of things we've been working on, goals we've been setting, so it's not some mystery behind a closed door."

However, some teachers, particularly those who specialize in older students, aren't keen on having parents at the lessons. "Once I had a situation where the dad was kind of manipulative and controlling and wanted to sit in on every lesson. He would tell the kid how to practice. That didn't work with me. So I said, 'I'm sorry, I don't really let parents sit in on lessons.' That father came around and saw that his fifteen-year-old was more mature than he thought," says William Wellborn, a member of the piano faculty at San Francisco Conservatory's Preparatory Division. "For a beginner, it's different, or a first lesson with an older student. But on a week-to-week basis with an older student, I don't like it because I want to develop a personal rapport with each student."

Injury Watch

"There's a lot of talk about playing without tension, but also a lot of pressure from some teachers to practice long hours," says Karen Rile. One of her four daughters greatly increased practice time on viola during high school and developed tendonitis so severe that it put an end to playing that instrument. "Not knowing anything about these issues when my kids were little, it never occurred to me that there could be a problem," observes Ms. Rile.

Several other of our parent advisors report that their kids developed muscle or tendon issues, too, but fortunately none were career ending. These difficulties often resulted from a sharp increase in practicing to help "cram" for an audition or a special performance. Serious, career-threatening injuries don't usually happen to "kids through the high school level because they usually aren't practicing enough yet to make such injuries happen," says Dr. Ralph Manchester, head of health services at the University of Rochester. However, it's smart for parents to know about potential problems that could develop later.

"I always worried about this," says Annette Radoff, mother of violinist Elena Urioste. "Especially when my daughter was very young, I read everything I could get my hands on—magazines, books, articles. Other parents were a great source of information, too. I made sure that my daughter did a lot of stretching and went to the community pool to swim as much as possible, both to be a kid and also to unknot everything. Once in a while when she was a teen, she would have sore muscles and would have deep tissue massage, which has been great. She has also been doing Bikram yoga."

Massage and taking breaks have also worked for violinist Anne Akiko Meyers. "I think every musician has experienced pain at one time or another. You take time off, read up about it," she says. "One plays better if you take time to rest your body, rest your mind. When I was younger, I was keeping the violin a little low so that my arm would have to support more of the weight. You learn to correct these things through experience and watching yourself play. Looking at videos of how you play can help."

Physical therapy plus some adjustments from private teachers made a big difference when Cindy Buhse's violist daughter developed a sore shoulder one time, and later on a sore wrist. "Physical therapy helped her understand her body better and know when to back off," says Ms. Buhse. "Her teachers showed what she had been doing wrong to help improve her technique."

For young people in rock bands, percussion ensembles, or other high-noise situations, parents should discuss with the teacher the value of using earplugs. "We recommend that kids wear earplugs. Some do and some don't," says School of Rock music director, Keith Fertwagner. "I wear earplugs when I'm rehearsing although I don't necessarily wear them when I perform. They take out certain frequencies that can be damaging to ears. They're not a hundred percent effective, but they help. You get used to them."

"The number one warning sign of a problem is if something hurts," says Cleveland Institute's Sandra Shapiro. "Playing music should never hurt—ever. If something hurts, kids should stop and take a break. If kids say their arms are tired, or their neck hurts, or with wind players that their mouths and jaws are sore or tired, take a break and then talk the problem over with the teacher at the next lesson. Also, if students are practicing more than an hour at a time—not good. They need to stop and take a break, do something else, and then come back. Your brain can handle only so much at one time. Practicing in spurts helps get more done." Pianist Jonathan Biss agrees, "When what you're doing during practice is truly rote, and you're no longer practicing with the specific intention of improving something, you should stop practicing. If it's mindless practicing, you're not going to get anywhere."

Ms. Shapiro recommends a special precaution to prevent sore muscles when a teacher has introduced a technical adjustment, such as a new finger position, a new bow hold for strings, or a change in mouth position for winds and brass. These changes involve youngsters using muscles in a new way. "The first few days, try the new technique for only five minutes," she says. "When that five minutes is over, that's it for the new technique for your hour of practice. If you take a break and practice for another hour, just five minutes for the new technique in the second hour, too. Make the transition slowly."

"I'm big on helping kids become self-observational as they play," says percussion teacher Ruth Cahn. "I constantly ask them, 'How does it feel?'" Some music schools offer courses that help students become aware of the physical side of their playing. Jennifer Roig-Francolí, an instructor at the University of Cincinnati's College-Conservatory of Music, teaches a course on Alexander Technique, which aims at lessening body tension. She offers an unusual suggestion: "One way to prevent overuse is to devote part of practice time to working *without* the instrument, mentally rehearsing something in your mind. You're still practicing, connecting your thoughts to your muscles so that when you pick up the instrument later, it's almost as if you had been practicing with the instrument."

Here are additional suggestions from Jennifer Roig-Francolí for signs that might indicate that a child is not playing in an injury-free manner:

- **Too fast:** "If a teacher is more interested in a child making rapid progress than in the child's overall well being."
- **Pushing:** "If the parent and/or teacher push the child to do something the child doesn't want to do, that will introduce a certain level of stress, which can lead to tension and possible injuries later."
- **Rigid:** "If any part of the body is rigid or fixed, even a part that seems to have little to do with playing the instrument, that's going to affect the rest of the body. If the knees are locked or feet are in odd positions, that can be a problem. Be on the lookout for postures that would look unnatural if the instrument were suddenly removed from the picture."

Special Needs—Special Planning

Finding a teacher who can be flexible in adjusting to a child's learning style is always important but especially so for kids with physical or learning issues. "The teacher and my daughter sort of made it up as they went along," says Charlsie Cartner, describing how her daughter, Catherine Getchell, blind from birth, learned to play trumpet at age ten. "When they started, he didn't know any more about doing this than Catherine knew about playing trumpet. He has a great sense of humor and that went a long way to making this work."

The teacher had been recommended by Catherine's piano teacher and used the same approach as the piano teacher—tape recording music for Catherine to listen to and play from memory. He worried that she might not learn good finger and mouth technique if she couldn't see what to do by watching him. "For his other students, he would use a mirror to show them what their embouchure [mouth position] looked like compared with what it should look like," explains Catherine Getchell. "He couldn't do that for me. I started lessons with him early enough so I hadn't developed any embouchure problems. I took lessons with him all through high school. At one point, I tried learning to read music in Braille, but it didn't work for me because I have to use both hands to play the instrument." In all the ensembles she has performed with, she has had to memorize the music she played, either by listening to recordings or having another trumpeter or her teacher record her part.

Enabling her to perform in school ensembles took a lot of preplanning. For high school marching band, she couldn't play and march at the same time because she needed to keep both hands on her trumpet, leaving no hand to handle her guide dog or to be led by a bandmate. It was important to find a solution because students who didn't play in marching band couldn't play in concert band. The band director agreed to let her stand on the field in an area called the "pit" with the marimba player and other musicians who didn't march. "If a kid really wants to participate, find a way," she says.

Careful planning is worth the time and effort, according to other parents of kids with special needs. "If you find the right music teacher, it can be so beneficial for kids who otherwise aren't doing well in school and may not think well of themselves," says the mother of a teen cellist with attention deficit disorder. "With my son, here's a kid who's not supposed to be able to focus, but he gets on stage and plays beautifully a five-minute cello piece he has memorized. His music teacher has been so much more accommodating than his regular school teachers in finding ways to help him learn."

A mother of a son with Asperger syndrome feels his success with piano helped him grow in self-confidence. His musical ability was evident from an early age, and the family was fortunate to find a community music school where teachers were eager to do whatever it took to make his classical and jazz piano lessons succeed. This required creative inventiveness on the part of the teachers, as well as a mother who sat in on lessons or out in the hallway for years. She would explain to teachers and staff that her son's meltdowns weren't behavior problems but part of the syndrome. The elementary school where he was mainstreamed "did a great job of using his strengths by having him play piano for assemblies so the other kids would see a child who clearly had academic weaknesses, but who excelled when he played piano," says his mother. He has gone on to earn bachelor's and master's degrees in music.

Whenever possible, Julie Novak tried to place students in mainstream situations when she was the music instructor at the Colorado School for the Deaf and Blind. She found that the teachers who were most likely to be successful with mainstreamed students "have high expectations, get students to do things for themselves, and think outside the box." These are terrific qualities for any teacher. Ms. Novak introduced Braille music to her visually impaired students during elementary school, earlier than Catherine Getchell tried it, and had success teaching it. "With deaf students, I focus on rhythmic skills, utilizing such teaching tools as movement, vibration, and visual cues. I taught a rock band unit for my middle school students, and they loved the vibration of the electric guitars, electric bass, and drums. Some people's brains are wired for music regardless of their hearing abilities. I have witnessed students with profound hearing loss enjoy music by whatever they can grasp from the vibration of the sounds. Deaf people have written their own music. The 'Gallaudet Fight Song' is a good example. It doesn't have a typical song framework, but students love it." (See Resources for a link to the song.)

The following strategies that parents and teachers used for special-needs youngsters could help others as well:

- **Prepare:** "Do as much as you can ahead of time to communicate with people who are going to work with your child as to what the issues are. Don't wait until the first lesson. I would print out articles on Asperger syndrome to give them beforehand. Also, become involved in the parent association. At first I didn't because when you have a child who's not the same as everyone else's, you feel like you might not have much in common. But they asked me to help with a festival, I had a great time and became involved. It made things go better at the school."—Mother of a pianist with Asperger syndrome.

- **Help with focus:** "When my son's cello teacher gives an instruction, he has my son repeat it back, which helps with his focus issues. I take notes during his lessons and type them up in bullet format so it's easier for him to follow. He has two lessons a week, instead of one, which also helps with focus. We came up with counting to ten or deep breathing as a way to help when he becomes frustrated. At home during practice, he jumps on a trampoline when he becomes frustrated, or I'll take the music book away and bring out our stash of fun music—*Star Wars, Harry Potter, Phantom of the Opera*—to remind him that we're doing this for fun."—Mother of a cellist with mild attention deficit disorder.

- **Specific:** "I am very specific with visually impaired students before performances, about where they'll stand, facial expression, taking a bow, what to wear, things other students learn from watching others but which our students have to be taught."—Julie Novak, formerly with the Colorado School for the Deaf and Blind.

- **Problem-solving:** "Use a problem-solving approach. If a school says no to participating in something, rather than demanding that your child has the right to participate, acknowledge the school's concerns and ask if you can address them together."—Catherine Getchell, Pennsylvania

- **Expectations:** "Have reasonable expectations, but don't be afraid to try new things. Children surprise you."—Charlsie Cartner, Virginia

SPOTLIGHT ON: ADRIAN ANANTAWAN, VIOLIN

No limits: Careful planning enabled Adrian Anantawan, born without a right hand, to start violin at age ten. His mother had a Toronto rehabilitation center build an adaptive device that let him use his right arm to move a bow across the violin. But the device wasn't ready when he started lessons. So his teacher had him spend two months learning to do pizzicato—plucking the strings. "I never got a sense there were things I couldn't do on violin because of my disability," he says. "I joined a youth orchestra the first year of lessons, before I could read music. It was one of the first ways I could participate in a group with other kids and feel I was really part of the group." After four years, he moved to another teacher and then went to Curtis. One summer during Curtis, he studied with Itzhak Perlman, another violinist who doesn't let physical limitations stand in his way. "We were making beautiful music. The disability was an afterthought," says Mr. Anantawan.

Cost Concerns

Music lessons are costly. Music schools may offer scholarships, many of which are need based. Some schools also offer merit scholarships. A few music schools have a two-tired fee schedule, charging less if the instructor is still a student or recent conservatory graduate. With independent teachers, some parents have bargained successfully to lower lesson fees or have opted for shorter lessons for their kids with a prorated fee reduction.

Several parents cut costs in another way by starting their children off with high school students. "When my son switched to bassoon in middle school, I got him lessons with a high school bassoon player. That was one of the best things we did. Kids relate better to high schoolers, who are good role models and they're cheaper," says Diane Cornelius. "After a while, the high schooler said she had taught him everything she could and told us to contact her own bassoon teacher, and my son started having lessons with him."

Another cost-saving strategy is to tap into the knowledge bank of a child's music teachers or youth orchestra officials to discover programs that offer low-cost or free lessons. That's how Toyin Spellman-Diaz's parents found out about the National Symphony Orchestra's Youth Fellowship Program for top high school musicians in the Washington area. It provides free lessons with a National Symphony musician. Other orchestras offer similar programs. Families in areas served by one of the new tuition-free El Sistema programs might see if there's any way their children could participate.

Musician parents sometimes teach their own children, both to give quality instruction and also perhaps as a money saver. This has its ups and downs. "I started playing piano when I was seven and my mother, a piano teacher, taught me for about the first five years," says New York Philharmonic bassist David Grossman. "She was a great teacher and taught me a lot, but at first I didn't want to practice. She made me have the discipline. At the time, I felt resentful, but now I'm glad she made me do it. But there came a point where we'd get into arguments during a lesson about why I didn't fold the laundry or do homework. It was clear that I needed an outside teacher." At age twelve, he began piano lessons at a New York music school and, while there, began lessons on the instrument that won his heart—double bass. He started on bass because the music school's orchestra needed a bass player. "There was also a scholarship there to learn bass. I tried bass and fell in love with it."

More Teacher-Search Strategies

- **Youth concerts and recitals:** "Go to concerts by other kids, see the kids who play well, and find out who their teachers are," says Kim Field, mother of two young string players and daughter of teacher Dorothy Kaplan Roffman. These could be youth orchestra concerts or concerts at local music schools. NEC professor Larry Scripp suggests that once you identify possible teachers, "Arrange to attend one of the teacher's recitals to see how the students play and how they seem to feel about what they're doing in relation to what the teacher is demanding of them." Follow up with a sample lesson.
- **Colleges and universities:** Cindi Russell found her daughter's first flute teacher by calling the flute professor at the state university near their Kentucky hometown. Her daughter studied first with one of the professor's students and later with the professor, until they had an artistic disagreement and she moved on to study with a graduate student at the conservatory in Cincinnati, a ninety-minute drive away. When that instructor graduated, her daughter studied with his teacher, the principal flutist of the Cincinnati Symphony Orchestra. Buzz Ballenger recommends trying community colleges, too, which "have a lot of good musicians who are adjunct teachers to earn a little extra money. We found they were also available to give lessons to kids."
- **Local orchestras:** Jiji Goosby found a flute teacher for her daughter by contacting the local symphony orchestra, one of whose flutists was glad to have a new student.

- **Patience:** By phoning around, France Couillard discovered who the best local double bass teacher was, but he didn't want to teach a ten-year-old beginner. So her daughter started with another teacher. Three years later, that teacher felt Lena needed to move on to more advanced training and put in a good word with the teacher who had turned the family down earlier. "By then Lena was thirteen. We met him. Lena played for him and from then on they have been working well together," says Ms. Couillard.

- **Competitions and summer programs:** Some youngsters found new teachers at summer music programs or even at competitions. It was at a competition that Dominique van de Stadt found an excellent teacher for her violist daughter. "I took to driving five hours each way two or three times a month so she could have lessons with him," she says.

- **Early start:** "If you want to begin lessons in the fall, start searching in the spring," says Ms. Odhner. "The most valued teachers have few vacancies. It may be too late to ask in the summer or fall."

SPOTLIGHT ON: SARAH CHANG, VIOLIN

Starting with Dad: "My father was my first violin teacher," says Sarah Chang, who started violin at age four. "A parent as a first teacher is OK, but it's not easy. You fight too much! For peace within the family and to lower the overall volume level in the household, it helps to have an outside teacher. My father gave me a great foundation and when I was six, he passed me on to his teacher, the late Dorothy DeLay, at Juilliard Pre-College. One or the other of my parents would drive me to New York from Philadelphia each Saturday to study with Ms. DeLay. Each student was assigned an assistant to work with, too. That was enough teachers. My dad took a back seat, but he would give advice when I asked."

Sarah Vautour in her fifth grade musical (top), at swim team practice holding the medal of an Olympic swimmer who visited her team, and at her high school senior recital.

6 On Singing

PARENTS OF YOUNG SINGERS deal with many of the same issues as parents of instrumentalists, but there are enough unique singing-related challenges to merit a separate chapter. One of our parent advisors starts this chapter by describing a major decision that young singers—and their parents—face during a singing-focused musical journey.

"My daughter Sarah loved to sing early on and was very dramatic about it. She sang in the children's choir at church and in the chorus at school. She auditioned for every solo she could get," says Laura Vautour. At the end of fifth grade, Sarah had the lead in a musical at her suburban Atlanta school and began voice lessons with the school's chorus teacher. But the summer after ninth grade, this young teen came to a fork in the musical road and had to decide which way to go.

That summer, she went to a musical-theater camp that gives kids a chance to polish Broadway-type song-and-dance skills. Great fun for lots of kids but not for Sarah. "It was the most miserable experience of her life," reports her mom. "Up until then she had been trying to do musicals and use the lower range of her voice." The lower register is what's often used for belting out Broadway showstoppers, but belting didn't seem to suit Sarah. "After she got into the program, she thought, 'What am I doing here?' The last day of the camp, agents come and give kids feedback. The agents told

Sarah that she had a legitimate soprano voice and that she would be doing herself a disservice if she didn't pursue that. That got her thinking that maybe she didn't want to do Broadway after all, with all that belting."

So Sarah switched to a teacher who had a degree in classical singing from a conservatory. "Sarah's voice improved tremendously when she started working with this new teacher," says Ms. Vautour. "They worked on songs that were appropriate for her type of voice. The teacher was very tuned into not straining the voice." Sarah continued to sing in choruses through high school, was in a school musical in tenth grade, and performed in a concert version of *Les Misérables* with her high school choir, but otherwise, she concentrated on classical repertoire. During her senior year of high school, she changed teachers again, after finding one who could help fine-tune her technique and prepare her for college auditions.

Having a chance to try out two of the main paths that singers can take—and to explore the differences in vocal production and instruction that each path involves—let Laura Vautour's daughter discover which kind of singing seemed right for her. Sorting out which genre to pursue is just one of the dilemmas faced by singers and their parents. There's also a debate about when young people should begin voice lessons and what they should study. This chapter lays out different sides on those issues and offers guidance from parents, pros, and educators on how to nurture and safeguard young voices.

The Anatomy of the Voice Lesson Debate

For many years, most voice teachers recommended that kids wait until age thirteen or fourteen to start private singing lessons. Recently, some teachers have taken the opposite view, maintaining that younger children can safely begin one-on-one vocal instruction. The divide occurs partly along stylistic lines. Both sides base their rationales on anatomy. To help parents with some of the lingo that crops up in this debate, here is a brief overview of vocal anatomy as it relates to children, followed by two sections of this chapter that present each side of the debate.

The sound-producing structures in a person's throat—the larynx and the vocal folds (the technical term for vocal cords)—usually don't develop fully until the early teens, after youngsters have passed through puberty. Overloading the vocal mechanism is bad news anytime but can be especially dangerous before it's fully developed or while it undergoes a marked growth spurt. For both boys and girls, the larynx and vocal folds increase in size during puberty, causing young voices to go a little haywire for a while, with boys' voices cracking and girls' voices becoming overly breathy. No matter when voice lessons begin, it's important to be sure that the voice teacher has studied vocal anatomy and knows a lot more about it than what has been provided in this brief overview.

Late-Start Advocates

Many teachers and music schools that focus on classical singing have traditionally preferred that young people not start private singing lessons until their early teens, recommending instead that younger children join a good children's choir or other choral group. That will allow the youngsters to have fun singing with others and learn some of the basics of good singing without overstressing their voices with too much solo performing.

These educators want to wait until youngsters have gone through puberty and their delicate vocal structures have settled down before teaching them the complex techniques that will allow them to produce a rich, classical sound. The ultimate goal for operatic performers and for many other classical singers is to create a sound that is so full and well-rounded, so rich with overtones, that it can be heard all the way to the last row of a concert hall without the singer having to shout or use a microphone. The whole body becomes a kind of resonator. Of course, when teens begin learning these techniques, they aren't expected to do that kind of self-amplification right away, but that's what they'll be working toward in private lessons.

It is possible for young children to imitate the full-bodied sound of an adult opera star, but to do so can put so much stress on the immature vocal system that lasting damage may occur, which could be career ending. A young child's natural singing voice tends to be light, airy, and thin—or as it's called in vocal-music jargon, "a light head voice." Trying to produce a fuller, bolder sound too soon can be risky. "The voice of an eleven-year-old isn't meant to do that," observes Allen Henderson, executive director of the National Association of Teachers of Singing. He cites the example of a celebrated young singer of a decade or so earlier who "hit it big when she was about eleven, sounding like a thirty-year-old opera soprano. You don't hear about her anymore." That's another reason classical teachers urge children to wait, to protect them from a misinformed coach or teacher.

The nature of the songs in the classical repertoire presents another reason that classically oriented voice teachers advocate a later start for private lessons. As Allen Henderson notes, students need a certain level of "maturity to work on that kind of music." Agreeing with that assessment is Elysabeth Muscat, director of the voice program at Peabody's preparatory division. "We start students at age thirteen because we're not teaching kids pop songs or musical-theater songs," she explains. "We're working on preprofessional repertoire of classical music and foreign language art songs in order to prepare students for college auditions. Many young children just aren't interested in that kind of music or in trying to understand the poetry in the songs or the foreign language diction. Even teenagers find it quite challenging. For younger children, we have a group children's class and chorus with appropriate repertoire for kids." As is typical of music-school choruses, Peabody's Children's Chorus includes youngsters from age six through high school, grouped in age-level ensembles.

Early-Start Advocates

Educators who endorse an early start for individual voice lessons tend to have more of a pop or musical-theater focus, although some classically oriented teachers support early instruction in certain situations. Pop singing might seem a safer choice for young voices because it doesn't require a singer to learn the complex techniques that are needed to produce the big, self-amplified sound of an opera star. Pop singers generally sing directly into a microphone, often in a conversational volume level, except when belting. Many musical-theater productions also use microphones. But because belting out heartfelt lyrics is such an integral part of pop and Broadway singing, these styles can pose risks for young voices. Belting out a tune without proper instruction or attempting to imitate the rough-edged, raspy growls and wails of a pop star can be tough on anyone's voice, especially a child's.

However, some teachers have come up with ways to work with young children, claiming to have figured out how to teach kids to sing pop tunes and other nonoperatic repertoire—and even how to belt safely—without overstressing a child's voice. They say that by understanding how a child's immature larynx and vocal folds work, they can design age-appropriate exercises and serve as vigilant guides to make sure there's no vocal damage.

"If a kid has been singing along with recordings by Miley Cyrus, Britney Spears, or Katy Perry, trying to copy an adult sound, the child may be doing things that are detrimental to her vocal health. This is where a voice teacher can be helpful," says Robert Edwin, a New Jersey singing teacher who specializes in teaching young children, many of whom work professionally in musical theater. "Kids can sing these popular songs safely, but they have to sing them with a child's voice. If children sing with a balanced sound appropriate for their system, their instrument is not going to fail them. But if their vocal folds are being asked to produce more sound or vibrations than they're capable of, that can cause an overload." Overloads can lead to vocal stress or, in some cases, damage that may need to be checked by a speech pathologist or doctor.

"If kids are only in a choral environment, they don't get one-on-one attention," explains Barbara Wilson Arboleda, another advocate of early voice lessons. This Massachusetts speech pathologist and singing teacher works with children who sing mainly for fun or to be in school musicals. "I see students who come in at age fifteen who have entrenched habits that are hard to get rid of." For children who want to do pop or Broadway-type singing, Ms. Arboleda feels that they need to work with a teacher who understands both the anatomy and how to do that type of singing. "You use the vocal mechanism differently for pop and rock than for classical. More teachers are becoming interested in learning how to do this, but it's still very new." She and Mr. Edwin have produced a video about their methods for young kids. (See Resources.)

The Middle View

Bridget Steele, head of the singing program at Pittsburgh's City Music Center, is classically trained and classically focused, but she has begun to provide early voice instruction for certain students. Ms. Steele recalls that when she began teaching at City Music Center, "It had a rule that the earliest students could start private lessons was in ninth grade. I'm a big believer in being careful about the developing young voice, but I've found that as with sports and everything else, kids are starting to do things younger. If parents call and ask for voice lessons for their seventh grader and you turn them away, they'll find someone else. The other reason for starting kids on lessons a little younger is they do musicals now in junior high. They want to audition." She has started offering voice lessons to preteens, while also encouraging them to join the school's choral groups. "I decide on a child-by-child basis. I don't have them do heavy music. We do

One of the ensembles of the Young People's Chorus of New York City.

light, classical French and Italian art songs and some musical songs. We steer clear of opera. For recitals, I have each student do one classical piece, one musical-theater piece, and one piece they sing with someone else so they learn to sing harmony."

"I fall somewhere in the middle of the great debate," says Robyn Lana, artistic director of the Cincinnati Children's Choir, whose members range in age from first grade through high school, grouped by skill and age into different ensembles. "If a teacher understands the young, unchanged voice, I'm all for starting children young, because good singing is good singing. There are many elemental things that can be taught to a young singer that can then transfer after puberty to a changed voice. I probably disagree with starting young children on musical-theater pieces or any repertoire that is too demanding and could do damage. But if the teacher understands that and is concerned with the child's long-term vocal health, there's no age that's too early to start, as long as the child has the right attention span." She notes, however, that many young children may not be ready cognitively for intensive one-on-one voice training. "In our choir, we do basic voice training—how to breathe, pronounce the vowels, sing musically—as part of an educational process that can work into a solo voice down the road."

Common Ground

So where does that leave the confused parent of a young would-be singer? It can help to know that not taking private voice lessons until the teen years worked out fine for many professional singers, including our pro advisors. Broadway star Kelli O'Hara was fourteen years old when she started private voice lessons in her Oklahoma hometown. Metropolitan Opera star Stephanie Blythe began singing lessons in high school in a group setting, taught by the school's choral director. She didn't see her first opera until she was sixteen, when her upstate New York high school took a field trip to New York City to attend a performance of *La Bohème* at the Met. Tenor Lawrence Brownlee, who also performs at the Met as well as at other opera houses around the world, was eighteen when he began private singing lessons.

However, all three of these pros knew a lot about music before their first singing lessons. They had been having fun singing in choirs or other ensembles. They also knew how to read music because they had been playing piano and other instruments.

Choral singing and playing instruments—these are two activities that both sides of the voice-lesson debate agree are terrific for young would-be singers whether they're taking private voice lessons or not. These areas of common agreement are discussed in the next two sections. Following that are tips from our parent and educator advisors on how to choose a good singing teacher at whatever age lessons begin. Educators also share warning signs that can help parents notice when a child might not be singing in a voice-healthy way.

Several ensembles of the Young People's Chorus of New York City in concert.

The Choral Advantage

"There is nothing better than choral singing when it comes to really learning how to make music, how to blend and be part of the whole, how to listen," says Broadway star Kelli O'Hara. "I was singing in church choirs from the time I was about ten. We also had music class in school, and I can remember being in an elementary school production as a kindergartner singing 'Good Ship Lollipop' with my class. My love of choral singing started in junior high, when I joined the school honors choir. I miss that kind of singing." She now usually sings showstoppers in *front* of the chorus of Broadway shows.

"I began singing in junior high when I started a barbershop quartet with three friends," says opera singer Stephanie Blythe. "But I didn't start singing every day until I went to high school and joined the mixed chorus. I sang because it was fun, a great group activity. Choral singing helps children develop musically. It teaches a student to be responsible to the group, to excel not only for yourself, but because good work makes the whole ensemble sound wonderful. There's a sense of satisfaction that comes when the group does well, much the same as a sports team feels after a game."

"For a young child, the payoff is performing," says Elizabeth Núñez, assistant conductor of the Young People's Chorus of New York City, whose singers range from age seven through high school. "A big motivator for youngsters singing in choirs is that the performance is so much stronger than if just one seven-year-old is singing alone."

Nearly all the young singers of our parent advisors sang in a children's choral group. This was true both for those who started private instruction early and those who waited until their teens. Many kept on with choral singing even after starting private lessons. Some youth choirs go on tour and perform in major concert halls, an incentive for staying involved.

Choral singing usually doesn't stress a child's voice, if the chorus is led by a skillful choral director. The blending of many voices together creates a sound that is big enough for an audience to hear, rather than requiring each child to produce a sound that will carry far. "A lot of choir directors have a rule, 'Never louder than beautiful,'" explains soprano Stephanie Meyer, who taught voice at the University of Missouri at Kansas City.

In choosing a choir for a young child, parents should speak with the choral directors to learn how they teach good singing and safeguard the young, developing voice. For an idea of what a parent might expect to find in a good choir, here's how Elizabeth Núñez describes what happens in her organization's choirs for her youngest singers. "We work on vocal technique from day one—sitting up straight, using breath in the proper way, singing beautifully and correctly," she says. "We also have children learn to read music from day one. We have a number of games we play the first few weeks, getting them to learn how to read a score." To make sure children are singing correctly, "at each rehearsal, especially with our younger divisions, we have about twenty children sing an eight-measure passage by themselves. We give a quick assessment right there of what they are doing well and how they could do it better."

Choral groups like hers often sing a wide range of music—classical, jazz, Broadway, folk tunes, and world music. "Good technique can be transferred through different genres. It's the articulation or vowel formation that changes," says Ms. Núñez. When her choir members hit their teens, she says, "We encourage our older students to study privately if they can." Twice a year, the chorus gives its older singers weekly private lessons for six weeks and keeps a list of local teachers parents can contact for additional lessons.

There's another kind of chorus that children can join if there's an opera company nearby—the children's chorus needed in many operas. "A lot of my colleagues who sing opera were in an opera children's chorus when they were little," says Brian Zeger, artistic director of Juilliard's vocal arts program. "They were able to learn the opera stories and see how opera singers sing."

Choral singing actually led tenor Lawrence Brownlee to his opera career. From an early age, he had been singing in the children's choir at the church where his father was the choir director and his mother sang solos. He also sang in school choruses from elementary school through high school. By tenth grade, he had won a spot in the all-city choir in his hometown of Youngstown, Ohio. That year, the director of music for the district was forming a different ensemble, a special show choir of twelve students from various area high schools. "My high school choir teacher suggested I try out," says Mr. Brownlee. Winning a spot

Lawrence Brownlee

Shy soloist: "My father made me sing solos in church choir, and I hated it. Who knew that he was preparing me to have a solo singing career? I was one of six kids. My father directed the church choir and had us all sing," says opera star Lawrence Brownlee, who also played trumpet and other instruments. "Music was in my head all the time. My father encouraged me, provided lessons in all the instruments I played. Whatever interest I had, he made it possible. But he'd say, 'I want you to sing this solo.' He was pushing me in a way that was supportive. I sang in school choirs, too. Singing in a group was OK. I could hide in the group. But I was shy about solos. Then in high school, friends told me, 'If you sing, the girls will think you're cute.' So I began to sing solos. I began to get some response from the girls. That's when I became less shy about singing."

in that show choir changed everything. "They gave voice lessons as part of the show choir, and in one of the workshops someone said, 'You have a real gift to sing classical music.' If it hadn't been for that, I might not be singing classical music today," recalls Mr. Brownlee. That led him to enroll in a program for gifted music students at Youngstown State University. A year later, he transferred to the vocal music program at Anderson University, where he saw his first opera and performed in one for the first time, as Tamino in *The Magic Flute*.

"In choir as a child, it was all natural singing, what came naturally," he says. "But 'natural' doesn't necessarily mean proper. In college, I started classical training and learned a different way to use my voice. It is such an involved process, very technical, a lot of things to think about." But he says the gospel singing he did as a child in church choir helped ease the way for some aspects of the opera repertoire. Gospel singing often involves "mellismatic" singing, a free-form, swooping style in which the singer sings one syllable while moving between several notes. It's similar to the vocal embellishment in classical coloratura singing. "You need a supple kind of singing to sing coloratura, which I do quite a bit now. It was helpful to have had the freedom to do that as a child."

The Instrument Advantage

Also helpful in preparing Lawrence Brownlee for serious voice training was the fact that he already knew how to read music from the many instruments he played as a child. "In school I played trumpet, in church I played drums, in junior high I added baritone horn, and I took piano lessons for a while," says Mr. Brownlee. "Music was all around me. Playing instruments and understanding music theory helps you as a singer in so many ways." Wind instruments can be particularly useful to singers in helping them develop breath control. Stephanie Blythe played two wind instruments in her school concert bands—flute and baritone sax. Kelli O'Hara was in the woodwind section of her school bands as a clarinetist.

"I started very early with piano lessons," says Ms. O'Hara, who in addition to doing Broadway shows also gives song recitals. "One of my biggest regrets is not sticking with piano longer. I could now accompany myself if I had." Voice teacher Jill Dew feels that having good piano skills can help a singer artistically. "When you're learning a new Broadway or opera song, if you can play the piano, you can play the song for yourself and learn it without always having to use a recording of someone else singing it. When you hear a recording, you're hearing the person's interpretation," says Ms. Dew, head of the voice division in the preparatory department of the University of Cincinnati's College-Conservatory of Music. By playing the tune on piano, singers can develop their own ideas for how to sing it before hearing someone else do it.

Instrumental experience can also make a singer a more well-rounded musician, something that Juilliard's Brian Zeger says may help during the college and conservatory admissions process. "We ask students auditioning for the vocal music program at Juilliard what instrument they play, whether they've been in an orchestra, if they like listening to all kinds of music," he explains. "We've found that part of the formula for students becoming mature singers with good skills is that they were around a lot of music growing up, have good ears, some music theory, and a broad base of musical skills."

Finding Voice Teachers

The basics of the voice-teacher search are similar to that described in chapter 5, with the same pros and cons coming into play in deciding whether to have an independent teacher or one connected with a music school. Two key advantages of going the music school route that are discussed in chapter 5 apply also to singing: the chance to perform in ensembles and take other kinds of music classes besides individual lessons. Among the classes a music school might offer that are especially useful for singers are sight singing—learning to sing a new piece just by reading the music—and also solfège, a kind of sight singing in which each note is sung using its musical name: do, re, me, etc. Music schools, of course, aren't the only places where students can work on sight singing and solfège; independent voice teachers and some children's choirs also teach these skills.

For Kristin Bond, living in a small Massachusetts town, the voice-teacher search was challenging. "We didn't know anyone whose children had ever studied voice privately," she says. The need for a voice teacher crept up on them by surprise. What started as a fun hobby for her older daughter—singing in church choir and middle school chorus—gradually became more serious after she joined a regional youth choir in ninth grade. Then she attended a summer vocal music program at a nearby university and decided she wanted singing to be "her life's work." Ms. Bond asked around for teacher recommendations, but she rejected some possibilities because her daughter "didn't have much interest in musical theater. She wanted to sing classical. She ended up taking lessons with the conductor of the regional choir," says Ms. Bond.

If the goal is to find a voice teacher skilled in teaching young children, the search can be especially tough. "There are many voice teachers who are teaching younger kids nowadays and doing a good job of it, but parents are going to be limited by where they live. They may have a lot of choices, or very few, especially if they're in a rural area," says Allen Henderson of the National Association of Teachers of Singing. Community music schools may be a good place to start because they may not be as centered on classical music as the preparatory divisions of conservatories. However, Peabody's Elysabeth Muscat suggests that schools like hers might still be worth contacting because faculty members may "know of teachers who are more into pop or musical theater, or who work with young kids."

Another option is to persuade a teacher who usually teaches older students to take on younger pupils. "Voice teachers who truly understand the vocal anatomy can adapt their methods," says Ms. Arboleda. She warns, though, that if a youngster wants to learn how to belt, parents should make sure the teacher has had experience teaching belting.

Using a teacher who usually works with adults helped Buzz Ballenger find a teacher for his daughter when she was eight years old. By contacting the music department at his local California community college, he found a piano teacher who was also a jazz singer. She was willing to work on both piano and singing with his daughter. After a few years, this teacher explained that it was time for a new teacher because his daughter's voice was "tending classical," and she needed a teacher with classical training. The parents went back to the community college and found a classical teacher who worked with his daughter from age twelve until she entered Eastman for her bachelor's degree in vocal performance.

As noted in the last chapter, it's wise to interview teachers and arrange for a sample lesson before signing up for lessons. This is the plan Joe Bianchi followed when his eight-year-old daughter performed in a musical at a community theater, loved it, and wanted to do more. He searched online to find voice teachers near their home in

New Jersey, interviewed them, and had his daughter take some lessons before settling on the teacher who seemed right—Robert Edwin. Beth Norden found her way to Robert Edwin by asking for advice from parents whose children were performing at the same community theater as her six-year-old daughter.

"There are people out there who claim to be singing teachers but unfortunately shouldn't be," observes Mr. Bianchi. That's why Peabody's Elysabeth Muscat warns, "Check to see if the teacher is a member of the National Association for Teachers of Singing or is affiliated with a music school, or what training the teacher has." The website of the National Association for Teachers of Singing site has a searchable list of teachers. (See Resources.)

Once lessons begin, another piece of advice given earlier for instrumentalists applies to singers: For young beginners, it's smart for a parent to sit in on lessons for a while. "I have no musical background. So if I wasn't at the lesson and didn't know how he's teaching her, I'd have no way of helping her when she's practicing," says Mr. Bianchi. "The parent and vocal coach need to be on the same page to help the child."

Warning Signs of Vocal Stress

News reports about pop stars having surgery to repair vocal damage can add to the worries of a music parent. Classical singers sometimes need surgery, too, but their health issues don't make the same kinds of headlines as those of an Adele or a Keith Urban. Many of the pop stars who end up with vocal damage do so because of the financial pressure on them not to cancel performances. Most of their earnings come from concerts, not from selling albums. That may tempt them to violate a basic rule of healthy singing: Don't sing when your throat is so sore that your voice sounds hoarse, a sign of laryngitis.

Young people may also find it hard to cancel a performance if they have a bad sore throat, especially if they have the lead in the school musical or are supposed to perform in an important recital or competition. Not all sore throats mean laryngitis, but if a sore throat causes "hoarseness in the speaking voice, or if they go to sing a phrase and there's cracking and the voice turns on and off unpredictably, or they can't sing something high and light like 'Happy Birthday' without cracking, then chances are they shouldn't sing that day," says Barbara Wilson Arboleda. "It's disappointing, but there's no reason to put yourself at risk for that level of performance. Recitals, solos in a choral concert, and school musicals are not worth singing when you're sick. Maybe for a high stakes performance like the *American Idol* finals, but not for the school play."

Hoarseness is a red flag for any singer, whether it's accompanied by a sore throat or not. If the speaking voice becomes hoarse after singing, "That's a warning that there's a problem with how the singing voice is being used," says Mary McDonald Klimek, a singing teacher and a speech and language pathologist who has helped a number of top stars with their rehab regimens after vocal surgery. "The voice is very resilient, but it's fragile, too," notes tenor Lawrence Brownlee. "It can take a lot, but you also need to be careful."

Here are other warning signs that could prompt parents and kids to check with the voice teacher or choral director to see if the youngster's vocal technique needs adjusting:

- **Pain:** "Watch for any pain or loss of voice," says Peabody's Elysabeth Muscat. Ms. Arboleda agrees, "It's a sign that something has overfatigued or been compressed. If that happens on a regular basis, it's something to be concerned about."

- **Overactive muscles:** "Watch the child sing. Do you see a lot of muscle activity on the outside of the throat? If so, have a discussion with the teacher. The muscles that you use for singing are inside the throat. Those other muscles, you don't need to use," says Jill Dew. "The goal is effortless singing. Do they look comfortable or are they struggling?"

- **Raised shoulders:** "When they breathe, do they move their shoulders? A good teacher will have the student breathe so the top half of the body never has to move. When you take a breath and the shoulders don't move, the neck is relaxed. That's what you want," adds Ms. Dew. "If they have good posture, they'll have a more beautiful, freer sound. I try to have students practice with a full-length mirror so they can watch themselves and see what their bodies are doing. Your whole body is your instrument."

- **Raised chins:** "If they extend their chins up, that's not good, as in the old Charlie Brown cartoons which had the Peanuts characters holding their little heads up to sing," says choral director Elizabeth Núñez. "If a kid is reaching up like that, the throat is tense and stretched. It's an indication that they're pushing."

- **Losing notes:** "They should be gaining notes, not losing notes, or at least staying the same. If their range is growing less, either from the top or bottom, that's a concern," says Juilliard's Brian Zeger. "There's no reason someone should lose a note, other than boys going through puberty."

- **Overly breathy:** "If it takes an enormous amount of breath to sustain a tone or if the voice sounds raspy or overly breathy, there may be swelling," says opera singer Stephanie Blythe. "Healthy singing is a well-supported, easy tone."

- **Tired voice:** "If a child comes out of a singing lesson with a tired voice, that's another warning sign. After a productive, voice-training session, a singer should come out feeling energized, wanting to keep on singing," adds Ms. Klimek. "If it sounds like your kid is screaming and not singing, he or she probably is and shouldn't be. Sometimes young singers dismiss discomfort—even pain—as something to be expected since others are feeling it, too. Singing should never hurt."

- **Straining:** "If a child is considering trying out for a show like *Annie* and can't sing the high notes, they're putting themselves at risk," says Ms. Arboleda. "Young kids believe anything is possible. That's one of the great things about working with kids. But they also believe they can sing anything they hear. For a nonprofessional kid who wants to sing a song like 'Tomorrow' from *Annie,* it's easy to find a version of the song that's transposed down low enough." But in order to sing the song as high as it's actually written, Ms. Arboleda says a youngster needs to be able to sing the highest notes without straining or screeching.

Switching Up

Mastering the technique of singing, particularly classical singing, deals with manipulating things in the throat and mouth that a singer can't see or really even feel. The learning process unfolds gradually. Several kids of our parent advisors learned the basics with one teacher and then moved on to another who delved into more advanced aspects of vocal technique.

Laura Vautour's daughter met technique-boosting teachers at Tanglewood's summer program for high school musicians, which she attended after her junior year in high school. Even though she was a capable singer—good enough to be admitted to that program—she discovered how much more there was to learn. "The teachers at Tanglewood worked with Sarah in a very technical way, giving her detailed instruction on what to do with her voice," says Ms. Vautour. "When she came home, she wanted a teacher who would be very technical, would give specific advice, pick her technique apart, work with her on her repertoire. Her regular teacher here at home was warm and nurturing, but after Tanglewood, Sarah's needs changed. She found that she could learn really well with detailed, technical instruction." By chance, one of the teachers she had worked with at Tanglewood was moving to Georgia that fall to be choral director at a performing arts high school near the Vautours. She became Sarah's new teacher. "The change in her singing was dramatic," says Ms. Vautour. "The other teacher was upset when we changed teachers, but in the end, it worked out and we stay in touch still. She was an integral part of Sarah's development, and Sarah is so grateful to have worked with her."

A summer music program provided a similar benefit for Susan Raab's son, who had been doing musicals since elementary school at community theaters and also in school, but he didn't have voice lessons until middle school. During the summer after junior year at his suburban New York high school, he attended a musical-theater program at New York University (NYU), where he worked with teachers who introduced him to tension-free singing. "Before then, I put a lot of pressure on my voice and tried to force it to make what I thought was a bigger sound. That started me down a path of tension," explains Jeff Raab. The NYU teachers gave him a different way to think about singing. "The body and your natural voice are going to work for you. If you learn to get out of their way and breathe comfortably, it becomes easier to sing," he says. During his senior year at high school, he had lessons with one of the NYU teachers, who helped him handle a demanding role in his high school's musical. "It was a hard role to sing—very high, with a lot of rock belting. I was able to get through it without destroying my voice thanks to this teacher," he explains. That led him to apply to NYU, where he earned his bachelor of music degree.

Juli Elliot's daughter, Corinne, also found a new teacher during her last years of high school. Her new instructor was a young singer, Jamie Jordan, who had just started teaching at Corinne's performance arts high school and who introduced Corinne to different aspects of vocal technique than her regular voice teacher. Corinne took lessons with the new teacher and with the regular teacher, too. "There was a nice connection between the two teachers. They were tending to different things," says Ms. Elliot.

Cross-Genre Singing

Versatility is highly valued in the music world these days, as will be noted also in later chapters. Vocal-style flexibility can be especially important for singers. It has been an essential element in the successful career of Kelli O'Hara, who sings a range of styles from classically lyrical to rambunctious Broadway showstoppers. "Every type of singing I did as a teenager led me to this point. There was a lesson in all of it," says Ms. O'Hara. "It taught me to work in an ensemble, to melt away some of my fears, and to learn different genres of music." As a youngster, she sang in her church choir, in the high school honor choir, and in high school musicals. She went to summer music camps and took private lessons in classical repertoire, while also going to dance class.

"My sister and I loved to sing together, doing country duets, like the Judds," she adds. "I didn't care where I sang. I just wanted to sing."

That attitude was reinforced when she became a vocal performance and opera major at Oklahoma City University, where she studied with Florence Birdwell, who specializes in training singers to handle both musical-theater and opera styles. Kristin Chenoweth, another versatile Broadway singer, also studied with Professor Birdwell. "Ms. Birdwell says that as long as the voice has the right technical foundation, it can be used for any genre, just as an instrument can be used in different genres, depending on the abilities of the musician," explains Ms. O'Hara. "Ms. Birdwell calls her technique Speaking on Pitch. It is the sentiment that counts, not the genre. Communication is communication, and as long as we are clear, a message can be heard."

Opera singer Stephanie Blythe also feels that a well-trained singer can handle a range of styles. "I sing many styles of music and have always done so," says Ms. Blythe, who played the lead in *Hello, Dolly!* at her high school. "I change the style, not the technique. An easy, supported tone allows for all sorts of fun styles." During her professional career, in addition to singing dramatic opera roles, Ms. Blythe has also performed in concert versions of Broadway musicals and has given recitals featuring Cole Porter tunes and Kate Smith's 1940s pop hits.

A number of college programs teach singers how to slip between genres. Parents who want to introduce the idea of versatility to youngsters might encourage them to explore different kinds of singing groups, as Buzz Ballenger's daughter did during high school. She performed in musicals and light operas with local theater groups, sang with a community jazz choir, was in her school chorus, and took classical singing lessons.

Kelli O'Hara

However, Kelli O'Hara notes that to succeed in having a cross-genre career requires "a lot of work earning trust within different musical worlds, as well as keeping certain aspects of the voice in shape." She spoofs the difficulties of having a cross-genre career in a zany song on her *Always* CD: "They Don't Let You in the Opera (If You're a Country Star)." What encouraged her to carve out her own special kind of musical career was advice she received from Mark Madama, director of Music Theatre of Wichita. "He told me that there is only one *me* out there. So that is my best selling tool. No matter what paths others take, I will have only my path," says Ms. O'Hara. "As a beginning artist looking at an entire world of competition in front of me, it meant the difference between fear and self-confidence."

Delivering a Song

The focus on communication regardless of the style that Ms. O'Hara learned in college supports another piece of advice that our singing pros emphasize—the importance of youngsters finding their own way of singing a song rather than copying another's style. As Stephanie Blythe explains, "Singers need to take time to develop their own 'voice,' not just a sound, but a vocal persona, so when they sing, they truly have something to say in their own voice. This comes from lessons, practice, time, and thoughtful study of the text and music, not from trying to sound like a singer you admire. There are too many singers out there that sound exactly like the last phenomenon that came along."

Voice teacher Jill Dew works on this with her students, encouraging them to create what she calls "Your Own Little Opera for the Song," by creating their own back story for a song. She explains to her students, "The more detail you can come

A teenaged Stephanie Blythe playing the lead in her high school's production of *Hello, Dolly*.

SPOTLIGHT ON: KELLI O'HARA, SOPRANO

A gift: "I grew up watching movie musicals with my mom. Being from a small Oklahoma town, I didn't see live theater. These movies were my inspiration," says Broadway star Kelli O'Hara. "I don't think I ever imagined I could make singing a profession. No one I knew had done that. My parents always supported me, but they also had never known the arts as a viable career. Singing was looked upon as a gift, a fun part of me. I never burned out. As an adult, that has carried over. As long as I have other things in my life that are important to me—family, friends—singing will remain a privilege, a joy. It has always been one of the most important parts of who I am, but it's not *all* I am. My parents helped me know that. Let kids sing. Get out of their way and listen. Then encourage them to do other things as well. Life experiences feed singing."

up with makes the song more uniquely yours. Nobody will sing it the way you do. You'll know why you're singing it, where you're singing it, what's going on, whom you're singing it to." Soprano Stephanie Meyer, who uses this approach in her singing, notes, "The audience doesn't need to know that I'm singing about my ex-boyfriend. But if I'm being very honest in my singing, that's what the audience gets. And then it's about *their* ex-boyfriend."

Different Timelines

"Our daughter wants to be an opera singer and thinks she realizes it will be a long haul, but I don't think you really understand that until you get into it," says Laura Vautour. "There was no way that we could hold her back from doing something that she's talented enough to do. The summer programs that she got into gave us feedback that she has the talent to do this. We can't deprive her of trying for that dream. We're going to help her go for it."

"Classical singing is a fairly long road," acknowledges Juilliard's Brian Zeger, although he notes that opera isn't the only path for classical singers. Classical singers are also hired to sing with professional choirs and choral societies or to perform as soloists with those groups. Others perform as soloists with orchestras or specialize in performing contemporary classical music. Teaching is another option, as it is for all musicians.

Some classical singers don't launch a performance career until their late twenties or early thirties. "The human voice takes years to cook," says mezzo-soprano Stephanie Blythe. "The actual vocalism doesn't fully mature until the mid-thirties, so there's lots of time to spend learning languages and becoming a solid musician." That's what many classical singers do—polish their skills in graduate school. Others audition for special training programs run by major opera companies, as Stephanie Blythe did, who won a spot after college in the Metropolitan Opera's Young Artist Program. This training program, which Brian Zeger leads in addition to his Juilliard duties, offers young singers expert coaching and the chance to perform small roles at the Met. At age twenty-four, Ms. Blythe sang an offstage role in one production and landed her first major role at the Met at age twenty-seven. Lawrence Brownlee earned a master's degree and participated in training programs at two opera companies. Then he won the Metropolitan Opera Auditions at age twenty-eight and began performing with other opera companies but didn't perform his first major role at the Met until his mid-thirties.

"These training programs, which most opera companies have, are often launching pads for careers," says Mr. Zeger. "Some people in these programs have already had good professional opportunities but are setting aside time for final levels of polishing. Virtually all the big careers come through these training programs."

Even after starting a vocal career, training may continue. "I have a voice teacher that I work with frequently. We all do," says Lawrence Brownlee. "There are things that I call my Achilles heel, things that will give you problems your entire life. You want to check in with those things so they don't become blaring issues. It takes a good trainer, a good coach to help you use your voice most efficiently, and to show how to reach the high notes in the right way. It's also not just singing the high notes, but singing them in a way so it doesn't look like you're killing yourself but also doesn't sound too easy either. It's a fine line between showing that it has effort in it but also that you could sing a hundred of those high notes."

The path for other kinds of singers can be long, too. Kelli O'Hara spent time after college taking acting and dancing classes in New York City, along with voice lessons.

Stephanie Blythe

That enabled her to become a "triple threat"—a performer who can sing, dance, and act. She began winning roles in Broadway musicals at age twenty-four, but for several years those musicals didn't make it big. She was nearly thirty before landing a breakthrough role in a big hit, *The Light in the Piazza*. That led to leading roles in revivals of *Pajama Game* and *South Pacific*.

Teens who are interested in pop or Broadway careers may be tempted to skip college. For pop, educator Robert Edwin notes that there may be some rationale for hitting the road. "Pop music is ruled by kids," he says, although some colleges are now offering training programs in popular music. For musical theater, how-

SPOTLIGHT ON: STEPHANIE BLYTHE, MEZZO SOPRANO

A different lesson: "I went to college to become a music teacher, but after a year and a half, I became a writing major and earned a degree in English composition. That was one of the best things I could have done for my voice," says opera singer Stephanie Blythe. She earned her degree at the State University of New York at Potsdam, while also taking voice lessons at the university's Crane School of Music. "I took my time and got an education, which gave me something about which to sing. My nonmusic study made me more keen to sing because I had something I wanted to express and knew that singing was the way to express my thoughts. Studying how to write helped me understand how to organize my thoughts and gave me a way of studying poetry and prose that would help me connect to opera and song texts."

ever, he encourages students to go to one of the many colleges that offer strong musical-theater training. He says that an eighteen-year-old who skips college to head to New York City to audition for Broadway shows will be "competing against twenty-two- and twenty-four-years-olds who look like they're eighteen but have had four more years of voice, dance, and acting training. The odds of being successful at eighteen are slim. They're still slim at twenty-two but greater if you've had more training, are more mature, and more ready to go out there. Plus you have a college degree." That degree can be a big advantage if not enough breakthrough roles materialize. (See chapter 11 for more on college and career concerns.)

Professional flutist Paula Robison as a teenager, playing a piccolo at her childhood home in California.

7 Dealing with Time Issues in Practicing

THIS CHAPTER FOCUSES ON how often kids should practice, for how long, and ways to coax them into a regular practice habit without major battles. The chapter's opening vignette features professional flutist Paula Robison, who describes how her father handled these issues when she was a preteen and teenager.

Ms. Robison began playing flute at age eleven, after four years of not doing very well on piano. "Piano just wasn't the right instrument for me. My father used to say they would never have known that I had a musical gift by listening to me play piano," explains Ms. Robison. Her father, who loved music and was an amateur violist, thought perhaps flute, with its high singing sound, would be a better fit for his daughter, who always loved to sing. He was right. She started lessons in school on a flute lent to her by a family friend. "It was like I was made for it," she says.

"My parents could see that I blossomed on stage. I think they saw a possible life for me as a musician. My father was a writer and knew how important it is to hone your craft. When I was about twelve, my father said to me, 'If you want to be the best flutist you can possibly be, you must practice very hard.' He didn't want to be one of those parents who forces their children to practice because of their own hopes and dreams. So he said, 'We need to have an agreement. Do you want me to make you practice? This is something you must decide. There are going to be times when you won't feel like practicing. If we agree on certain hours for practice—from 4:00 to 6:00 p.m.—and you're not practicing, do you want me to say you have to practice?' I said, 'Yes.' We shook hands on it," recalls Ms. Robison.

"Then a day came, when I was thirteen or fourteen, when I was lounging around on the couch after school and he said, 'Paula, you said you wanted me to make you practice. So now you have to practice.' I was furious. I threw down my book and stomped up the stairs. I whirled around and shouted, 'Some day I'm going to thank you for this!' I don't actually remember this, but he used to love to tell this story. There were definitely times during junior high when I didn't really want to practice. At one point I changed my practice time to getting up at five o'clock in the morning to practice before school because that was the only time I had the energy to do the kind of practicing that I really needed to do. I was so tired when I got home from school. The passion for music was always there. The joy was there. He wanted to instill in me the discipline, the feeling of responsibility toward my art, that it was wonderful to be an artist, but that I also had to be a craftsperson and learn to play the instrument well. You can never express the music as the composer wrote it, along with whatever is in your heart, if you don't constantly practice your craft. I kept our agreement. I practiced every day. I thank my father every time I pick up the flute."

Many Routes to Regular Practice

As Paula Robison's father realized—and she came to accept—regular, daily practice is an important goal for a serious musician. But many kids, even those who love music, find that the daily work of practicing falls into the same category as homework, something they aren't always thrilled to tackle. They may have fun playing music and even like practicing much of the time, just not necessarily every day.

"It is absolutely as normal as the sun coming up each morning that children do not want to practice every day a hundred percent of the time," says Norma Meyer, piano teacher and mother to professional bass player Ranaan Meyer. Most of our educator advisors agree. "Even professional orchestra members and conservatory professors tell me, 'My child is reluctant to practice.' I tell them, 'That's normal,'" observes Larry Scripp, a music dad who is also a professor at New England Conservatory (NEC). Something else that's normal—teachers can tell during a lesson when a student hasn't practiced much. "You hear that there's been no progress on whatever piece is being worked on," says Carol Prochazka, former head of piano instruction at Peabody's preparatory division.

Our pro advisors didn't always want to practice every day when they were children either but eventually became regulars. So did many of the youngsters of our parent advisors. Their parents used different strategies to encourage the practice habit—from strict oversight to a more relaxed approach. These varied strategies undoubtedly reflect the parents' basic parenting styles. This book, with its anecdote-based research, is in no position to wade into the child-rearing debate, especially since there's no agreement on this topic among parenting experts. Instead, our advisors present a range of options.

As Carol Prochazka came to realize from her many years of piano teaching, a variety of approaches can work. "Parents need to devise ways that let music fit into the general system they've found to be successful in how they raise their children, how the parents usually motivate, how they usually reward," she observes. But, as she and others have discovered, a method that works for one child may not suit the youngster's brother or sister. Nor does one approach work over the whole course of a child's musical development. "There is absolutely no formula," notes NEC's Mark Churchill. "It's a step-by-step, trial-and-error process. Of course, you map out a plan, but it needs to be a very flexible plan."

"Practicing is always a challenge for kids," observes conductor and music parent Marin Alsop. "There will be good days and bad days. Understand that, be sympathetic, but also be consistent in expecting regular practice. However, don't mistake a lack of desire for practice as more than simply that." It doesn't necessarily mean a youngster has lost interest in music.

This chapter and the two that follow present practice ideas that our advisors found helpful. This chapter focuses on timing issues. The next chapter—chapter 8—discusses parental coaching and how to make practice seem like less of a chore. Chapter 9 presents coping strategies when cracks appear in the practice routine.

First Step: Understanding Why

No matter what approach is used to encourage regular practice, the task is easier if kids understand why it's important. A sports analogy can help. Musicians, like athletes, depend on having toned, flexible muscles that are ready for action. The muscle groups that singers and instrumentalists rely on aren't as big as those needed to ace a tennis serve or win a marathon, but without a regular workout, those tiny music-producing muscles in fingers, lips, face, and throat may not come through when needed.

"I tell my students they're like marathon runners and Olympic athletes who need to practice the same movement over and over," says Dana Myers, violinist, music mom, and violin teacher. "The repetition is needed to develop muscle memory. For example, with violin, after you practice making a shift enough times, it becomes a given. Your muscles know what to do to make the move without you having to think about it. It's like after you've walked up a flight of stairs enough times, you know automatically how high to raise your foot. Your body needs time to get the muscle memory by doing repetitions." To show her students how important Shin'ichi Suzuki thought practicing was, Ms. Myers explains that he said to practice only on days that you eat. Music mom Theresa Chong tells her kids that it's like brushing your teeth—you don't skip.

Some studies have shown that it takes a whole lot of practice (by some estimates 10,000 hours) over many years (ten years in some studies) to turn out not only a top-level musician but also expert performers in other fields, such as sports, chess, art, and writing. Books by Malcolm Gladwell, Daniel Levitin, Geoff Colvin, and Andrew Solomon (see Bibliography) describe several studies which can be used to support the idea of a 10,000-hour or ten-year rule. Often cited is a 1993 report of a research project that focused on students at a German conservatory. This study investigated the practice habits of violin students who were all in their early twenties, had been studying music for at least ten years, and had similar training. The top performers had put in about 2,000 more hours of solo practicing over their years of training than those in the middle skill level, and about 4,000 more hours than the least accomplished. The top students, who averaged more than two hours a day of practice, were also better practicers.

A 10,000-hour or ten-year rule probably won't make an impression on young, reluctant practicers but might catch the attention of older ones who dream of becoming musical stars. However, for many parents and children, the point of music study isn't to produce the world's next Yo-Yo Ma but just to have fun. For such families, logging in thousands of hours of practice may not seem like a goal worth pursuing. However, studies show that the more time invested in any activity leads to the development of more skills. More skill may yield more enjoyment, as youngsters know from personal experience with video games. "Our kids become expert at video gaming because they put in the hours," says Marin Alsop. "Redirecting some of those video hours into mastering an instrument will give them a lifetime of possibility, not just sore thumbs."

Getting to Regular

Practicing every day is the ideal, but for some parents, it's a goal rather than a mandate, especially in the early years. They focus on helping children get into the habit of practicing rather than insisting it be done every day. "I believe in practicing each day, but I'm not strict in the sense of practice or else," says Melissa Tucker, an instructor at the Longy School of Music and mother of a teen flutist. "I tried to help her develop the habit of playing a little every day. When she was young, she had fun making a practice chart and put stickers on it for each day she practiced. If she practiced five days out of the week, that was good enough. After a while she didn't need to put the stickers on the chart. She just practiced for herself. She got in a routine." Some teachers, including piano teacher Carol Prochazka, accept the fact that everyday practicing might not happen for beginners or for older students who are doing music as a hobby. She was fine with five days a week.

But many parents, especially those with children in Suzuki programs, try to achieve daily practice right from the start. "There was always the expectation in our family that they were going to practice every day, but I never got into a combative, forced relationship with my kids over practice," says Sarah Odhner, the Pennsylvania mother of several Suzuki kids. "It was a matter of saying to them, 'When do you want to do it?'"

Some parents take a more assertive stance. "I pretty much made my kids practice every day at first," says Dr. Jeanny Park. She started them on piano at age five because, "As I fully admit to everybody, I never played piano as a kid and always wanted to. If I had given them the option to quit at the beginning, they would have. They didn't like the everyday discipline. But it wasn't a horrible thing. By the time they reached fourth grade, they had been doing it for so many years that it was part of their routine and they did it independently." This California mother took another firm stand by saying that her son and daughter had to continue studying piano until they graduated from high school. However, she relented on this after her son began playing trumpet. "He became so involved in trumpet that when he started high school, I said, 'You can drop piano.' He said, 'No, I like it now.' My daughter never grew to like piano, although she says it helped with singing, which she loves."

NEC's Larry Scripp also gave his children "no choice whether to study music, just as they had no choice of whether to go to school or not. It was something they needed to do as part of their education. I required them to practice every day but always tried to instill a love of learning in it." Like Dr. Park, he set a timeline for their music study. "I said the intensive study of an instrument had to continue until age sixteen, although, by about age fourteen, you're not able to tell an American teenager what to do anyway." Dominique van de Stadt, mother of four musical kids, also had a time mandate: "Quitting was not an option—at least not until the child was an older teenager who found other valid, time-consuming pursuits, maybe varsity sports, ballet, science fair, math competition, chess."

Other parents who took a hard-line approach made use of their kids' love of music to encourage practicing. "We have a general rule that applies to most things in our family, that if you commit to doing something, you see it through. That applied to music and to sports, too," says California dad Buzz Ballenger. "We also had another pretty simple rule: No practice, no lessons. That may sound harsh, but we didn't have to say that often because our kids liked music and practicing." Several other families discovered that for kids who love music but are in a slump, the threat of stopping lessons snaps them into shape. This works best, however, if also combined with figuring out why they're in a slump and what can be done to try to get them back on track.

Some parents kept lessons going even when kids weren't practicing much. Marion Taylor generally took a hands-off approach to her daughters' flute and clarinet practicing, noting that they "practiced on an as-needed basis," never very much, but enough to do well in the ensembles in their upstate New York schools and also in all-state competitions. She tried to toughen up at one point, but it didn't fit the family's style. "I went through a period during middle school where I heard another mom say she had her kid practice every morning before breakfast and I thought I was supposed to do that. So for one month I told the girls they had to do that. They looked at me as if I were crazy," says Ms. Taylor. So the girls went back to being in charge of practicing, doing it as long as they felt was needed. However, during seventh grade, her younger daughter's practicing slowed down more than usual. "She came to me and said maybe she should stop because she wasn't practicing much," recalls Ms. Taylor. "I told her, 'We don't mind continuing to pay for lessons. Let's just keep music as part of your life.' The teacher kept plugging away, and Becky rode past that hump." Later, she managed to win a full music scholarship to the University of Miami.

Ann Turner appealed to her children's sense of fairness, explaining to them that "a certain amount of practicing was expected each week to be fair to the teachers who were investing their time with our children." The junior high band directors in their Ohio hometown helped, too. "The band directors had a practice sheet that went home

Erika Nickrenz, at age eleven, in one of the recitals at the music school she attended as a child.

with each child. It had to be filled out and returned each week to the teachers. Eventually both of our children's inner drives kicked in and motivated them to practice, without the parent being the taskmaster. But with all of the things our kids were plugged into, finding time for everything was a challenge." Her daughter, now a professional French horn player, became a self-directed, regular practicer, but her saxophone- and bassoon-playing son required reminders all through high school. "He would probably say I was a nag. Finding a way to get children to practice without giving reminders would be great, but I'm not sure there is a way."

Laura Vautour seconds that observation. She notes that she tried her best "to be supportive and not add to the pressure" with all the things her young soprano was involved with during high school. But this Atlanta-area mom admits she was tempted to intervene. "You see them procrastinate and waste time, but then I'd remind myself, 'They're teenagers—they do that.'"

Let Kids Take Responsibility

Nagging and its counterpart— unsolicited advice—stopped pretty early for one New York couple when they discovered, rather by chance, another way to turn their son into a regular practicer. "When he was about six, for a while he was just going through the motions of practicing cello, not really working on it," recalls Anne McCollough, whose son, James, had started cello enthusiastically at age four. "Neither my husband nor I play the cello so we didn't know all the things he should be doing, but we had gone to the Saturday morning group lessons at his music school and knew a little. So I said, 'James, I think you should do a little more.' He got really angry at me. So I said, 'OK, I'm not going to be involved. Fine.' We let him have a couple of lessons where he was unprepared.

SPOTLIGHT ON: RANAAN MEYER, DOUBLE BASS

Late Bloomer: At first, Ranaan Meyer was an on-and-off music student, taking piano lessons now and then with his mother, playing cello for a few months in third grade and then quitting. In middle school, his mom said he had to do either chorus, band, or orchestra because she felt music kept teens more grounded. He admits that he picked double bass because "there was a popular kid who played bass, and I wanted to be popular." After two months of not becoming popular, he wanted to quit, but his mom didn't let him this time. He took lessons but never practiced until, at age fifteen, a friend introduced him to jazz. "I went from zero hours of practice to two hours a day because it was so awesome." His mom found him a new teacher who taught classical and jazz bass. Soon this high schooler was playing jazz gigs.

At group class those weeks, James was horrified that he wasn't doing as well as everyone else. After that he was self-motivated. He became self-conscious in a good way and wanted to figure out how he could do better, so when it was time to play in the lesson, he'd get it right."

Other parents also employed a let-them-learn-the-hard-way approach. "There have been times when we've been a little overinvolved in ensuring that our son practices enough, but it's important for him to develop his own relationship with his piano teacher and suffer the consequences of not having accomplished enough in the week. It's a delicate balance," says Jackie Yarmo, whose son studies with a classical teacher and is also in a New Jersey School of Rock program. Washington state dad Joseph Rakosi notes, "Once we let our kids take more responsibility for their own practice and ultimate results, they took more ownership of the process."

How Long to Practice

In many families, children's first practice sessions are pretty short. Shirley Bell's son, violinist Joshua Bell, practiced for about fifteen minutes a day as a five-year-old beginner. His practicing reached only thirty or forty minutes a day by the time he was eleven and had already performed a concerto with a community orchestra and been accepted into a high-powered summer music program.

"How much time students practice each day depends on the age of the student, what instrument is being studied, and what level music they're playing," says Cheryl Melfi, a clarinet instructor and former assistant director of the Community Music and Dance Academy at the University of Missouri in Kansas City. She says most instructors at that school would probably agree that "for beginners, about twenty to thirty minutes is enough. But for teen cello students in high school, working toward college or conservatory auditions, a cello instructor would probably want them to practice three hours a day. A vocal instructor, however, would say practicing that long would be inappropriate." So might an instructor for brass instruments, whose students shouldn't practice for too long at a stretch, so as not to strain delicate lip muscles.

"For kindergarteners, we want the child to practice a half hour a day, and that half hour can include getting the instrument out of the case and having a bathroom break," says Jenny Undercofler, director of a music-oriented public school in New York City. "After that, I tell parents that practice should gradually increase, but I don't put too fine a point on it. By third grade, they should practice around an hour a day. By middle school, about two hours."

"My rule of thumb was: If you have a thirty-minute lesson, thirty minutes of practice five days a week. If a forty-five-minute lesson, then forty-five minutes five days week, and so on," explains piano teacher Carol Prochazka. She agrees with our other educators, however, in feeling that teens who aim to go to a conservatory need to log in two hours or more "because that's what everyone else is doing who's trying to go to a conservatory."

Violin teacher Dorothy Kaplan Roffman, who specializes in teaching beginners, doesn't recommend an exact number of minutes. "I just say it should be every day," she explains. She assigns specific tasks, often quite small ones, and it's up to parent and child to work out how long it takes to do them. Her daughter, Kim Field, takes a similar task-oriented approach to managing her young daughters' violin and cello practice. "Practicing should be about 'little wins,' new bits of pieces learned or a tricky technical challenge mastered or musical emotion emerging in a phrase," says Ms. Field. "If we have time, we have several little wins a day. If it's a busy day, practicing may consist of one or two little wins. It's about the success. The more time we have, then the more little wins we get to rack up, which is fun."

"I put a lot of responsibility on my students to achieve the goals they set. I don't see my job as making them practice. My job is to teach them," says Larry Williams, a French horn player and head of the brass department at Peabody's preparatory division. "I tell them, 'You'll get as good as the work you put in. Every time you see me you'll improve. I'm going to meet you where you are and get you a little better that day. If you don't practice, it won't be as much fun. But if you do practice, we'll take big steps forward.' Each week, I ask, 'Have you practiced?' They know not to lie. If they haven't, I'll say, 'Are you sure you want to take lessons? If you don't, that's OK. I'm still your friend. We have plenty of French horn players. You're not letting us down.' Once they see that I'm not going to take responsibility for their success or failure, they usually start to take it on themselves and get to work."

John McCarthy tries to involve his piano students in finding solutions to practicing slowdowns. "When someone hasn't been practicing, it's important not to be nasty about it. They value that we can talk through why things are not going well. Maybe there's trouble at school or they're jealous of so and so. They're teenagers. This is part of life," says this San Francisco Conservatory faculty member. "But I'm no Mr. Softee, either. We do want to get the job done. I might set a realistic goal for the next day after finding out what their day will be like and let the kids say when they can practice. Then I ask the student to e-mail me to say if that happened. Report to me rather than have the parent involved. At first they feel terrible because they haven't done it. I clarify that I'm not going to be upset or happy, no judgment. I just want them to be conscious that they did a video game instead. It seems a turning point for some of them when they have to be accountable."

Using Rewards—or Not

"At first, I paid my younger daughter to practice, a penny a minute. It worked for a while, but it got to be kind of juvenile so I stopped when she turned nine years old," says Thanh Huynh. "I changed to 'paying' her for performances by writing a 'certificate'—an index card with her name, date, and the piece performed. Each card was worth five dollars. She saved them up and redeemed them. When she was younger, she redeemed them for toys. In high school, she was more interested in clothes or electronics. Over the course of nine years she earned approximately two hundred certificates. Some people might say, 'That's horrible. The kid should be self-motivated.' I have no problem with paying her. After all, professional musicians get paid for performing," says this Baltimore research scientist.

"There are different schools of thought on rewards," says Sandra Shapiro of the Cleveland Institute of Music. "Some people say rewards are bribes, that practicing should come from the heart. I think that's idealistic. Everybody likes a reward at the end of work. For an adult, your reward is your paycheck, aside from the gratification of doing what you love, of course. Children get to the point of wanting to practice for itself, but rewards can give them something to hold onto, to get them through the rough patches."

"My kids practiced for all kinds of things when they were very young—M&Ms, Fruit Loops. Later it was for computer time, whatever the juiciest thing was for the child at the time," says Sarah Odhner. Lis Bischoff-Ormsbee used a point system with her kids when they were young, letting them rack up a certain number of points for their practice minutes that could be used to get something special. "Yes, it was bribery," says this upstate New York mother. "At that age it worked, and we didn't make the rewards easily attainable."

The bargaining that parents do with older kids is another a kind of reward. "When my daughter was thirteen, she was very social, and so I said she had to practice for an hour before she could go online or on the phone with her friends," says New Yorker Julia Castro, whose daughter and son both play double bass. "My

> SPOTLIGHT ON: MARK INOUYE, TRUMPET
>
> **Time out:** "I was a pretty rowdy, hyper kid. When I would get in trouble, I had to sit in a chair in my room and do nothing. No speaking, no moving, no nothing. Just sit there and think about why I was being punished. It was usually only a five-minute penalty, but if I talked back, the time doubled. If I continued to talk back, it doubled again. There were a few occasions I sat for over two hours in that chair. When I started trumpet, the rules changed. I could sit in the chair and do nothing—or I could sit there and practice trumpet. I got in a lot of practicing," says Mr. Inouye, now principal trumpet of the San Francisco Symphony Orchestra.

daughter would stomp off, but she did it. After eighth grade, I've found that kids go back to normal, and I didn't have to bargain with her like this anymore. But thirteen-year-olds, they're trying to figure out who's running the household and bargaining helps." Rationing video game time became a bargaining chip for other parents. "When our son became interested in video games, we suggested that he practice piano first, and then he was free to play his games for the length of time he had committed to his practice. This resulted in some excellent practice time," recalls Maryland mother Karen Rayfield.

Education experts acknowledge that rewards can work "in the short term," as long as you "use them sparingly and wisely," writes Deborah Stipek in her book *Motivated Minds*, a guide to helping children feel motivated to do homework. She used rewards to encourage her own daughter to do math homework. Her book notes that while some research studies show that rewards can encourage kids to do schoolwork, other research shows that working only for rewards can interfere with a child's creativity.

The Ten-Minute Plan

"Once my kids start practicing, they don't want to stop, but it's getting them started that's the problem," says Marie Green, Illinois mom of four musical youngsters. Cheryl Melfi has a solution: The Ten-Minute Plan. "Getting kids to practice is similar to getting yourself to do an exercise routine. The standard advice that you hear about exercise is: Just start. Promise yourself that you'll exercise for ten minutes and then you'll decide if you really want to keep on. I find that works for my clarinet students," says Ms. Melfi. "There's a mental barrier to opening the clarinet case, getting the reeds ready, putting the clarinet together. I ask the parents to tell students to play for just ten minutes. Usually if they do that, they'll go on to complete their half hour because once they get started, they find it's fun."

John McCarthy uses a variant of the Ten-Minute Plan for his piano students. "I don't give a total number of minutes needed for practice," he explains. "I'll often start with an outline of things that I'd like to have happen in the course of a practice session. I break it down to ten minutes of sight reading, ten minutes of technique, ten minutes of maintaining your repertoire, ten minutes on a new piece, ten minutes of polishing and memorizing. That's almost an hour. Ten minutes doesn't seem like much. Actually, ten minutes is not nearly enough for any of these things. It takes ten minutes to get engaged. Ideally the ten minutes will trigger a real appetite to practice more. To have clear goals in practicing is the key and then the time takes care of itself."

"If my daughter is really busy and doesn't have time for a full practice, I'll suggest that she play a song she loves or start a new piece and just get the notes down," says

Melissa Tucker. That helps keep her daughter's flute-playing muscles toned. Trumpet teacher Wes Sparkes notes, "It's especially important for brass players to put their lips to the horn and practice at least ten minutes if that's all they can get in, so they don't lose the shape and structure of the embouchure [lip position] that they've built up." Another tip for brass players: If they can't take their horns on vacation, bring along the mouthpiece and buzz their lips a few minutes a day to keep those lips in shape.

Some parents have their own Ten-Minute Plans. "When our daughter was five years old and starting piano lessons, I would set a timer for ten minutes. She was to practice until the timer buzzed and then she could do whatever she wanted," recalls New Yorker, Lisa Sgouros. A timer also removes the parent from the role of taskmaster, letting the timer be the bad guy. As youngsters increase in age and ability, so can the minutes on the timer.

Finessing the Schedule

Brass teacher Larry Williams may be flexible about how long a student practices, but he feels that whatever the schedule is, it "needs to be set. It doesn't work if it's floating, fitting practice in whenever you can," he says. "It can be different each day, but if possible the times should be the same each week, so it becomes a routine." That isn't always possible with all the other things kids do, but that's the goal. "The kids I teach are way overprogrammed, doing marching band, sports, karate, community service, foreign language, AP courses—typical overachievers. I'm not interested in burning them out and breaking them down, but they need to set up a schedule."

"I work out a schedule that lets homework, music, and fun fit in comfortably almost every day," says Jennifer Ingerson, Chicago mother of two young music students. "I try to make sure that music isn't a burden. I don't have my kids practice

> SPOTLIGHT ON: JONATHAN BISS, PIANO
>
> **Laissez faire:** "My parents took a hands-off approach. It wasn't like they had to convince me to practice. I loved the piano," says Jonathan Biss, who started piano at age four and whose parents are violinists. "I didn't practice a huge amount when I was young and sometimes needed to be reminded, but if they said, 'Go practice,' which wasn't often, it was always accompanied by 'if you want to do this.' Their point was that you don't have to do anything you don't want to, but if you choose to do it, you have to do it well. My parents created this atmosphere that I didn't feel I was doing it to please them or because it was good for me. I was doing it because I loved music."

too late in the day or when they're hungry. If children are stressed about how much time music takes up in their day, they will begin to dislike it. After all, music is supposed to be an optional, fun activity."

Some parents, at least in the early years, try to have practice occur at the same time each day. "We made practice part of their daily chores each afternoon," says Linda Schnur of St. Louis. That worked when her sons started on trumpet but became more difficult to accomplish during high school when her sons became involved in more activities.

"I never told my kids that they had to practice," says Vivian Weilerstein, mother of cellist Alisa Weilerstein and Joshua Weilerstein, a professional violinist and conductor. "My role was to help with organization and create an environment where it's comfortable for them to practice. My son wanted to play violin, but it was just one of many things that he did as a kid. I tried to set it up so that he had a schedule that enabled him to have time to practice violin in the morning before school, so it became a very natural thing for him to do. Violin wasn't as huge a part of his life as cello was with Alisa. I never had to organize a practice schedule for her. She was self-motivated and wanted to practice." Before-school practicing worked for other families, too, although Paula Robison notes that when she did this during high school, "A neighbor would turn on his radio full blast and point it at our house because the sound of the flute is not dolce when neighbors live too close."

In some families, setting up practice time involves reorganizing household activities. "I might take on some of my daughter's chores so she can practice more," explains Beverly Berndt, Kansas City mother of a teen bassoonist. The McColloughs use a similar approach. "We fix our son's breakfast so he can practice before school and move dinner either early or late, to accommodate evening practice," explains Anne McCollough, whose son has a lot of rehearsal times to juggle each week because he is in several youth ensembles. "He plays cello and piano. He practices one instrument in the morning and the other at night. It's too much to do them back to back." Splitting practice into separate segments can also help youngsters who play only one instrument, by allowing them to find spare chunks of time in a busy day. In addition, splitting practice into a few separate sessions can make it less likely that any one session goes on so long that the youngster slips into a loop of mindless repetition.

Time-management assistance can also lighten a jam-packed roster. "I try to manage his workload in terms of activities so my son doesn't get overextended," says Lydia Zieglar. Fellow Marylander Margaret Cureton explains, "By the time they were teens, my job was to keep their schedule free. The practicing was up to them. They know how difficult a career in music is. They have to want it and do what it takes."

Positive Peer Pressure

"What ultimately turned my children into regular practicers was their involvement with other kids—playing in group classes and youth orchestras—plus their commitment to their instruments," says Sarah Odhner. The positive peer pressure that comes from performing with a group helped many of our other advisors' sons and daughters catch the practice habit, too. As Ms. Odhner notes, "After all, nobody wants to let a friend down."

The peer benefits of ensemble playing can arise in all kinds of groups—youth orchestras, marching bands, choral groups, jazz bands, chamber music groups, rock bands, and so on. Omaha School of Rock music director Keith Fertwagner explains, "If you have one person slacking off on a song, that kid is kind of ruining it for everyone else. Everybody else in the band needs to say, 'Hey, buddy, you're messing it up for all of us.'"

A father of two young jazz musicians observes that "being around other musicians who are as good as or better than my kids pushes them to practice," says Wayne Matthews. His kids have performed in a New York youth jazz band sponsored by Jazz at Lincoln Center.

In addition to not wanting to let the group down, musical friendships made in those ensembles can encourage practicing. "If our daughters took only private lessons and had just occasional recitals, I suspect neither would have continued with music," says Heather Gange, mother of two string musicians who began studying at Peabody at a young age. "Playing in orchestras and chamber music groups let them develop musical friendships, see that 'cool' people play at a high level, and kept my daughters interested and motivated to practice."

Musical friendships—"that's what it's all about, for my daughter anyway," says Melissa Tucker. During middle school, playing in a flute trio at music school was her

The brass section from the St. Louis Symphony Youth Orchestra in 2010. Trumpeters Casey Keller and Aaron Krumsieg went on to be performance majors at conservatories.

daughter's "favorite thing and what kept her going on flute, playing with the other girls." During high school, the social glue has been marching band, which has so many after-school rehearsals she no longer had time to get together with her trio. "She misses the flute trio, but she started making friends in marching band and loves it. It's a big social thing."

The social aspect has been important for Lis Bischoff-Ormsbee's daughters, too. "My girls joined jazz ensembles, orchestras, bands, pit orchestras for shows, sang in musicals—all opportunities that gave them a good feeling about continuing in music. It's a lifelong passion for them, even if not a profession," she says. Friends made in youth ensembles can be long-lasting. Professional oboist Toyin Spellman-Diaz still keeps in touch with friends she made in youth orchestra. So does violist Lauren Chipman, who notes, "My best friend in the whole world is someone I met in youth orchestra. We still talk three or four times a week."

A different kind of peer motivation comes into play with the auditions that are required to join some youth ensembles. Kurtis Gruters, a neuroscientist, started percussion lessons at age nine while growing up in Arizona. "My freshman year in high school, I was an on-again, off-again practicer," he recalls. "That year, I tried out for the all-region band and orchestra and missed by one point. This made me sufficiently angry, via my competitive streak, that it got me practicing more. As I practiced more, I truly began to understand and love the work, which completed my transition to being a regular practicer."

Jazz bassist Christian McBride knows the power of peer competition from his own teen years and from working with young musicians at Jazz House Kids, a program his wife, singer Melissa Walker, runs in New Jersey. "People say music isn't about competition, but it is when you're a teenager, playing in a jazz band," notes Mr. McBride. "You want to set up an environment where they can inspire each other and also goose each other on. The ones that get their butts kicked one day are going to go home, practice harder, and the next day they'll be back, 'Come on, I'm ready for you now!'"

Other kinds of group experiences can also spark an interest in practicing, such as the regular monthly recitals at the music school that pianist Erika Nickrenz attended as a young girl. "When you have only one recital at the end of the year, there's not as much impetus to practice," she notes. "My piano teacher had recitals once a month. I almost always played in them so I was always practicing for something." Clarinetist Anthony McGill makes a similar observation about the impact of being in several youth ensembles. "I began to practice more because I had more to practice for," he says.

There are many kinds of ensembles that our advisors' young musicians joined. In addition to ones at a youngster's regular school or that are part of a music school's offering, there are others that are sponsored by professional orchestras, music-related organizations, or places of worship. In addition, there are all-state, all-county, or all-city ensembles that are often sponsored by music teacher associations. Community theaters offer performance outlets for singers and for instrumentalists skilled enough to play in a pit orchestra. Quite a few of our panelists' teens formed their own rock bands, jazz combos, or chamber groups. Ensembles that aren't part of regular school have an added bonus in often playing more challenging repertoire than school groups. The more exciting music may inspire practice.

Although ensembles may produce an increased interest in practicing, their rehearsals and performances can crowd youngsters' busy schedules. High school marching bands are especially time consuming, dominating the fall season with so many rehearsals and games that some teens have trouble keeping up with the practice they need to do for private lessons on their instruments. As Ms. Tucker and other of our advisors note, most kids love marching band. However, spare-time trumpeter Catherine Getchell offers a dissenting opinion. "I don't want to knock marching band, but it wasn't my favorite thing in high school," she says. "For a brass player, you're basically blowing your brains out in marching band, and it kind of killed my chops until the season was over. I would spend a month or two recovering my embouchure. If I could have done just concert band and not marching band, I would have, but so would every other serious musician in the school and then there wouldn't have been a marching band."

Some outside-of-school youth ensembles charge fees, although our parent advisors report that scholarships may be available. There may also be fees with a high school's marching band, as is true of the St. Louis high school where Gary Borkowski has been a parent volunteer. "Marching band is expensive for the kids and families, but with a strong parent organization like ours, there are plenty of fundraising opportunities," says Mr. Borkowski. Kids at his school sometimes find summer jobs to help with the expense.

Ensemble Volunteering

There's another downside to ensemble participation, besides fees. When kids join an ensemble, that often means there will be a lot more work for mom and dad, who will need to make arrangements to get kids to rehearsals and performances. In some cases, parents will be expected to do fundraising and other volunteer work. Although some parents may not be thrilled about the volunteering, many who have pitched in are glad they did.

"Yes, it's time consuming, but worth every minute. It's a way to share the experience with your kids," says Gary Borkowski. Sherrie Neumeier, another St. Louis parent, adds, "Getting involved supporting the marching band gave us an opportunity to serve the school and the students, not just our own daughter. It gave us the added benefit of being more directly involved with her during high school and seeing how she had grown in responsibility and integrity. Don't be a 'drop-off' parent. Life with your kids being around is too short as it is."

Janice Fagan did many kinds of volunteer work when she served as head of the parent association for the pre-college division of Manhattan School of Music, where her daughter studied piano. In addition to fundraising, she arranged information sessions and programs that would interest parents who often travel long distances to bring their kids to the school each Saturday and spend the day hanging out there.

Sue Jones took on an advocacy role to support music programs at her daughter's Texas high school, recalling that "when the PTA was deciding how to allocate funds, I argued for the music programs because there were always ten people arguing for football dollars to my voice for music. I wrote the newsletter for the band parents' booster club, testified at the school board, wrote letters. We also raised money for orchestra and marching band contests."

Being a band mom was practically a full-time job for Betsy McCarthy. She headed the jazz parents association at her son's Seattle high school, whose bands participate in jazz festivals around the country and overseas. The parent group raises money for travel and to support the whole program. Scott Brown, the school's director of

bands, explains, "We're an urban, public high school and get little funding support from the school district. There's no way we could do all the things we do without the parent groups." Their money-raising projects include an annual auction as well as selling tickets for the band's performance each holiday season of a jazz version of the *Nutcracker*. Ms. McCarthy adds, "We arrange for kids' jazz combos to get hired through the jazz band's website to play private parties. Kids keep half the money and the program gets half." The parents also sell hats, aprons, CDs of past band performances—and they do bake sales, too. "Most parents are pretty

Betsy McCarthy's son, Chris, performing with drummer Max Holmberg during their high school jazz band's European tour, summer of 2010.

invested in their kids' experience and are excited about participating," adds Ms. Mc-Carthy. "It's a close-knit group because we go to see the kids perform all the time."

However, Mr. Brown notes, "The band director needs to be clear with parents as to what their role is. I let parents know that I'm appreciative of their help, but they're not going to choose the festivals we go to or the music we play. It's important to define roles clearly. It's also important to respect what they do and be thankful all the time that they spend so much time supporting the program and their kids."

Summer Programs as Practice Boosters

Summer music camps, workshops, and festivals can also play a role in sparking a youngster's interest in practicing more regularly. These summertime music-centered experiences let young people learn more about music, make friends with other kids who love music, and have a chance to work with exciting new teachers and conductors. Youngsters can also see how much they improve by participating in a program where music is the focus—not just an extra squeezed in after finishing homework—and where practicing is something that the other kids are doing, too.

"The summers my daughter spent at music camp were probably the single most important factor in her wanting to excel at music," says Massachusetts mom Francine Bernitz. Her daughter's commitment to excellence led to her majoring in both violin and viola performance at Oberlin.

There are many kinds of summer music programs for young people, including ones that are close to home, such as the music-oriented day camps that are often sponsored by music schools, arts organizations, or local recreation and education departments. There are also sleep-away camps that offer music activities—some have music as just one part of the camping program, while at other sleep-away camps music is the main event. In addition, Suzuki associations often hold summer camps, as do marching bands. For advanced students, there are high-powered, by-audition-only summer music programs and festivals.

"For a first camp, you probably don't want to send kids to a boot-camp type of situation where they practice all day," says Sandra Shapiro. "You might start with a camp that's more of a traditional camp but with a music emphasis. There are many fine camps like that. Once your child has done that, then you can think about more advanced programs." Tuition can be costly at some programs, but scholarships are frequently available.

At the time this book was written, there was no central website with a comprehensive listing of summer music programs. To locate summertime possibilities, parents could ask for recommendations from a youngster's music teacher, other parents, or music school officials. Music school bulletin boards often feature advertisements for summer programs.

"It can be humbling to go to music camp and discover that you are a big fish in a little pond at home—but not at music camp," says Annette Radoff. "That can provide a reality check and the kickstart that a student needs to move on to the next level." Ann Turner notes another benefit: "The children are on their own, meeting other kids with the same interest, and they're learning from kids—*not* from a parent—how important practice is." Music camps also give youngsters a chance to try something new they might not have thought of before, such as play in a jazz combo, take composition lessons, sing in a musical, or play a different instrument.

Summer programs, by immersing youngsters in performing challenging music, can have a big impact even for a child as enthusiastic about music as Shirley Bell's son, Josh. At age eleven, he attended a high-powered summer string camp, Meadowmount School of Music in upstate New York. It was a "major turning point," says his mother, both in terms of practicing and in boosting his passion for music. "Before then, he was practicing at most forty minutes a day," she says. "At Meadowmount, they make you practice five hours a day. He goofed around a little there, but he practiced. Having to practice that much made such a difference in his tone and technique. He became aware of what practicing does and how good you can become. Not only that, he fell in love with music that summer, from listening to the others play, listening to his own sound, getting positive feedback, hearing recordings of great violinists, and beginning to have the idea that music was going to play an important part in his life, one way or the other. That's what it's all about, developing that passion for music. When he came home from that camp, he was a different person and a better violinist."

However, as Ms. Bell recalls, "The re-entry process when your kid goes away to an experience like that is profound. It took a while for him to re-enter our world. I lost something of what I had before. When he came back, I wanted to know all about what had happened. He wouldn't communicate that to me. The experience at that camp was so intense, there was no way he could share that because it would lose in the sharing. It was like I was intruding into his world. In retrospect, I can recognize some of the tensions, and so I tell parents to try your best to recognize and respect your child's boundaries and not be too intrusive. It's not easy. It was important for me to recognize how much my personal needs were being met by my child's gifts and successes." He didn't necessarily practice five hours a day after returning home and even went through a period during his teens of overdoing it on video games. He had two more summers at Meadowmount and attended other summer programs—the Aspen Music Festival and the Marlboro chamber music festival—but his mother feels his first summer at Meadowmount turned him into a musician.

Growing Into It

The transformation that Joshua Bell experienced is typical of many kids who become serious musicians—going from liking music to loving it. This change occurred during the early teen years of the young pianists profiled in Benjamin Bloom's book, *Developing Talent in Young People*. That book quotes a statement the late violinist Isaac Stern made in a 1979 *New York Times Magazine* article in which he observed that at some point from age ten to the early teens, "The child must become possessed by music, by the sudden desire to play, to excel."

Our parent advisors have noticed this metamorphosis in their sons and daughters. "It took many years of us encouraging and asking him to practice for him to do it on his own. He became a regular practicer when he realized he could be—and wanted to be—good," says Damian Conrad, Oregon dad of a trumpeter. The same happened with Laura Vautour's daughter, an accomplished singer. "She loves to sing and when she started getting recognition for it, with solos and entrance into special programs, she started practicing more on her own because she decided she wanted to be one of the best," says Ms. Vautour.

For Vivian Weilerstein's son, Joshua, the change came when he was sixteen years old. Despite her efforts to arrange a workable schedule for him, he didn't practice much as a youngster. "His intensity started when we moved from Cleveland to Boston when he was sixteen, and he joined a youth orchestra at NEC—the Young Philharmonic Orchestra," his mother explains. "His life suddenly changed. He became completely immersed in orchestral music, began practicing much more, and did it on his own."

For some young teens, the practice pendulum may swing all the way over to the practicing-all-the-time level. "I tried to get my son to stop practicing sometimes during high school and do more homework, but we couldn't seem to win that battle,"

SPOTLIGHT ON: JOSHUA BELL, VIOLIN

Different wiring: When Joshua Bell began to be seen as a young violinist with potential, his mother says, "I felt a responsibility to get him to practice more. Before then, it was all fun and games. But our wiring is different. There were conflicts. Maybe I thought he should practice two hours, and he thought one was enough. He knew himself better than I did. He was able to focus and learn on his own terms. I had to learn to listen—and preach less. Let children be who they are without imposing your needs on them. Avoid power struggles—not an easy task." He admits he should have practiced more at times and played video games less, but he's glad his parents let him have other interests. "There was plenty of 'Mom, I don't want to practice!' Normal banter between mother and kids," he says. "They were good parents. We're still close."

says Betsy McCarthy. "We backed off on homework to some extent. We weren't OK with him getting less than a B, and he didn't. He wants to be a professional musician. It's his passion, and we just tried not to squelch it." After high school, he headed to NEC to major in jazz performance.

Percussionist Payton MacDonald was so interested in music as a teen that he begged his parents to let him practice more. "My parents did these big home-improvement projects and roped my sister and me into them," he says. "I remember many Saturdays working until four in the afternoon doing something like putting in a sprinkler system, saying, 'Please, Dad, I really want to practice. I'm tired of digging ditches for the sprinklers.'"

Mega-practicing doesn't have to lead to slacking off on homework, however. Payton MacDonald, despite all his practicing—and yard work—kept his grades high enough to gain admission to the University of Michigan. Alisa Weilerstein and Marin Alsop both logged in many hours of daily practice but did well enough academically to attend Ivy League colleges.

A Gift

"For kids who are serious about music, it's such a gift for parents to make sure the kids practice every day. The kids won't always see it that way when they're young, but it's a gift because they can't recapture those years when they have the time to put in," says music educator Jenny Undercofler. Marin Alsop agrees, but says that in addition to hoping that her son will grow up "understanding what achievement requires, knowing how to motivate and inspire himself to do things that he may not always want to do, I want him above all to love music and get pleasure and satisfaction from playing an instrument." The next chapter explains how parents try to mix joy and fun into the practice routine.

Theresa Chong's son, Chase Park, age eleven, at a master class taught by professional cellist Steven Isserlis (top), and a few years later playing in a concert as a teenager.

8   Fine-Tuning the Parent's Practice Role

"FINDING THE RIGHT BALANCE between helping and being overbearing—I think I finally learned my lesson," says Kristin Bond. That was the number one "lesson learned" for many of our advisors and the central topic of this chapter: Figuring out how to help—not hinder—in offering practice-time assistance. Joining this Massachusetts mother in launching this chapter's discussion is Theresa Chong. Together they lay out some of the main issues with their frank accounts of mistakes made while trying to walk the music-parenting tightrope.

"My daughters started piano when they were about seven years old, regular lessons, not Suzuki," recalls Ms. Bond. "I play piano a little, and thought I could offer helpful hints as they practiced. That didn't work out so well. My intervention into their practicing backfired. I was perceived as a nag. I don't know if that in and of itself deterred them from practicing, but they wouldn't practice piano unless they were pretty much forced." Later, both girls went on to be better about practicing when they found new musical interests that their mom had less experience with—singing for the older daughter and trumpet for the younger. Not only did their mom have fewer insights to offer, but she had figured out better ways to deliver her suggestions.

For Theresa Chong, the balancing act was especially tricky because she was required to help with her children's practicing because they were taking Suzuki lessons.

Her role as a practice coach began when her son, Chase, began Suzuki cello at age four. Soon, she was also supervising his younger sister on Suzuki violin. At first, things went fairly smoothly. "But once you're in it, you just get sucked into trying to get your kids to do it right. The lessons are expensive. There's an incentive to get the kids ready for the next lesson," notes Ms. Chong. "One day when Chase was about six, I saw myself on tape telling him what to do when he was practicing, telling him he's not holding the bow the right way. I couldn't believe my tone of voice. It was so mean!" She had recorded his practice so he could see how he was doing, but instead she saw what *she* was doing. She began to rethink her role. "I didn't want to be overbearing, but it's so easy to be overbearing as a mother. You care about your child and want things to go well."

Before Chase turned nine, she realized she had to pull out of the practice-coach role. Her son's teacher worried that he might make slower progress without his mother supervising. "I told the teacher that it may take more time, but he has to learn to practice on his own. We were spending more time arguing than practicing. Otherwise we'll be enemies," says Ms. Chong. She reorganized the situation so she could step back and Chase could step up. A helpful assist from technology made this possible: They began videotaping his lessons. "A lot happens in a lesson and the teacher covers things very fast. Now he could watch the lesson by himself to know what to do." A few years later, positive peer pressure nudged him to practice even more after he attended a high-powered summer music camp. The commitment to practicing that he saw in the program's highly skilled older students rubbed off on him.

It's Not Easy Being a High-wire Artist

Ms. Bond and Ms. Chong have a lot of company among our other parent advisors, many of whom have also struggled to find their practice-time role. "I often get trapped into trying to have my kids live up to their piano teacher's expectations instead of letting them do it for their own enjoyment," says Sandra Johnson, Chicago mother of two young piano students. Tamara Dahling, Indiana mother of an aspiring singer, warns, "Taking kids to lessons, listening to them practice, it can be difficult not to let your child's life become your life."

Even professional musicians have trouble monitoring practice with their own kids. "I would hover too much over him in his piano practice, and it created conflicts between us," says rock musician Jim Skrivan, who teaches at the Omaha School of Rock and started his son on piano at age five. Brent Samuel, cellist with the Los Angeles Philharmonic, reports that when he tried to help his four-year-old with her piano assignments, "I found I had absolutely no perspective on what to expect of her. I got frustrated because it seemed that she was having trouble with something that was very simple. I had to remind myself that I had no idea what 'very simple' was for someone just learning how to play piano—maybe it was in fact very difficult."

"Sometimes even I don't follow my own advice," admits an advocate of non-pushy parenting, Larry Scripp of New England Conservatory (NEC). "I can get so wrapped up in wanting my daughter to finish a piano piece that I have to remind myself that, as she tells me, 'I'm just a kid, remember?'"

"It's a fine line to walk, because kids vary in the amount of input they want from their parents," explains Dr. Yeou-Cheng Ma, pediatrician, youth orchestra director, and music mom. Her independent-minded daughter was a preschooler when she announced her no-input preference. "When she was four, practicing cello, we heard her play a wrong note and called across the room, 'No, that's an E-flat.' We heard this scream, 'And who do you think you are? The masters of music?' We backed off," says Dr. Ma, whose husband is also a musician.

Complicating the issue, kids change over time in how much help they're willing to accept. When Juli Elliot's daughter started on piano at age seven, "She was receptive to having my help. As she got older, we had some stereotypical mother-daughter clashes. She would say, 'I'm going to practice now, and I request you not make any comments,'" notes this upstate New York mother. Melissa Tucker, Massachusetts mom of a teen flutist, observes, "There's a learning curve for any music parent. You hear the mistakes, the hurried practice, but have to balance your reactions. I'm still learning how to give feedback in a way that she can take it in and hear it in a positive way."

For Sarah Odhner, the learning curve went the other way—figuring out how to be *more* involved. "I have six kids, six tries to learn how to do it," explains this veteran music parent from Pennsylvania. "I learned what *not* to do with my first son. I thought I could just tell him to go practice. But he was very young, would get stuck and not be sure how to fix things. I'd be cooking dinner, dealing with five children, and I'd yell, 'Try it again.' That wasn't a good way to make him feel nurtured. He got discouraged and dropped piano. I became more hands-on during practice after that."

A hands-off approach, however, worked well for other parents. "My kids love what they do, want to be good at it, and so the drive to practice comes from within," says Wayne Matthews. Even though he has been hands-off in terms of supervising practice, he has been hands-on in finding opportunities for his teen woodwind players—locating private teachers for them, and enrolling them in music camp and in a youth ensemble.

A self-motivated learner is the goal of all music parents, whether hands-on, hands-off, or somewhere in between. In this chapter, our advice team shares strategies on how to make practice less of a hassle for everyone.

"An Outside Pair of Eyes"

"Practicing music is an art in itself," says violinist Dana Myers. "When students are at a lesson, the teacher is in charge, showing what to do. But when students practice at home, suddenly the student is at the helm, making decisions." It's hard for children to know if they're doing what the teacher wants. That's where parents come in.

"Correct development of technique is so important in those early years, but children can't watch themselves to check on technique. Parents are an outside pair of eyes to help the students at home," explains music educator Jenny Undercofler. Most of our educator advisors—Suzuki and traditional—recommend that in the first years parents need to find a comfortable way to assist during practice. "The parent is there as a support, to help the child use the practice time well, following up on whatever the teacher's instructions are. It's just like with regular homework, the parent will oversee without doing it for the child," says Cleveland Institute's Sandra Shapiro.

"There has been a dramatic difference in our son's practicing after we started sitting with him and focusing on what he's doing rather than us walking around doing the laundry or other things, and expecting him to get through it," says New Yorker Bradley Detrick. He didn't help with his son's piano practicing the first few years because his son's first piano teacher didn't suggest it. Then they switched to a new teacher who insisted on parental involvement, partly to fix some technical gaps the first teacher hadn't addressed. "I find the best practicing happens when I'm seated in a chair next to the piano, right after dinner, to establish the idea of a routine, that this is what we do," says Mr. Detrick.

No matter what the level of practice involvement, parents don't have to figure out on their own what needs to be accomplished. Either the teacher writes that up on a practice chart or in the student's assignment book, or the parents take notes if they're sitting in on lessons. Later in this chapter, there are suggestions for figuring out what to say. Equally important, however, is how the coaching is delivered, preferably with a light touch, an abundance of praise, and the understanding that soon the need for this kind of assistance will fade. "It's like weaning a baby, little by little it dwindles. The dwindling may take a few years, but parents gradually transition themselves out of practicing," says violin teacher Dorothy Kaplan Roffman. "The idea is for the child to have learned how to be comfortable when something doesn't work and to know how to make a plan to fix it."

The transition isn't always easy, as Ms. Roffman discovered when one of her own daughters was about eleven years old. "Practicing with her was not working out," Ms. Roffman recalls. "My husband said, 'You have to remove yourself from the situation.' That was difficult for me to do, but I did it, and she became a violinist.

She had a passion for music. If the friction between parent and child is too great, that can end it. I learned a lot about teaching from my own children."

A Fun Start

Young kids learn through play, as education experts tell us and any parent can confirm. That's as true for music as for any other subject. Parental coaching for beginners should aim at making the practice experience fun—or at least have elements of fun in it.

Conductor Marin Alsop knows from her own childhood what can happen when practice isn't fun. She started piano at age two. Her practicing was carefully supervised by her mother, a professional musician. "That was the kiss of death," says Ms. Alsop. "Practicing piano with my mother was grueling because she was very demanding and critical. The fun factor was definitely too low." Ms. Alsop quit piano. She switched to violin at about age six and had a much better time, partly because she got to play in ensembles with other kids, but also because neither of her musician parents practiced with her. "I was old enough by then to take charge on my own with violin."

Her less than enjoyable early piano experiences have influenced the way she has supervised her son's music lessons. Although she tries to have him practice regularly, in the early years she added an element of fun by using kid-oriented motivators. "For a while, to reward good practicing, we used 'reward' minutes on Wii video games that he could cash in on weekends. But we don't really need to do that much anymore."

Scavenger hunts added fun to some families' early practice sessions. "When my twin daughters were young, we would put the little songs they're supposed to practice on index cards. One of them would hide the cards around the house and then the other would go find them. When she found one, she'd have to play that song," says Rebecca Henry, a Peabody violin teacher whose daughters started on cello and violin as preschoolers. Flute teacher Vanessa Mulvey recommends a grab-bag approach. "Write on pieces of paper something that has to be done in the weekly assignment and place the papers in a hat or in a plastic egg. The child draws out a paper and does that part of the assignment."

"When my younger daughter was five, she'd say, 'If I play it right, will you chase me?' As silly and undignified as it seems, we'd spend practice time away from the piano to chase around the room," says NEC's Larry Scripp. "If that's the release she needs to go on with music, the small sacrifice in practice time is worth it. Now she's older and takes ballet. She asks me to play a piece on piano that she's learning so she can dance to it. If she loses ten minutes of practice time so she can see music fused to dance, are we really losing anything?"

Ms. Henry would sometimes accompany her daughters by playing the piano part for the string pieces they were learning. So did Shirley Bell when her son Josh was starting violin. This is a great way to engage with kids and make those easy, early pieces sound richer and more impressive to the kids. Lis Bischoff-Ormsbee and her husband formed a rather unusual backup section to accompany their three kids when they were learning to play saxophone, drums, and cello. Mom would play piano and her husband would play trombone or pound away on a makeshift drum (hitting a basketball with sticks). "The kids had fun having a 'family band' and felt as if they were really making music, even though what they were playing was very beginner stuff," she says.

One fun part of practicing for violinist Robert Gupta, now with the Los Angeles Philharmonic, came from learning new tunes before the other students in his Suzuki class, with his mother as co-conspirator. This was particularly noteworthy because he reports that his mother was basically a strict monitor, "always reminding me what the teacher said and making corrections. She wasn't a musician, but she sat in on the lessons taking notes and learned what to say and do." However, she let him do something a little daring, in Suzuki circles, at least. "I loved listening to the Suzuki tapes and always wanted to play the pieces in the next Suzuki book. The teacher wouldn't let me do that. But my mother would. So I always knew the music that only the older kids in our group class knew because I learned it at home."

Another way to add some zip to pieces that need to be practiced is to "make up stories or operas about them," says Rebecca Henry. "I also encouraged my daughters to be creative and make up new sounds or songs on their instruments." However, she admits that she and her daughters didn't always do imaginative things every day. A few days they even skipped practice altogether. "There were days when everyone was tired, and I'd let it go to minimize household trauma. Of course, I wanted them to practice every day, and we were usually quite consistent. Everyone has to find the right balance for their family."

More Ways to Liven It Up

Here are a few more ideas for adding a bit of fun to practicing. The first three are mainly for young children. The next four would also work for older youngsters.

- **Toy audiences:** "We kept early practice sessions short, with stuffed animals cheering them on."—Marilyn Resmini, Virginia
- **Pet performances:** "My daughter would practice and give concerts to the family dogs until she was ready for us to listen to her. We pretended we

hadn't heard the early stuff so she could perfect it before playing it for us."—Beverly Berndt, Missouri

- **Art work:** "My mom drew a picture with all the notes of a piece. As I learned the piece, I could color in each note as I went along."—Jamie Raudensky Doyle, Massachusetts
- **Loud music:** "We made going to lessons fun. We played loud music on the way and stopped for ice cream afterward."—Pam Conrad, Oregon
- **Favorites:** "Every practice session should include time to play pieces that are already polished, so they can add a bit of musicality to them to make things interesting. Where's the pleasure for a child of always practicing only pieces that are new, tricky, and need work?"—Kim Field, London, UK
- **Talk it over:** "We talk about the pieces they're playing. I share my ideas about the pieces—the images, colors, and stories that I hear in them—and compare my thoughts to their ideas so they can develop their own ideas about the music."—Jiji Goosby, Tennessee
- **Extras:** "In addition to their regular lesson music, we got music for pieces they could play on their own for fun, like *Star Wars* music and the *Pink Panther* theme."—Diane Cornelius, Oregon

Play Around

"We let our son 'play around' on the piano and count some of that as practice time," says Chicago mom Sandra Johnson. Alisa Weilerstein's parents also used this approach, allowing their young cellist the freedom to explore and improvise. "Up until I was about nine years old, I'd do my structured practice, mostly with my mother, about thirty minutes or so," says Alisa. "But I loved cello so much that I would then take the cello up to my room and improvise, without the music, trying to play pieces by ear that I loved listening to on recordings, like the Dvorak cello concerto. I begged my teachers to let me play those pieces, but they said I wasn't ready. Even though I knew they were right, it was my little escape to go up to my room and play whatever I wanted without anyone telling me I couldn't. Some parents forbid this so kids won't develop bad habits. My parents encouraged it. I did develop some bad habits which I had to undo later, but it was worth it. I'm so grateful I was given this freedom."

Her mother, Vivian Weilerstein, agrees, "Every child is different, but it was definitely important to let her be wild and free and play through the Dvorak concerto by ear in any way, shape, or form that she could. Improvising when you're young is essential." That concerto became a part of AlisaWeilerstein, making it easier years later for her to learn to play it for real when her skills finally caught up with her imagination. However, even she admits, "Sometimes I didn't feel like practicing, but I knew I had to do it to become the cellist I wanted to be. When there was any friction over practice, my parents would say, 'Well, if you want to do this, that's what you have to do.' It was a very rational discussion." So she would practice—and then follow up with musical experimenting.

The No-Nonsense Approach

Although violinist Robert Gupta's mother let him have fun breaking the Suzuki rules by learning new pieces on his own, hers was basically a no-nonsense approach. A few of our other musician advisors also had strict parental oversight. Some children liked it. Others chafed under the tight control. Robert Gupta is a fan of his mom's approach. "She was extremely strict. I'm so happy that she was," he says. "I needed that structure and guidance. If she had not been strict and let a teenager be a teenager, I wouldn't have gotten this far. She enforced a certain number of minutes of practice each day. If you're done early, do it again. After I started Juilliard Pre-College at about age eight, she let me practice on my own."

"Discipline is important for any child's development," says violinist Anne Akiko Meyers. She started Suzuki violin at age four and is glad that her mother served as a firm supervisor in the early years. "It's hard for a child to focus on something that takes away from playtime. I remember my sister got to hang out in the sandbox while I had to practice—the ultimate drag. I wasn't damaged. I haven't been in therapy over it. It's part of growing up. I was so happy with violin, and it's lucky I was good at it. I didn't come from a family enmeshed in the music industry. But my parents felt it was important to find the right teachers, to cultivate the potential, put me on a path of trying your best and seeing where that leads."

However, other pros have mixed feelings about the strict parental monitoring they received. An accomplished classical musician who prefers to remain anonymous explains, "My parents started me in music at a young age with no expectation that I would pursue a career in music. To them, music lessons were something good for a child, a way to develop discipline and add to a well-rounded education—on the path to becoming a doctor or scientist. So early on, music was my parents' idea, and they pushed and pulled me along for about the first ten years. There were some mild struggles. While I didn't hate practicing, other things were naturally more attractive—like joining my friends for a game of football or basketball. Ironically, the roles reversed during high school. I began to find a certain degree of success in music, and thus I started taking more initiative in my musical activities. This caused my parents to fear that I was becoming serious about music, and for years they expressed strong reservations about my pursuits.

Somehow, these different stages of conflict with my parents have brought me to where I am today. Looking back, I realize that even if a career in music was not what my parents had in mind for me, music would not have been possible without the immense sacrifices they made with their time, money, and energy. And had they not pushed me early on to practice more than I had wanted to, maybe I would never have discovered my own potential."

Most parents probably do a certain amount of "pushing." It depends on how it's done. The late violinist Isaac Stern, who helped guide many prodigies, noted in a 1979 article in the *New York Times Magazine* that the young musicians he taught all had someone pushing them, often a parent, "sometimes gently," but sometimes not. He warned that the nature of the pushing would influence the outcome, whether the child would develop and mature as a musician or would end up leaving music.

"As a teacher, I try to balance whatever the students are experiencing at home," says Peabody violin teacher Rebecca Henry. "If home life is fairly unstructured, I tend to provide more structure in my lessons with that child, giving clearer expectations for what to do in practicing. If the home is very structured, and I can count on consistent practice and oversight by a parent, I can broaden the concepts in the lesson. If I sense excessive expectations and tension from a parent, I spend time emphasizing that studying music is a complex, beautiful process that takes time, helping the parent relax and enjoy the process. However, I find that in many families that have high expectations of the children, their children are used to this and some can handle a lot of detailed expectations in the lesson. I try to meet the students where they are and offer what they need."

SPOTLIGHT ON: ALISA WEILERSTEIN, CELLO

A touch of humor: "I started practicing with my father when I was nine. He was strict, but he made it fun," says Alisa Weilerstein. She would practice first on her own and then with her violinist father, Donald Weilerstein. He created silly characters to deliver his advice. "One would talk in opposites, using a high falsetto voice, getting madder the better I played," recalls Ms. Weilerstein. "I was a rusher and this character would say, 'Play faster!' So I would play slower. With string instruments, you're supposed to play close to the bridge to have a clear sound. This character would kick and scream, 'I hate it when you play close to the bridge!'" Her father says the silliness "took the tension out of it. In a round-about way, I was pointing out what she should do. Alisa liked that the characters were strange, and she could defy them. There were also good characters that would fight with the bad ones, like a children's puppet show, without any puppets. Gradually the practicing became more conventional, but if tension began to build, we would call in the characters again."

Yoko Segerstrom, mother of two musicians who are headed for professional careers, used a fairly strict approach with her kids but has had second thoughts about it. "My attitude now is totally different," she says. "Practice was always a struggle with my kids, especially in elementary school. When I look back, I think I was too strict with my kids. It all worked out, but it wasn't always pretty. My daughter was very dramatic. There were a lot of tears, although she says now that she thanks me. I feel I could have introduced music in a different way." This music mom isn't a professional musician but can play piano and now teaches piano to young students in an after-school program. "I'm more laid back with my students than I was with my kids. I changed quite a bit because of my kids' musical endeavors."

What to Say—or Not—as a Practice Coach

Although new music parents who aren't musicians may wonder how they can possibly have anything useful to say as their children practice, our advisors note that it's not as hard as it seems. "Even if they don't know how to play the instrument, parents can be extremely helpful by guiding the child's inquiry and discovery process, asking good questions, and collaborating with the teacher who does know what to do," explains NEC's Larry Scripp.

Mei Carpenter, a nonmusician who raised three accomplished musicians, explains that at the beginning, "They were starting at such a basic level that it was pretty straightforward what to do and say. I went to their Suzuki lessons, took notes, and knew from the teacher exactly what they needed to work on at home."

As noted earlier, non-Suzuki parents who aren't sitting in on lessons can refer to the weekly assignment book or have a quick chat with the teacher after a lesson about what the child is supposed to accomplish that week. "Look at the child's assignment book a few times a week and say, 'Oh, I see your teacher wrote such and such. Can you show me how that goes?' That gives the child independence while also showing interest," suggests piano teacher Carole Prochazka. "Or if the parent hears the child playing the same section over and over, getting stuck in the same place, ask if the teacher wrote anything about that in the assignment book. The parent could also ask the teacher after the next lesson how the child could handle problems like that." Baltimore mother Lynette Fields encourages her children to do the asking. "If my daughter is having trouble with something when she's practicing flute, I say, 'Wait until you go back to school and ask the teacher.'"

Regardless of what kinds of suggestions a parent may offer, the mode and timing can make a difference in how they are received. As Sarah Odhner and Dr. Yeou-Cheng Ma discovered, shouting commands from across the room isn't ideal. Nor is interrupting the child to make corrections while the youngster is playing a piece or a section of it. "My daughter did not react well to my interrupting her playing to remind her to use proper technique. It created anxiety in her as she played. I've stopped doing that," says Kim Hanna, New York mother of a young violinist. Interruptions can make children lose a sense of the flow of what they're doing.

"At one point when my daughters were about five and six years old, I was so annoyed with myself for interrupting that I told them I'd do five push-ups if I interrupted again," notes Kim Field. "Once I actually had to do the push-ups. Most of the time now, I listen when they are playing, and if I have ideas and corrections, I type them on my laptop so I don't forget. Not only do I tell them my ideas right after they have finished the passage (or piece), but I also save the notes and print them after practicing. Since my children now often practice on their own, they have my notes to help them when I am not around."

However, even if you wait for the child to finish, launching in right away with corrections can be disheartening. Dana Myers, a St. Louis Symphony Orchestra violinist whose piano-teacher father supervised her childhood practicing, recalls, "Sometimes I resented that he could be heavy-handed and negative with me. Being critical can sour the whole experience. He took it as a personal insult if I dared to play a single note out of tune. However, my father had a lot to do with the fact that my intonation is solid. I have him to thank. If you're criticized too much, you get to the point where you're afraid to make mistakes. Sometimes you have to let kids make mistakes, and then talk it through."

Violin teacher Dorothy Kaplan Roffman recommends delivering suggestions in a way that encourages children to think about what to work on next in the piece, to prepare them to take charge of their practicing. "If there is a troublesome measure, the parent can ask, 'What was it your teacher said to do about that?' This helps the child remember what happened in the lesson," says Ms. Roffman. "It's good not to feel that everything has to be fixed at once, to work on one thing even when other things aren't working."

Erika Nickrenz tried to help her son think about how to solve his practice problems in the coaching that she did with him during the first year and half after he started trumpet at age eight. "I let him play through a piece without stopping. Then we would talk about what was good about it first," she explains. "I'd praise him a lot for what he did well. That's better than always saying, 'Oh, this is wrong' and being negative. He can feel good. He knows that I see he's trying. Then I'd ask if he thought it was perfect or if there was anything that needed a bit of work. As a teacher, I do the same with my piano students. I want kids to learn to think for themselves and listen to what's coming out of their instruments. Sometimes my son would say it was perfect even if it wasn't. Other times he'd say he missed this

Professional pianist Erika Nickrenz helping her son practice trumpet.

or that. If it was a rhythm thing, we'd work on counting. If he wasn't playing in tune, I'd say, 'Can you make that sound more in tune?' Now, he practices by himself, but I can hear him from another room and I'll come in and out, to help or not, depending on his mood."

Targeted Comments

Once teens and independent-minded preteens take charge of practice, figuring out what to say—if anything—requires masterful diplomatic skills. Anne McCollough would wait until her son, James, asked for comments. Then she would frame her responses carefully. "We learned not to comment unless asked," says this New York mother. "His music is his music. I would often cook dinner while he practiced. We'd wait until he said, 'What do you think of this?' Then I would say what was good or maybe that one part could be smoother. It would never work to tell him it was all great because he would know we hadn't really listened."

Larry Scripp agrees that it's important to give targeted comments—"smart praise, instead of empty, pro forma praise. The way you praise matters," he explains. "Pick out something specific to say about their playing that was good. Or you could ask the child, 'Is there something about the piece you thought you couldn't do and now you can?' You want to celebrate their learning, not their 'talent.'" For example, parents could say that they like the way one particular phrase was played, noting that the child's hard work on that section paid off.

According to education researchers, studies show that praising the *work* a child does on a task is more effective than just praising them for being smart, talented kids. Complimenting innate ability can make kids reluctant to tackle hard challenges, because they might be afraid that if they should fail at a particularly demanding task, that might tarnish their reputation for being "smart" kids. Whereas kids who are praised for being hard workers are more likely to keep up the effort.

Different Kids—Different Strategies

Some parents find that effective practice-coaching is not one-size-fits-all. Different children require different strategies. Mei Carpenter's older daughter, a violinist, was more amenable to suggestions than her younger daughter, a cellist. After the relatively easy early years of helping her cellist practice, "We'd get into such battles about what and how to practice. I realized I needed to step back and let her do her thing, that I can't be so invested in this. I didn't want to live through my kids," says this Ohio mother. "I decided this is hers. It's up to her to practice. I'm not there to make sure she's perfect."

Rebecca Henry used different approaches with her twin daughters. "I might suggest the same kinds of things to each of the girls, but their reactions and learning styles were completely different. One has perfectionist tendencies. If anything wasn't right, she'd get mad and stop, instead of playing it through and working on it. My other daughter would play a piece through ten times and be happy whether it sounded good or not. I found these differences fascinating as a parent and as a teacher."

Another mother was already familiar with using different strategies with her two children because her younger child has mild attention deficit disorder, while her older one does not. This mother uses similar approaches in helping the younger child with music as with regular homework. Mom is there to keep things on track and talk things through if the child gets frustrated, although this youngster is not shy about sometimes saying, "I'm a musician, thank you, and would like to just play now with no comments." The older child practices alone although sometimes asks a parent to sit nearby, to listen or to read a book.

Raising three string musicians and a guitarist called for great adaptability on Dominique van de Stadt's part. "One child preferred to practice wherever I was, mostly in the kitchen preparing dinner. Another practiced in the bedroom with the door closed. The other two were more flexible and changed their routines according to their moods," explains this Arizona mom. "Some liked input, some only praise, and some nothing—only a willing ear. I tried to accommodate these styles while requiring a certain standard of work. I commented or made observations when I could not help myself (too pointed at times, I admit)."

Practice—Not Just a Run-Through

Many of our parent advisors report that it isn't easy for kids to grasp the idea that zipping through a piece from start to finish isn't the best way to practice. "No matter what I or their teachers said, it took all of my children time to figure out that slow, focused practice with extra work on the technically difficult passages was more effective than playing through pieces a little too fast, over and over, with frustrating stumbles along the way," says Ms. van de Stadt. Seconding that is New Yorker Lisa Sgouros, who notes, "It took a while for our daughter to realize that when she practices more efficiently, she enjoys it more."

"That's one of the things that a good teacher does—show the child what effective practice is and model it for them in the lesson," says Carol Prochazka. "You work on it with students in a certain way in the lesson and they see the results. I'd say, 'This is what I want you to do at home,' knowing that it still probably won't get done because it's hard. It's about setting specific goals." San Francisco Conservatory piano faculty member William Wellborn explains, "When we start a new piece, no matter how talented the students are, I show them the best way to practice it."

"There was never a problem getting our daughter to play her violin. Actual practicing, however, as opposed to amusing herself by playing, took longer to figure out," recalls Annette Radoff, mother of professional violinist Elena Urioste. "It's fun to noodle around on the violin. It's less fun to hammer through something, time and time again very slowly, doing the labor-intensive, nitty-gritty work that it takes to play the kind of repertoire she wanted to play. Eventually it sinks in. When Elena was young, we had a 'warm fuzzy' jar. After each practice session when she did the kind of hard work her teachers wanted and didn't just play around on the violin, we would put a cotton ball in the jar. When it was full, Elena would choose an activity as a reward, like watching a movie, going on an outing, or baking things together. She began to set specific goals for each session. Having teachers who helped her understand how to do this was critical."

There are many techniques that can help kids become more effective practicers. In addition to slow, focused practicing and working on a new piece in small, manageable chunks, it's also useful to do "smart repetitions." That involves repeating a trouble spot correctly several times after the child has managed to figure out how to play it right. The repetition helps cement the correct moves into muscle memory.

Keeping careful notes during a practice session has helped some youngsters. Betsy McCarthy, Seattle mom of a jazz pianist, says that during high school her son became "extraordinarily disciplined in his practicing. He kept a notebook of what he did each day." The same strategy worked for trumpeter Mark Inouye of the San Francisco Symphony Orchestra. "I would write down my problems and my progress, almost like I was keeping score. Every wrong note was a point for the 'other team.' I would listen to my playing so I could catch problems," says Mr. Inouye. "I wanted to shut out the opponent. Zero points for the other team! I was able to chart small improvements, note by note. I saw the value and fun in hard work because I could see and hear improvements, even if they were small—especially if they were small. Success overnight might not be realistic, but improvement overnight is definitely possible."

Attending master classes can also let kids (and parents) learn effective practice techniques. In master classes, a professional musician or master teacher critiques performances by a few students who serve as guinea pigs. These classes are usually done before an audience and are often held at music schools. Watching a master teacher zero in on problems in a student's performance and offer practical suggestions for the student to try on the spot—often with dramatic improvement—provides a glimpse into how to practice. "It doesn't matter if the master class is for the instrument a child studies. The child can learn so much about musicality in general," says Michael Steger, who has taken his violinist and cellist daughters to master classes for many other instruments at their New York music school.

"Practice is something you're always learning how to do better," says pianist Jonathan Biss. "I practiced better when I was at conservatory at the Curtis Institute than I did during high school. I practice better now than I did at Curtis." Many musicians actually come to like practicing. "When you practice well, you feel so centered, as I imagine runners must feel," says Dana Myers. Cellist Adrienne Taylor adds, "Practice is an essential part of my life. I don't feel right if I don't practice. It's such an interesting time to have to yourself each day, to really work on something, think about something, to focus. It's almost meditative." (The Bibliography notes books that offer practice suggestions.)

SPOTLIGHT ON: ISABEL TRAUTWEIN, VIOLIN

Energy: "The first time I had fun with violin, I was eight years old and went to summer music camp," says Cleveland Orchestra violinist Isabel Trautwein, who began Suzuki violin at age five. "I love my mom, and I'm grateful that she practiced with me, but it was joyless—counting mistakes, doing things ten times." At music camp in her Alabama hometown "music came to life." The camp director used easy arrangements of classical pieces. "She would get in front of complete beginners and within an hour had us making great music. It was fantastic. It was fun." Ms. Trautwein tries to instill that feeling in the kids' programs she started in Cleveland, including El Sistema@Rainey, a free after-school program; and also TACO—The Awesome Children's Orchestra—which on one day a year has kids and pros perform together, "re-creating the energy of that first camp I went to as a kid."

Students in one of Isabel Trautwein's El Sistema programs—El Sistema @ Rainey—performing with kids from a similar program in Cincinnati— MYCincinnati—conducted by violinist Eddy Kwon.

An Assist from Technology

As Theresa Chong discovered, taping a lesson can help a youngster know what to do when working on a piece at home. Cleveland Orchestra trombonist Shachar Israel requires his students to record their lessons. "I have students who practice a lot but don't practice right. So I say, 'No recording—no lesson.' I also have students record their practice. Listening to their own practicing is part of practicing."

Making recordings doesn't require elaborate systems. Some students use cell phones, laptops, or inexpensive tape recorders. Peabody's Rebecca Henry uses a cell phone to take snapshots that students "can take home as a reference. If a student is holding the bow just right or doing something else fabulous, we take a picture of it and e-mail or text it so they can see that when they go home."

A computer program helped instill good practice habits in Kristin Bond's younger daughter after she switched to trumpet. "She practices trumpet without being asked," says Ms. Bond, who gives partial credit to SmartMusic, a computer program used in the local middle school. "Her grade was dependent on using SmartMusic at home with her computer to record herself practicing. She'd record herself playing a passage, and the computer gives a score on a 100-point scale. She kept trying to get high nineties. The scores went to the teacher." In addition, her daughter "has fallen in with a group of kids who love trumpet. They work really hard on it, learning challenging pieces to audition for district and all-state bands."

Going Solo

Some youngsters, either by necessity or choice, do well without any parental monitoring of their practicing. "By the time I was nine, I was getting up at 5:00 a.m. to practice violin before school. That got me out from under my parents' critical ears because they were still asleep," says Marin Alsop.

Violinist Jennifer Koh also practiced solo much of the time. "My parents couldn't be looking over my shoulder all the time because they worked full time," she explains. "I'd take the bus to and from school and come home alone. A lot of it was self-discipline. For me it was also a personal thing. I loved reading, and I loved violin. Now looking back on it, I realize the things I loved were solitary things. Even swimming, which I did until I was ten, if you're on a swim team, it's not like basketball where you're interacting with people all the time. These things seem to suit my personality."

Professional pianist Gloria Cheng handled practicing on her own, too. "I was born with a strong sense of self-discipline. It's not something I'm proud of or not proud of—it's just a fact. I had a watch that I hung on my piano lamp, and would begin practicing at 3:27 p.m. each weekday after returning from school. My goal was to get in two solid hours of practicing before my mother returned from work, usually at 5:30 p.m. The extra three minutes were in case the phone rang (no answering machines then) or if I happened to get a cookie. I don't know where this part of my personality came from, and I don't know if those two hours were productive in any real sense, but I did put in my time. Nowadays, thankfully, I'm much looser about the situation!"

Self-taught rock musician Keith Fertwagner practiced on his own, too, but not exactly "solo." When learning to play drums, he recalls, "I'd make tapes of music I liked and come home after school and play for hours a day in the garage banging away on the drums, listening to those recordings, figuring out how to do what the drummers on the recordings were doing."

Listening Counts

"We let listening count as part of practice time," recalls Dominique van de Stadt. "We would have our kids listen to performances of pieces they're learning and watch excellent musicians play the pieces on YouTube."

"Listening to music is incredibly important," says Dorothy Kaplan Roffman. "I'm constantly telling my students to download some CDs, get into a comfy chair at home, turn the lights down, and listen. Think about the sounds you're hearing and try to recognize the different kinds of sounds that different performers have. Is it a crunchy sound, a heavenly sound, a singing sound, a ringing sound? Then think about how does that happen?"

Keith Fertwagner gives the same advice to his School of Rock students. "Listen to a lot of different styles of music," he tells them. "Everybody has different methods, different ways of writing and playing. There's a lot of information in that music. Listen and figure out what someone is doing on the guitar part. Once you know, you can try. It's impossible for anyone to match a song one hundred percent. You do your rendition, let your personality shine through while keeping true to the song."

Broad-based listening as a teenager helped prepare Christian McBride for his cross-genre performing and composing career. "My uncle plays acoustic bass, and when my mother told him I was taking acoustic bass lessons in school, he was overjoyed and had me come over to his house," says Mr. McBride. "My uncle pulled out a big stack of albums and force fed me jazz all day. That could have been risky. Sometimes people beat you over the head with this, that this is something that's good for you, almost like medicine. But the way he did it was perfect. He was so cool. He always had hip clothes, the quintessential cool cat. He's sitting there listening to these recordings and would have a jolt of excitement if he liked something. He'd say, 'Give me five! Isn't that hip!' I didn't know what he was talking about, but I thought if he's enjoying jazz that much, there's something there I need to pay attention to. Before then, I was into pop culture, listening to whatever was on the radio—Michael Jackson, Prince." His uncle's enthusiasm inspired him to begin listening to jazz, but he kept listening to all the other music he liked as well—pop, rhythm and blues,

Wynton Marsalis

soul, and classical. "As much as I loved jazz, I never stopped listening to soul. To me, James Brown deserves as much attention and study as Miles Davis. Music is music, no matter where it comes from."

Listening to jazz albums turned around trumpeter Wynton Marsalis. His father, Ellis Marsalis, explains, "I was able to get a trumpet for him when he was six, but it mainly sat in the closet for about six years." Basketball was more important to Wynton than trumpet until he heard an album by jazz trumpeter Clifford Brown and decided he wanted to play that way. After that, "Wynton would practice consistently, set goals for himself, have schedules that he would make up every day," says his father. His trumpeter son was also listening to classical music. During high school, after sitting in on a rehearsal of Beethoven's Fifth Symphony with a community orchestra, he became a Beethoven fan. In addition to perfecting his jazz and funk skills, he was also playing classical music. He analyzed Beethoven's symphonies and wrote his senior term paper in high school on Beethoven's string quartets.

Pianist Erika Nickrenz also advocates wide-ranging listening. "If your kids are studying piano, don't just have them listen to piano music or go only to piano recitals. Open up their ears to all instruments. My mother took me to lots of kinds of performances and had the radio on all the time, blasting music out all day long. Hearing and loving other music helped me stay passionate about piano."

Role Models

"My son has a pretty good attitude about practicing trumpet, but he has an advantage in hearing his parents practicing all the time," says Erika Nickrenz, whose husband is a professional clarinetist. "My son has accepted that it's part of the routine. In hearing how we practice, he knows that you can't instantly learn pieces unless there's slow playing and lots of repetition." The same was true for jazz drummer Ali Jackson. His parents were musicians. Being involved in their musical world made practicing seem like a normal everyday activity. "My parents involved me in their daily routines, which included rehearsing and performing. Practice was something I enjoyed. After the passing of my father when I was twelve, my passion for music was engrained. I was self-motivated, moving forward."

Marin Alsop had the same advantage. "My parents practiced for hours each day. That was the example always present in our home. This was good and bad. It made me understand that practicing is necessary in order to be a high-achieving artist, but sometimes I felt in competition with their practicing for their time. My parents also always played music with me. Music drew us together and became a source for sharing and enjoying each other." When Ms. Alsop developed an interest in

SPOTLIGHT ON: ELLIS AND WYNTON MARSALIS, PIANO AND TRUMPET

Lead by example: "People ask, 'Did you make your kids practice?' No, I did not," says Ellis Marsalis. "I was never a stage-door dad because I was doing the same thing myself, trying to figure out how to play this music myself. I was a practicing musician. Whatever my sons took away was hearing the music I was working on." He was playing jazz gigs while also teaching at the New Orleans Center for Creative Arts, which his sons attended during high school. His son Wynton Marsalis notes, "My daddy kind of taught all of us to play on some level. We grew up with his sound." His father's gigs made an impression. "I grew up always watching my father and other jazz musicians playing. They never played for that many people. They were always struggling. They didn't make any money. They played clubs—there'd be five people in the club." This famous son, by founding Jazz at Lincoln Center, has helped spark a jazz revival that has created a huge new audience for jazz.

conducting at age nine, "My parents were extraordinarily supportive. They told me, 'You can do anything you want to do.' My father even bought me my first set of batons."

Professional musician parents aren't the only ones who can serve as role models. So can parents who play an instrument as a hobby or who sing in a choir. "My daughter, who plays flute, convinced me to start flute lessons. I love it," says Heather MacShane, a Massachusetts mother of a flutist and a harp player. "I think my taking flute lessons validated music for everyone." Kristin Bond pulled out the French horn she hadn't played in years to join an ensemble at her church. "Both my girls have played in that ensemble with me," she says. "It's a small group of mixed ages, some high schoolers, along with adults of differing abilities. I hadn't played my horn for almost twenty years. I started again, really awful at first, but it was good for my girls to see adults performing, some proficient and others less so. They see there's a place for every level of ability to enjoy music."

Thanh Huynh, who explained in an earlier chapter that she started jazz piano lessons as a hedge against an empty nest, notes, "My daughter could see that I practice what I preach with regards to practicing." Before long, her daughter caught the jazz bug and added jazz lessons to her violin lessons. The summer after her junior year in high school, this young violinist heard Ranaan Meyer's trio, Time for Three, perform its blend of bluegrass, rock, and classical. She switched from jazz lessons to free-form improvisation lessons. "She's not going to be a professional musician, but training in improvisation in any form is a useful skill in life," says her mom.

Being There

At some point in a youngster's development, the role of "appreciative listener" may be exactly the right way to encourage practicing. According to Sue Jones: "When my daughter was young, up until about age twelve, she always wanted me there to listen to her practice flute. I didn't comment. I have no real knowledge of music. I never had any music lessons. I just enjoyed listening to her." Clarinetist Richard Stoltzman had an appreciative listener when he was starting out—his grandmother, who would sit with him as he practiced. "She wouldn't say anything, other than sometimes she'd say, 'Oh, that's pretty. Play that again.' She'd never say, 'Oh, that's not good.' Sometimes you practice and nobody's listening—*you* aren't even listening. You go on automatic pilot and don't accomplish anything. Having the feeling that there's somebody there, even though she wasn't critical—or maybe because she wasn't critical—was very nice." Violinist Adrian Anantawan, who practiced on his own as a kid, says, "I would come into my parents' room after I practiced. They might be in bed, late at night, but they would listen to me play whatever I had been working on and were always encouraging."

"I never miss their performances, no matter how small," says Sue Woods, St. Louis mother of three young musicians. She feels this helps keep alive their interest in music. Flutist Paula Robison still remembers that her parents "came to all my concerts. They were my cheering section." High school band director Matthew Ceresini has seen how this kind of support plays out in his band room: "I find that the students who are good players and practice a lot are the ones whose parents come to all the concerts. They're invested in what their kids are doing instead of just buying an instrument."

However, a few educators warn that sometimes parental enthusiasm can edge into "stage mom and dad" territory. As one teacher says, "The parents who aren't so helpful are the ones who know their child hasn't been practicing and still want to know why the child didn't get a solo. The parents who are enormously helpful are the ones who listen to their kids practice, come to performances, and encourage their kids to get better."

Joining a youth ensemble may help adolescents stay as excited about music as these members of the Young People's Chorus of New York City.

9 Managing the Ups and Downs

MUSICAL JOURNEYS HAVE THEIR UPS AND DOWNS. Even the most enthusiastic young musicians can struggle when they hit a rough patch. In this chapter, our advisors share ideas on how they helped their youngsters pick themselves up after a tumble and keep moving forward. To start the discussion, here's how one mother handled a common stumbling block—sibling friction.

"Our older daughter announced during middle school that she didn't want to play violin anymore," says one of our parent advisors. "It's not uncommon for an older sibling to be overtaken by a younger one and that's what happened to my older daughter." Both sisters had been playing violin since they were about six years old. They studied with the same teachers, played in the same group classes and youth ensembles. The older girl would "get so frustrated when it was clear that her younger sister had caught up and surpassed her. She also didn't like some of the music she was playing."

Realizing that her threatening-to-quit daughter really loved music, this music mom found a way to ride out the storm. She scoured the Internet for people who distribute sheet music for a special kind of music that her older daughter liked and acquired a batch of it. "My daughter said that was the only kind of music that interested her. So when she would say she was going to quit, I would pull out a piece of this music and say, 'Oh, why not sight-read this,'" explains this mom. "We did that for a couple of months. Her teacher was on-board with this because she realized that my daughter was trying to provoke a showdown, and if we did anything else, she really would quit. Her teacher is a mom herself who went through the adolescent phase with her own children and understood what was going on."

Another teacher who knew both sisters suggested that the older girl could switch to another instrument. "That could sidestep the whole competition issue," says the mom. "This teacher thought my older daughter could become an excellent violist. I spoke with her violin teacher and orchestra director and they thought this was a wonderful idea. My daughter was OK with this, too, and now plays nothing but viola and loves it."

After switching instruments and teachers, this young violist was willing to play other pieces in addition to her favorite tunes. She still wasn't thrilled about practicing, but did well enough to win a place in an advanced youth orchestra and make all-state. Her mom realizes that having both girls play the same instrument with the same teacher for so many years may not have been a good idea. "We should have known or someone should have pointed out to us that they should have had different teachers." But thanks to the creative collaboration between teacher and mom, a discouraged youngster found her way back to music.

"They'll Thank You"

The timing of that young violist's musical crisis is typical of many threatening-to-quitters, coming as it did during middle school. "I find that the most dangerous time for kids wanting to quit is from around age twelve to fourteen," says Sandra Shapiro, dean of the Cleveland Institute of Music's preparatory division. "By then, some kids have decided that music is what they want to do. But for kids for whom music has become a burden in some way, that's the hardest age range to keep them going. Maybe they feel pressured and don't want to live up to that pressure anymore. Or maybe they want more time with friends. Once they're over that hump, they're fine. But it's tough, because just handing out stickers doesn't cut it any more."

Helping adolescents trudge on through the rough spots puts parenting skills (and tempers) to the test, but many of our advisors rose to the challenge. "You want to do everything possible so the child doesn't give up music because they'll thank you at some point," says Mark Churchill, cello teacher, conductor, and former dean of the Preparatory School at New England Conservatory (NEC). "I've never met an adult who studied music as a child and gave it up who didn't say, 'I wish my parents hadn't let me quit.' Thousands of people over the years have told me that. Parents are given a real guilt trip by kids. On the one hand, kids say they want to quit, and then later on they'll say, 'Why did you let me give it up?' It's tricky because as kids become teenagers, you can't force them to do much of anything. If you try, it will backfire."

Child psychiatrist Dr. Gene Beresin warns, however, that parents can't always count on a they-will-thank-you-someday outcome. "There are scenarios where parents force kids to keep on with music and the kids say, 'My parents ruined it for me. If only they had just let me have fun with it.' Those kids didn't want to be forced to do another thing by their parents," says Dr. Beresin.

A successful outcome depends on how it's done. According to NEC's Mark Churchill, parents need to be "tuned into why the child is finding it hard. At the same time, you need to create an environment in those crucial adolescent years when kids start to build their own identities and pick their own activities, so that they will come to make the choice themselves to do music and continue to devote themselves to it."

The first—and often hardest—step involves figuring out what is really bothering the youngster. "Kids may say one thing but mean something else, or they may feel one thing one day and change their minds the next," says Missouri mom Sherrie Neumeier. "Talk with their teachers to get both sides of the story and then help the kids identify what really is the rough spot and help *them* find the solution. Give time to allow things to come to pass."

Earlier chapters have dealt with two approaches used by that young violist's family: changing instruments and teachers. (See chapters 4 and 5.) This chapter focuses on other ways parents have revived a kid's wavering interest. Our advisors also suggest how to handle other hurdles that may not necessarily cause youngsters to quit music but may take the joy out of it, such as having performance anxiety or a tendency toward perfectionism. In addition, there's a discussion of the often painful

Switching to a new teacher helped Betsy McCarthy's son find the aspect of music he became passionate about—playing in jazz bands.

conclusion some parents reach, that for some kids, it's best to send them forth to pursue their nonmusical interests.

Strike a Deal

"One of our daughters got tired of playing cello and wanted to stop. We didn't want to force her to keep playing, but we didn't want her to stop because we felt she'd miss it," says upstate New York mom Lis Bischoff-Ormsbee. "So we said she had made a commitment to the school orchestra and had to keep playing in orchestra but could stop her private lessons. That kept her playing. She still took group lessons in school with some older boys. In a couple of months, she was ready to study privately again in order to keep up with those boys."

William Wellborn made a special arrangement with one of his piano students. "He's smart and likes music, but he's not going to be a concert pianist," explains this San Francisco Conservatory faculty member. "He had lots of other interests, was very busy, and so we decided during his senior year of high school that he could have a lesson every other week. This is unusual. Most kids need the weekly lesson. Either I could be a monster and drive him away, or I could work with him where he is and help him have a great experience with music. Amazingly, he started playing better."

Harriet Wingreen, who for many years was the pianist with the New York Philharmonic and is profiled in *Meet the Musicians* (see Bibliography), lost interest in practicing piano during high school when she became involved in a drama group. Her wise piano teacher at the music school where she had a full scholarship encouraged her to keep coming to lessons even if she didn't practice. Instead of assigning pieces to be worked on at home, the teacher spent the lessons letting this teenager sight-read exciting new music. That turned Ms. Wingreen into a master sight-reader, which helped a few years later when she returned to music and auditioned successfully at a conservatory. (See Resources for an online video about her.)

Give Them a Break

Julia Castro didn't just lower the pressure on her daughter by lightening her practice schedule. She gave this teenager a break from music. Her daughter, like the violist described earlier, had sibling issues. She played the same instrument as her older brother—double bass—and felt frustrated that she couldn't keep up with him. She had chosen to play bass in elementary school because she thought her brother could help her, and he did. "Because he was doing so well on bass, I think she thought it would be easy, not realizing how hard he was working on it. Her brother knew right from the start that he wanted to be a musician and has worked toward that and practiced a lot, but my daughter was never as motivated to practice. In her midteens, I think she felt that she was never going to be as good as he is. So she took a year off," Ms. Castro explains. "Then she found that she missed it. She has gone back to bass, at a different New York music school than he attends. It was her decision to go back. We said that if she goes back, she has to practice. Now she realizes this is important to her, and I don't have to force her to practice. She's even thinking of going on to a conservatory or becoming a teacher. She's not sure. I don't want to push her."

Change the Music

"Our younger daughter played piano, hated the pressure of performances, and so we allowed her to quit. What we should have done was find a better teacher, one willing to let her play popular music instead of classical," says Kyle Todd. Several of our advice givers managed to do what this Massachusetts dad wished he had done. They found teachers who gave students a broader range of music to study, which revived the youngsters' interest.

"If children don't like the music they're playing, speak with the teacher and try to find an alternate, an equivalent piece in terms of technical challenges and musicianship," says Dominique van de Stadt, the Arizona mom who has had a lot of experience maneuvering her four kids past their musical hurdles. "If the hated piece absolutely has to be learned, balance it with a piece the child really likes."

Several of our educator advisors who focus on classical music say they are fine with including nonclassical tunes. "Almost all of my cello students have two lives," says Mark Churchill. "They're serious classical musicians who practice a lot, but at the same time they're listening to popular music on their iPods. They need to bring those two worlds together. I encourage them to improvise, compose, play jazz and other genres." He notes that in the new El Sistema programs, students perform classical standards as well as pop tunes arranged for orchestra. He recommends a book that shows how a New Jersey piano teacher incorporates many kinds of music in her lessons: *Note by Note* by Tricia Tunstall. (See Bibliography.)

"I involved my students in the choice of pieces," says Carol Prochazka, former head of piano at Peabody Preparatory. "I'd play them a few possibilities and have them rate the pieces on a scale of one to ten—from 'I love it' to 'I hate it.' There's so much variety, even in the classical repertoire, so many choices. If the child isn't interested in the classical repertoire, there are plenty of well-written popular types of music that could be taught, that are pedagogically sound and might engage them more."

However, handing out pop tunes may not excite youngsters whose frustration stems from wanting to play classical pieces that are too difficult. "Some students haven't advanced far enough to be able to play music that's as sophisticated as they are, especially if they're late beginners," says Peabody violin teacher Rebecca Henry. "They may want to play Beethoven, but there may not be any pieces by Beethoven that they're ready to play. Maybe there's something else from that period they can play that taps into their musical sophistication."

Quadruple Play

April Hansen changed everything—teacher, instrument, type of music, and learning environment. "Our daughter had started on piano in fourth grade. It was her choice, not something we forced her to do. She liked it at first. But when it got hard, she'd get frustrated. If she couldn't get it the first time, she'd stop practicing. When she would practice, she'd do well in her lesson but getting her to practice was so stressful, a battle of wills. I didn't want to force her to do something she didn't want to do. By seventh grade we realized something had to change," says Ms. Hansen.

"A friend opened a branch of the School of Rock here in Omaha, and we thought that would be more fun for her. It's music she's familiar with." They signed her up for rock keyboard. That didn't work either. "My daughter kept saying she wanted to sing," says Ms. Hansen. "I tried to persuade her that playing piano can help if you sing, but I met with more resistance. So she switched from keyboard to vocals. She loves it! We love to hear her sing. At the School of Rock, each kid has a forty-five-minute lesson a week, and they're also put right away in a band group. So it's not an individual thing—it's a group thing. They learn how to listen to each other, how a rock band works as a team. Once they're proficient enough, they move into a performance group and use the skills they're learning to put on shows. They do a new show every three or four months. The first show she was in was about the Beatles. The school makes it fun. They're actually learning about music and music theory without realizing they're learning. It fits her learning style. She was bored with the traditional learning process, using lesson books. Every kid is different and every family is different. What works for one doesn't work for all, but this works for her."

Help with Plateau-ing

"As my son and daughter transition from intermediate to advanced (or beginner to intermediate), transitions can be difficult. When they find they cannot play the new level, it's frustrating and they want to give up. It's important to be patient and supportive," says Donald Tam. This California father of two piano students is describing a common problem: how hard it is to move from a comfortable skill level to one that's much more demanding.

If being supportive and encouraging doesn't work, Beverly Berndt has found it helps to let her daughter take a break from working on the hard, new piece that's causing difficulties. "I let her not play the instrument for a while and work on something else," says this Kansas City mom whose daughter plays several instruments. "Then when she goes back to it, she starts on scales and a favorite piece that she can play until that gets her ready to conquer the rough one." Also helpful is a reminder about practice strategies that have worked in the past, including a key one that impatient youngsters often skip—slow practice. In addition, parents or kids could ask the teacher to suggest specific practice techniques geared to the troublesome piece.

"Even kids who are serious about music have times when they hit a plateau and are stuck," notes Rebecca Henry. She has found that teens and preteens are especially prone to this. "A lot of students that age become self-conscious and self-deprecating. Their bodies are changing. They're concerned with how they appear to their friends. Sometimes they lose their sense of progress on their instruments. I try to give them perspective. Although they might feel that they are not progressing or wish they were playing more advanced repertoire (or whatever the issue is), I point out that the quality of their sound is much more beautiful or that they are expressing themselves more emotionally now. I also let them set their own goals. I might think the student needs bow-arm work, but she may not be open to that right now. Instead of my having this objective agenda of the sequential things that a student should do (which of course I have in my head), I'll see what the student is interested in improving. Some

SPOTLIGHT ON: JENNY UNDERCOFLER, PIANO, EDUCATOR

Turnaround: As a piano student at Juilliard and Eastman, Jenny Undercofler enjoyed playing pieces by contemporary composers. As music director of a New York public school that offers classical music training, she started Face the Music, an after-school group that performs the kind of new music she likes by such composers as Philip Glass. "At first, Face the Music was a home for students who were disaffected with regular practicing. For some, it was a complete turnaround. It hooked them on repertoire they found more motivating and got them taking their instruments out of the case more." No longer limited to students from her school, the ensemble has grown to more than seventy kids. It performs in concert halls and clubs. "Playing in different places and meeting contemporary composers gives them a taste of what they could do later as musicians."

may wish they could play faster or sight-read better. I find out what they are interested in improving or playing and use that window of opportunity to get them remotivated."

Make It Social

For youngsters who are in a slump, joining ensembles can provide a friendly boost. Marion Taylor notes that the social aspect of music helped rekindle her young flutist's interest in music, in addition to having a chance to coast a bit in her flute lessons for a while, as described earlier. "A major turning point was getting into honor bands, such as all-county or all-state," says Ms. Taylor. "The bands were fun. She liked seeing the same folks year after year at all-state festivals, and unlike the sports she played (soccer and lacrosse) there were boys in the honor bands. Boys from the honor bands became her new, nonsports friends. She'd go to music events with them."

"The start of adolescence is a very social time. If they don't have friends who are musicians, it can be hard," explains Sandra Shapiro. "With large ensembles there are often picnics or parties." Some ensembles go on tour or take part in music festivals, offering more opportunities for a musical social life. Some musical activities actually put teens right in the center of a high school's most important social events—the school musical and football games. In addition, as noted earlier, ensembles that aren't part of regular school have the added advantage of usually playing more exciting pieces than school-based groups, which can provide a boost for teens who are bored with their school ensemble's repertoire.

Joining outside musical ensembles can also help those youngsters whose musical interests are so intense that they may have trouble fitting in at their regular schools. "Our son's serious interest in and understanding of music began at such a young age that it made him different from other children," recalls one member of our advice panel. A few other parents report that their kids had similar friend-making issues. Not many use the word "bullying," but even if difficulties didn't rise to that level, several youngsters felt a sense of isolation because they were so committed to an artistic pursuit that their classmates didn't share or understand. The parents of these kids all found the same solution: They involved their children with others who were equally enthusiastic about music, either by enrolling them in a program at a music school, signing them up with a youth ensemble, or sending them to summer music camp. As one mom notes, "Music camp was the first time my son met other kids with a similar passion for music. He didn't feel as alone."

"The hardest period for our daughter came during the 'tween years," says Annette Radoff, mother of violinist Elena Urioste. "Elena felt as if she had a foot in each world—the music world and normal school. Elena knew that in order to be accepted at her public school, she had to keep her music to herself. Many of her school friends were simply not interested or didn't understand her commitment to violin. She did what she could to fit into their world, but there was a loneliness. Fortunately, we found the Center for Gifted Young Musicians." This program, offered by the preparatory division of the Boyer College of Music at Temple University in Philadelphia, is one of the by-audition-only programs for advanced youngsters offered at music schools and conservatories. Elena spent her Saturdays there from age twelve until she entered Curtis at age seventeen. "Temple Prep gave her a peer group of other gifted young musicians that she was able to learn from and socialize with," explains Ms. Radoff, whose daughter earned a partial scholarship there. "These were kids to share stories with and not have to explain why her fingers were calloused, or what that creepy mark on her neck was [from where the violin rubs on the neck]. Her social life centered around Temple Prep."

Bassist Ranaan Meyer agrees that regular school can sometimes be hard for musical kids. He and the other members of his string trio, Time for Three, made a video about bullying that has become a YouTube hit: "Time for Three—Stronger." He notes, "We all experienced a certain amount of bullying growing up. It wasn't just one person who gave us a hard time all through school, as in our video, although we know people to whom that happened. But there was always some knucklehead who would say something. With me it was sometimes random because I was carrying a

Ranaan Meyer (center) performing with his Time for Three string trio.

funny-looking instrument. Some person would think it was fun to ridicule me in front of their friends. I went to a public high school, and most students didn't know what a double bass was. In junior year, I began winning competitions, got into all-state jazz. All of a sudden I went from people not understanding to people celebrating. We made the video to make sure that in the music world we celebrate people and their uniqueness." (See Resources.)

Concertgoing

Attending live concerts can be a morale booster for youngsters who find themselves in a musical slump. If those concerts are a little out of the ordinary, even better. They can open kids' eyes to enticing, new possibilities. "The more you expose your children to interesting players and kinds of music, the better. We're in a music world now where people can't just do one musical style," says Melissa Tucker. "Look at Yo-Yo Ma, all the styles of music he plays." She took her flutist daughter to see a performance by boundary-breaking flutist, Greg Pattillo, who does what's called "beatboxing." He's a classically trained flutist who plays snazzed-up versions of tunes on flute—some classical, others not—while making popping noises with his mouth, to provide a driving beat for the song. "She loved it," says Ms. Tucker. "He also did workshops on improvisation and beatboxing. She was nervous about doing the workshop but really liked it. With experiences like this, the interest meter goes sky high. Here's a classical musician playing in this cool, funky style."

SPOTLIGHT ON: JOSHUA BELL, VIOLIN

Popularity: "I wasn't one of the popular kids at school, but I wasn't unpopular either," recalls Joshua Bell. "I don't think people knew what to make of me because I was also playing sports and didn't fit into any one category. For me, it's always been more important to have a few really good friends than being liked by everyone in school or anywhere else. If someone thinks you're weird because you play the violin, that person is an idiot. It's tough, though, those school years. But I've noticed that people who were popular in those school days don't always wind up being popular as adults."

To make the concert experience even more of a thrill, try going backstage afterward to meet the performers. "Many people don't realize that it's pretty easy to go backstage," says former artist manager Edna Landau. "Sometimes you need prior arrangement, but sometimes not. Meeting these role models is so important for young people. The mystique goes away. It reinforces the reality of what it means to be a performer, that they're not unreal but just like anyone else." It can also make youngsters feel that they're becoming part of the music world.

Going to a live performance completed the turnaround for Marion Taylor's flutist daughter. After she survived her middle school practicing slowdown, she still thought of herself as an athlete who played flute on the side. She had been thinking of doing premed. Then she saw a performance of the musical *Wicked* in New York City during the spring of her junior year of high school and was overwhelmed by the show's flutist. She sent her mom a text message during intermission to forget about med school, she wanted to be in the pit. That summer she made a return trip to Manhattan, met some of those pit musicians, and even sat in with the woodwind section. The text message to her mother that day was, "I'm in flute heaven."

Sports Issues

"We're feeling our way through the sports issue," says Heather Gange, who is trying to figure out where she falls on the worried-mom spectrum—from "I don't worry about sports at all" to "My child can never do sports or pick up heavy objects that might hurt a finger." To stake out a position, Ms. Gange consulted the orchestra teacher at her violinist daughter's Baltimore school. "We talked about sports you can expect to have injuries with and others where, if you're careful, there should be no problem," reports Ms. Gange. To complicate the situation, Ms. Gange's daughter is devoted to two sports that are among the most risky for a violinist: field hockey and soccer. "She wears her field hockey gloves, which we know will do no good if somebody bashes her hand. She is good at sports and is very social. Her friends play sports. For her, sports are a good thing." She's also pretty young. Her parents have decided to keep their fingers crossed and hope things will sort themselves out.

Julia Castro's son broke his collar bone playing soccer in seventh grade and couldn't play his double bass all summer. "He was devastated," she says. "He had auditions coming up. We told him, 'You have to give up one or the other.' He chose bass. It's hard because you want them to experience everything." Many of the kids of our parent advisors who played sports through high school focused on activities that were less likely to cause injuries to music-producing fingers and lips: swimming, track, cross country, tennis, golf, karate, tae kwon do, fencing, and figure skating. Dance provided an exercise outlet for several youngsters. Others did sports in a low-key way, not on official teams, but in pickup games.

"Find a balance," says Jiji Goosby, who has tried to do that with her violinist son Randall. "In elementary school, he played flag football. For a time, football was more important to him than violin. He said, 'I love playing violin but don't like practicing.' Instinctively, I knew he had something special with violin so I stayed stern and said, 'Whether you like it or not, you're going to practice. Let's get it over with in the morning before school so the afternoon is your free time.'" During middle school, violin became more important when he had heard about the Sphinx competition and decided to practice enough to enter it. He won the junior level at age thirteen. After that, he did sports just for fun, mainly pickup basketball games. "I tell him to be careful, not to jam his fingers, but I don't want to restrict him too much," says Ms. Goosby. "It's important to let him be a normal kid. If violin is everything, he'll go crazy and not enjoy it as much."

It wasn't fear of injury but waning interest that persuaded flutist Alice Jones to drop sports. She had been heavily into sports through middle school in her Texas hometown. "I did basketball, volleyball, kickball, and track," she says. "I realized over time that I didn't like them as much as playing flute. I would be in a basketball game, and I would feel nervous, not knowing if I can make the shot. But with flute, I didn't feel that kind of self-doubt. The decision was made for me by my reaction to what I was doing. I didn't keep up with sports after I started high school. Actually, there were weird scheduling things at my high school. You couldn't be on a varsity team and do anything else."

That brings up the other major sports hassle—scheduling conflicts. "Music teachers have always been more accommodating than coaches," reports Diane Cornelius. Several parents agree. When sports and music schedules conflict, it might help to involve the school music director in negotiations with a coach, according to Scott Brown, band director at Seattle's Roosevelt High School. "We try to find a way to compromise with our student athletes on performance and after-school rehearsals," he says. "We have a lot of clout with the athletic department because we bend over backward to support the sports teams. We have a marching band that plays at football games, a pep band at basketball games and volleyball matches." In addition, the school's jazz bands win prizes. "The coaches recognize that if someone is involved with our jazz bands, it's a prestigious thing. They're generally willing to make accommodations."

If team sports fall by the wayside, physical exercise still needs to have a place in a young musician's life. Cellist Alisa Weilerstein has tried to go jogging every day, both as a kid and as an adult. Violinist Anne Akiko Meyers notes, "Keeping in shape is imperative for a musician. I was on the track team at school and played soccer when I was younger. Now when I have to travel to perform, I always try to find a place to work out."

Lessen Perfectionism

Becoming a polished musician is a self-critical undertaking. However, for some youngsters, the pursuit of excellence can lead to such an excessive concern with spotting and correcting mistakes that making music loses its pleasure. "Perfectionism is an occupational hazard for musicians that we need to guard against," says San Francisco Conservatory's John McCarthy. Cleveland Institute's Sandra Shapiro agrees, "We musicians can be our own harshest critics, focusing on what goes wrong rather than saying, 'Wow, I really nailed that one passage.' It's important to be pleased with what goes well and say that next time, you'll take the next step, keep adding on layers of improvement. Of course, you won't ever be really satisfied because you'll always be reaching further, but you have to be in it for the joy of what you're doing."

Teachers and parents can contribute inadvertently to perfectionism, but they can also help keep perfectionism in check by modifying the messages about music making and performing that they send out to their youngsters. "Teachers can be a problem who are never satisfied and communicate that to their students, rather than emphasizing what the students have done well," says Ms. Shapiro. Parents can get caught in this trap, too, "by focusing on the wrong notes their children have played rather than on everything they're doing right."

It's important to emphasize to youngsters that mistakes happen, even to the pros, both in performances and especially when they're practicing. Pianist and music educator William Westney feels that mistakes can actually help musicians. The trick is to become interested in why they made the mistake rather than beating up on themselves for not being perfect. They can explore different adjustments to try until they hit on a way to correct the error. He has written a book on the topic, *The Perfect Wrong Note: Learning to Trust Your Musical Self*. (See Bibliography.)

Cellist Alisa Weilerstein observes that the way parents define a "successful" performance can make a big difference in a youngster's attitude. "I practiced a lot as a kid, and everyone made sure I was well prepared for concerts. But my parents taught me that a great performance isn't necessarily a perfect one," she explains.

SPOTLIGHT ON: RICHARD STOLTZMAN, CLARINET

Thank you: "It took me a while to realize that when I came home after a performance and spoke with my wife and kids, I'd talk only about what went wrong," recalls Richard Stoltzman. "My kids helped me see that I never said anything positive about this experience that we were all involved in all the time. It took several years to learn to shut up about all that went wrong and say something positive about the concert, at least when I was with the kids. They wanted to know I liked what I was doing. Save the critical assessment for later. I also learned that when people come backstage to congratulate me after a performance, they don't need to know what I'm dissatisfied with. All they want to hear is, 'Thank you.'"

Richard Stoltzman

"They told me it's better to have a performance that's interesting musically, where you've really communicated. It's always about communication. That's the important thing."

Piano teacher Sandra Shapiro agrees, "You want someone to tell a story up on the stage so that the music resonates with the audience. Live performances are not recordings. Things happen in a live performance, even to the most accomplished performers." That's why it's helpful to take youngsters to lots of concerts, so they can see that even if there may be a missed note now and then, a performance can still be enjoyable. Also helpful is to let kids know that the seemingly perfect performances on CDs have had all the errors edited out.

Of course, there are audiences that pay close attention to mistakes—the judges at a competition or audition—but even they may be won over by a performer's musicality despite a few glitches. Sandra Shapiro recalls an international piano duet competition that she and a partner won even though she lost her way in one piece. "The judges decided that despite my memory slip, we were head and shoulders above everyone else musically and in interpretation," she explains. "They weren't going to let a memory slip eliminate us because we recovered and went on to play well in the other rounds." (More on competitions in the next chapter.)

To reinforce the idea that absolute perfection isn't the goal, it's important to go easy during after-concert critiques, especially if there was a mess-up, so kids don't feel parents are out there keeping score. "We celebrated the things they did well with lots of sincere enthusiasm and praise. Then several days later we casually discussed things that could have made a good performance even better," notes Karen Rayfield.

"It is often hard for students to verbalize things they feel good about in a performance, but it's important for them to say what was good—that their memory was solid, or they felt improvement in some way, or that they said what they wanted to say in the music," says Rebecca Henry, violin teacher and music mom. "Later, when they talk through the performance either with a parent or with a teacher, they can talk about what they didn't like and how they would practice that section before the next performance. They can learn to take information objectively from each performance and use that to prepare for the next performance without being personal in their judgments of themselves, saying neither 'I am amazing' nor 'I am horrible.'"

San Francisco Conservatory's William Wellborn has noticed that in some situations, "the parents are creating problems without realizing it, putting on too much pressure. Sometimes it's a matter of me telling the parents that maybe they can be supportive in a different way. I find the old saying to be true, that you catch more flies with sugar than with vinegar."

Several of our parent advisors realized they needed to lighten up. One dad found a way to redirect the energy he had been putting into trying to have his son practice and excel. This dad channeled his efforts instead into doing research on the summer programs his son wanted to attend, handling the logistics of rounding up applications, keeping track of deadlines, and doing other back-up organizing, while letting his son take charge of the practicing and performing. That freed his son to enjoy the music making more.

Performance Jitters

Performance anxiety may crop up as part of perfectionism but can also develop for other reasons, such as the general self-consciousness that adolescents often develop, as happened to violinist Joshua Bell. "I don't remember feeling nervous when I started performing because I began playing violin so young, but nervousness started kicking in during my teen years as I started worrying more about what people were thinking about me," he says. He adds that before long, he was able to get those worries under control. "I always get nervous before a performance. It's just that you learn how to play when you're nervous."

That's one of the messages pianist Erika Nickrenz conveys to her son—feeling nervous before a concert is normal, as she knows from her own career. "There's usually a nervous excitement when you perform," she says. "The more experience you have as a performer, the more you learn how to use that nervous energy to your advantage. You play with more energy when you're a little nervous. Sometimes your fingers move too fast, but you learn to slow them down. That comes with experience."

To gain that experience, it helps if youngsters have chances to perform a lot. "If students perform only once a year at a recital, that performance is the be-all and end-all," says violin teacher Rebecca Henry. "If they perform more often, they learn that not every performance is the same, that earlier performances are rougher and that things gel over time."

Joshua Bell began playing violin very young—and performing at a young age, too. He feels that helped him not have performance jitters as a youngster. He gave his first orchestral performance at age seven in his hometown of Bloomington, Indiana. Here he is at about age twelve, also performing in Bloomington. The other photo on this page shows him around that age at the Meadowmount summer music program, with renowned violin teacher, the late Ivan Galamian, Meadowmount's founder.

In his teen years, Josh began moving onto the national arena, winning national competitions, including one that led to a performance at age fourteen with the Philadelphia Orchestra. Three years later, he had his Carnegie Hall debut. It's not surprising that, as he notes in this chapter, "nervousness started kicking in during my teen years," but he managed to bring it under control by learning "how to play when you're nervous."

Teachers often help by providing frequent performance opportunities. "My daughter's early violin teachers had monthly studio classes in which several students would perform for as many of the other students and their families as were able to attend," notes music mom Annette Radoff. "This provided an invaluable opportunity to get accustomed to performing publicly from an early age."

If teachers don't schedule regular performance experiences, Ms. Radoff suggests that parents can "create performance opportunities for your child, whether at school, retirement communities, churches, synagogues, or in your living room for assembled family members."

Many families hold at-home run-throughs before a child's recital or other performance. Dominique van de Stadt recommends making these informal tryouts as much like the real thing as possible by having the children wear their concert clothes and shoes, so they get used to playing in that outfit and can find out whether it is comfortable. She added another element to her living room run-throughs by having her kids "get totally winded from running up and down stairs and then have them play their piece immediately after that, to mimic having an adrenalin rush." Videotaping these simulations can let youngsters see if there are things they want to change—such as remembering to smile.

"I put chairs out with pillows on them in the living room so my daughter can imagine herself on stage with an audience as she plays her piece," says Theresa Chong. Piano teacher Hiroko Dutton did something similar during her own student days. "I'd put record jackets of famous pianists on the sofa so that I felt like those great people were listening to me as I played," says this Connecticut teacher. "For my own students, before their recital I have them practice bowing, both before and after they play their piece. In bowing before, I tell them to make eye contact with someone and smile, to win the audience over before you even start. That makes things easier. I also tell them never to stop if they make a mistake. The audience is listening to your music, not picking on you and noticing your mistakes."

Erika Nickrenz gives her son a similar message; "People in the audience aren't there to judge you but to have a good time and enjoy your music." She encourages him to get in the habit of "playing out and not go inward, because you're there to entertain."

Young performers aren't the only ones who need to learn to control performance nervousness. Their parents do, too. "My daughter is used to being on stage, so she just kind of does it, but it's a stress for me. I've heard her piece so many times from when she practices that I'm going through it with her, note by note, every breath. I always sit in the back so she can't see that I'm nervous for her," says Julia Castro. Even Erika Nickrenz admits, "I get just as nervous as if I were performing myself to see my son up there playing trumpet. It's nerve-wracking—and exciting. I try not to show I'm nervous because I don't want him to get more nervous. I'm usually smiling ear to ear, rooting for him every second."

Parents can manage their own jitters and help their kids at the same time by keeping busy providing backup. Here are suggestions for doing that, plus other jitters-control tips that can help everyone—parents and kids alike:

- **Preconcert details:** "The most constructive thing I did when my son Ben was under stress at a performance or audition was to be a nonanxious presence. I would take care of things beforehand that would make him anxious—ironing a shirt, giving him a haircut, getting some food, etc. I'd encourage him to let me know what would work best for him and then do it. At the performance, I'd bring something to do before it starts—needlework or a book—so he is not my only focus, and he doesn't see me sitting around waiting for him."—Sarah Odhner, Pennsylvania

- **Checklists:** "We tried to remove any distractions or worries for our daughter, such as figuring out when to leave to get there on time, is her outfit ready, do we have a water bottle or snack, is her flute in proper working condition, and does she have her music. That's because while driving her to a competition that she was playing with her flute trio during eighth grade, we're in the car, almost there and my husband asks, 'You have everything? Your water, your music?' From the back seat she says, 'Um, I don't know if I have my trio music.' She didn't have it. She had to read her part off one of the other musician's music. We decided from then on, we're writing a checklist and look at it before we leave the house."—Gail Caiazza, Massachusetts

- **Snacks:** "I learned from repeated experience that low blood sugar can be a problem before a performance or audition. Note to self: Carry bottled water and energy bars. Pack a sandwich."—Karen Rile, Pennsylvania

- **Pep talks:** "I remind my daughter that she has practiced the piece and done it well so many times that this is just another run-through, only with more people."—Beverly Berndt, Kansas

- **Quiet time:** "My daughter does not like to be disturbed doing her preperformance concentration. It's like an athlete warming up. She knows she must be ready physically and mentally."—Buzz Ballenger, California

- **Bite your tongue:** "One thing for sure, try not to argue or contradict kids right before a performance. They are stressed out. Give them some slack. Don't walk away either, which is just as bad. I know. I've done it. Give the lecture about manners and rudeness after the performance, quite a while after."—Dominique van de Stadt, Arizona

Curve Balls

Unexpected curve balls may require special problem-solving efforts. Parents of young-sters with learning issues have to bat away curve balls all the time, such as the challenge that the mother of a third grader with Asperger syndrome faced when she discovered that his music school's summer day camp required students to get themselves from room to room throughout the day. He couldn't do that on his own, but he didn't want his mom to shepherd him. She hired a teenager to escort him. This young lady could blend in with the camp's teens, making it not seem so obvious that her son had a monitor.

Alisa Weilerstein's family had to cope with an extremely challenging curve ball when she was diagnosed at age nine with type 1 diabetes. This disease requires people to limit sugar-containing foods and have daily injections of insulin. "The doctors were optimistic, saying that if I was careful and controlled it properly, I could live as I wanted and be a cellist," says Ms. Weilerstein. Her mother partnered with Alisa in managing the details, but let Alisa do a lot of the organizing. Her mother notes, "Our mantra for Alisa to say was: 'This is some-thing I can handle. This will not get in the way of anything I want to do.'"

When Alisa began to travel to other cities as a young teen to perform, her mother went along until Alisa was seventeen, but she let her daughter help manage one of the hardest tasks: restaurant food. "I was an independent kid," says Alisa, "and wanted to do things for myself, including eyeballing carbohydrates in restaurant food to juggle the dose. I would consult with my mother. It was always a joint effort." Initially, she had to receive several insulin injections a day until she went on the insulin pump at age sixteen, which "streamlined my control and made me more independent." Despite her positive attitude, she says, "I didn't tell anybody professionally about this for a long time. I signed with a manager at age fourteen, but I didn't tell her for three years. I didn't want anyone to know in the music world until I proved that I could carry the same schedule as anyone else."

Her advice to young musicians with physical challenges: "Go for it. What I wasn't prepared for was the peer pressure to eat when you're out, and everyone is ordering dessert or pizza. When questions would come, I realized I didn't have to answer them. You can say, 'Thank you for your concern but this is what I have to do.' People usually realize that you don't want to talk about it. I don't mind talking about it with friends, but with others, I just answer in a factual way and that's the end of it. There's nothing to feel embarrassed about."

Letting Go

"Knowing when to let a child quit music is tough," says Lydia Zieglar, who tried sev-eral strategies to keep her older son involved with music. He started with a preschool music-and-movement class at a Baltimore music school. Then came piano lessons, which he liked at first but lost interest in during middle school when he played drums in the school band. "Piano was too solitary for him. He enjoyed the band experience," she says. She made a deal, that he could start drum lessons if he continued with piano lessons. "After a year I backed down, and he quit piano." By then, ice hockey had become "his true passion," she says. "At his high school, there was no way to do band and sports. He chose ice hockey. I offered to let him continue drum lessons, but without the band experience, it wasn't as much fun. Practice time and missed lessons became an issue because of his sports schedule and academic workload. There are only so many hours in the day. He quit drum lessons. He is a more well-rounded person for having played an instrument." After a few years, he edged back. During his junior year, he needed to take an elective and took a music class, playing a little piano as part of that class. However, her younger son, a cellist, made the opposite choice, dropping organized sports to have more time for cello.

Several of our parent advisors have similar sibling splits—one child becomes increasingly devoted to music, as others develop other interests and quit music or pursue it in a less high-powered way. "I'm very nonjudgmental about whether people stick with music," says Peabody's Rebecca Henry. "Once someone has had some exposure to music, it's in you. It alters the way you think and sense things. Most parents truly want what's best for their children and follow their gifts, but some parents have to learn to accept that their child may have changed. If a child between the ages of six and ten loves to play, but at eleven or twelve starts getting involved in something else and music goes more on the back burner, that may just be part of the natural development of that child. Maybe they can have music in their life some other way. Maybe they can let it go for a while and come back to it later on their own terms." That happened with her own daughters.

"Neither one of our twins is going on with music professionally, which is fine with me," says Ms. Henry. "One daughter started on violin and ended up with viola. She enjoys viola, played in her high school orchestra and now plays in her college orchestra, while majoring in social work." Ms. Henry's other daughter kept switching instruments—from cello to piano to oboe—while gradually discovering that visual arts were her thing. "She quit band to take art. Kids are good at a lot of things and often have to experiment to discover what really turns them on. When she got into art, she blossomed." However, this young art enthusiast found a way back to music later by teaching herself to play a flute that her father, not a professional musician, sometimes plays. Toward the end of high school, she pulled out that flute a few times to jam with friends. "Music is still important to her," says Ms. Henry, who notes that this daughter has been pursuing varied interests during college. "She is a varsity swimmer majoring in biochemistry but has said she wants to join the steel drum band. You never know how music will fit in down the line."

Sometimes finding a way back to music involves becoming audience members, as happened with the grown children of pianist Emanuel Ax. "Both of our kids took music lessons," he says. "They did OK but didn't especially take to it, so we didn't push it. They know a little about music, and maybe down the road they'll get more involved. My daughter is starting to become interested in opera. It's such a personal, individual thing. It depends so much on the kid's personality. Some families have generations of musicians and some don't. Our family is one that doesn't." The Marsalis family has a lot of musicians, but one of Ellis Marsalis's sons chose a different path. "Our third son, Ellis Jr., did a couple of instruments, but music wasn't his thing," explains Mr. Marsalis. "We didn't bother him about that. I'm just as proud of my sons who don't play music."

Richard Stoltzman's two kids also went in different directions. His son is a jazz pianist, composer, and professor of music. His daughter cycled through a series of instruments—piano, violin, and flute—but has become an organic farmer. "As a child, her impression of me was that I was always in the basement practicing clarinet," he says. "Now her life as a farmer is almost completely outdoors. She taught herself to play a perfect instrument for an outdoors person, banjo. When she goes on hikes, she can make up songs on her banjo."

To lessen some of the pressure his kids may have been feeling about music, Mr. Stoltzman says, "When they were teenagers, I wrote both my kids letters. I wanted to tell them my feelings about what music means to me, why I'm doing it. I also told them that I loved them and that they didn't have to become a pianist, or a violinist, or any kind of musician to please me. Music is in you whether you go into music or not. My message was, 'Do what *you* want to do. Fulfill yourself. I'm ecstatic with how you've turned out.' Neither of them ever answered back. But my son told me recently that he remembered that letter, that it helped him understand me better and helped him understand better how he feels about music."

Anthony McGill during high school as a
student at the Interlochen Arts Academy
(top) and in a more recent photo.

10 Getting Serious

AS YOUNGSTERS BECOME INCREASINGLY SERIOUS about music, a whole new array of decisions and challenges arise, both for them and their parents. Clarinetist Anthony McGill turned serious at a fairly young age, as he describes in this chapter's opening vignette.

"When I was still pretty young, taking clarinet lessons at Merit Music School in Chicago, a man came to the school and spoke to all of us and asked an important question," recalls Mr. McGill, principal clarinetist of the Metropolitan Opera Orchestra. "He asked if we could imagine ourselves doing anything else besides music and whether we'd be happy doing that. He said that if we'd feel OK about our lives doing that other thing, then it would be OK to do that because doing music is so difficult. My reaction was that I didn't want to do anything else. I want to do music. That's when I realized how serious I was about music. I loved it. It was a part of who I was. I understood from a fairly young age that if you love something as much as I loved music, then it's OK to try to go into music. That's the same message I was getting at home from my parents. If you love it and work really hard at it, then it's OK.

"That's not to say everything always went the way I wanted. My parents were positive and encouraged me when I was down. They expected me and my brother to do well in school and in all our activities. They never told me they were worried that I couldn't earn a living as a musician. They were visual artists and art teachers who met at art school. The idea that you follow your passion was OK in our family," observes Mr. McGill, who was taking lessons at Merit Music School within a year of starting clarinet at his elementary school at age nine.

He had a good role model—his older brother Demarre, already a flute student at Merit when Anthony started there. They followed similar paths, for which they had some scholarship help, although their parents also had to take out a second mortgage to cover the substantial costs involved in raising two sons who were both very serious about music. These young musicians had private lessons, played with youth ensembles in Chicago, spent a few summers at the Interlochen Summer Arts Camp, followed by Interlochen's boarding school for some of their high school years. Then they each studied at Curtis and landed terrific orchestra jobs; Demarre McGill is principal flutist of the Seattle Symphony Orchestra.

Concerned adults frequently pose variations of "The Question" that Anthony McGill was asked. It's directed not only at would-be musicians but also at youngsters thinking about becoming visual artists, actors, dancers, writers, or other occupations that require single-minded dedication with shaky financial prospects. The message: "Can't you think of something else—*anything* else—you wouldn't mind doing?"

Some kids realize early on that they're as serious about music as Anthony McGill. Others take longer to reach that point. When they do, it may not mean that they see themselves heading for a musical career. "Some teens are highly invested in music, they spend so much time on it, it's their favorite thing, and yet it's not always going to play out that it's what they'll do as a career. But it's what they love," says Peabody violin teacher, Rebecca Henry. She discusses "The Question" with her teen students to help them think about how music can fit into their future—and into their present lives as busy high schoolers. In this chapter, our advisors offer suggestions for helping serious-about-music youngsters navigate the way forward, while keeping options open in case their answer to "The Question" should happen to change.

A Different Stage of Learning

When young people become serious about music and have reached a fairly high skill level, they're ready to benefit from professional-level teaching. This kind of instruction goes beyond the basics to focus on the nuances of musical understanding and interpretation, subtleties of phrasing, and details of technique that only accomplished students are ready to master. Youngsters and their nonmusician parents may be startled to discover that there is this whole new realm of higher-level skills and ways of thinking about music that advanced students are expected to tackle.

"I love challenging my students who think they've learned how to play correctly, showing them that they're playing only half the music. They're playing the stuff on the page, as opposed to the stuff that's not on the page," says oboist Toyin Spellman-Diaz, who teaches in Manhattan School of Music's Pre-College Division. "I tell them to pick up their instrument with commitment and intent, to not be afraid to dig down deep to figure out what they want to say with their music. I love to see students realize that so far they've mainly been playing with fear—the fear of making a mistake or not playing the right way. They have to overcome that fear and bring out their personalities."

Becoming aware of these beckoning musical horizons may occur when youngsters interact with new teachers or conductors at a music school, summer music program, youth ensemble, or in a master class. Some teacher switching may occur, as happened with Joshua Bell. His second year of summer camp at Meadowmount introduced him to a new style of teaching when he took part in a chamber music group led by Josef Gingold, the violin professor at Josh's hometown school, Indiana University. "What Josh experienced in that chamber music class, with Gingold's style and method, made Josh realize that's what he needed and wanted," says his mother, Shirley Bell. He liked Mimi Zweig, the teacher he had been working with for a few years, "but now he begged us to talk with Gingold about studying with him. For a while they both taught Josh, until Josef Gingold became his primary mentor."

To find new, higher-level teachers, our parent advisors used many of the same search strategies as discussed in chapter 5—asking for suggestions from teachers, music organizations, and other music parents. For the Bells, contacting a university proved effective, as it did for Jonathan Biss. He is several years younger than Joshua Bell but grew up in the same town and made an almost identical change: moving from a teacher who specializes in young children to a piano professor at Indiana University. This switch was easy for his parents to arrange because they're violinists who teach at that university, but other parents without such a direct link did well by cold-calling a nearby college.

Many serious-minded teens, as noted in chapter 5, wind up with a few extra teachers, who help with different aspects of technique. As a teen, Wynton Marsalis had several teachers that his father helped him find. In addition to receiving jazz instruction at the New Orleans arts program where his father taught, this teen trumpeter had both a regular, private teacher and another musician who taught him to play piccolo trumpet. A New Orleans Symphony Orchestra trumpeter gave him pointers on orchestral trumpet playing.

"My son Ben had two secondary teachers," says Sarah Odhner. His main teacher, a violinist in the Philadelphia Orchestra, introduced Ben to one of those extra teachers and also set up opportunities for him to have sample lessons with teachers at various conservatories. During his senior year of high school, Ben added lessons with his chamber music coach at his music school, "who drilled him on practical things for auditioning for conservatories: how to walk into an audition, how to present yourself, what pieces to play."

Bassist Ranaan Meyer found a secondary teacher on his own during high school, when he took a trip into New York City from his New Jersey home to attend a concert honoring legendary jazz bassist Ron Carter. "Just about every famous jazz bass player was in the audience. I was like a kid in a candy store," says Mr. Meyer. He saw a famous bass player who taught at a New Jersey university. "I got the courage to introduce myself, saying I was sixteen and would like to have a lesson. He said, 'I'm in the phone book.' I went home, looked up his number, and called him the next day. He called me back. I took a two-hour lesson from him and then started studying with him about once a month."

The Pre-college Option

Enrolling in an advanced by-audition-only pre-college program offers another way to find professional-level instruction. Alisa Weilerstein attended such a program at the Cleveland Institute of Music. Pre-college programs offer a wide array of activities—private instruction, ensemble playing, music theory, and other courses—providing an efficient way to broaden a student's outlook on many fronts at one location. The Cleveland program meets on weekday afternoons. Because the Weilersteins lived in Cleveland then, Alisa did mornings at her high school and afternoons at the Cleveland Institute, which offers two pre-college options: the Young Artist Program for high school students, and the Junior Young Artist Program for students in seventh through tenth grades.

Other pre-college programs meet on Saturdays, such as Temple Prep, which nurtured Annette Radoff's violinist daughter at Philadelphia's Temple University. Many families took on long commutes to let their children have pre-college training. For many years, Sarah Chang's parents made the four-hour roundtrip drive each weekend between Philadelphia and New York so she could study at Juilliard Pre-College. As noted earlier, Randall Goosby's commute to Juilliard Pre-College has been by air, flying from Memphis to New York on weekends.

The reputation of some of these programs can be a powerful magnet. "People got on our case for not having Elena audition for Juilliard Pre-College," says Ms. Radoff. But she and her husband decided to have Elena's music instruction be based closer to their Pennsylvania home, "so she could mature and develop. I'm sure great things happen at Juilliard Pre-College, but we felt that wasn't for us."

For families that live beyond reasonable commuting distance to one these programs, parents sometimes let their teenagers relocate to the city where a pre-college program is held. Juilliard, Cleveland Institute, and a few other schools allow out-of-town teens to make such a move. Students from around the country—and around the world—have done so. Dana Myers's older son spent his last year of high school at Cleveland's Young Artist Program. "We thought it might give him a chance to spread his wings a little, in case he was getting too dependent on us to help him to practice," explains Ms. Myers, a violinist with the St. Louis Symphony Orchestra.

Both the Cleveland and Juilliard programs have strict rules that require families to make appropriate arrangements for housing and schooling if students relocate, so that the youngsters have good supervision and aren't stranded on their own. That's wise, because when Sandra Shapiro attended Juilliard Pre-College in the 1970s, there must not have been such strict rules. When she was fourteen, she moved by herself from Milwaukee to New York. "My parents rented a room for me in an apartment with an elderly woman. I was on my own. It was exciting but scary. I had grown up in a sheltered environment and didn't know how to shop, manage money, or make decisions, other than musical decisions. People ask me whether I would allow my own child to do that—live on her own—and my answer is, 'Absolutely not,'" says Ms. Shapiro. "But I would allow her to commute to another city for lessons. For families that live too far to commute, if a parent is able to relocate with the child, they might consider relocating, if that would benefit the entire family. For our Young Artist Program, teens have to live with a guardian, parent, or other family member," says Ms. Shapiro, who oversees Cleveland's Young Artist Program.

Anne Akiko Meyers also relocated as a fourteen-year-old to New York for Juilliard Pre-College, about ten years after Ms. Shapiro. Her move was different because her

Anne Akiko Meyers

mother and younger sister moved with her. By then, Anne had achieved a certain amount of success back home in California. She had already performed with the Los Angeles Philharmonic and the New York Philharmonic. While attending the summer program at the Aspen Music Festival in Colorado, she met Dorothy DeLay, the famous Juilliard violin teacher, who offered Anne a full scholarship to attend Juilliard Pre-College. After starting at Juilliard, she had trouble at first adjusting to Ms. Delay's teaching style, which emphasized technique, leaving interpretation to the student. "I had gone from a teacher in California who focused on phrasing and color to this new, almost free-range approach. It was disconcerting," she says. "Her method was that you have to find your own sound, your own soul, after she gives you the tools—all the technical stuff. I think, 'How did I survive?'" But she did survive, adjusted, and did well.

> **SPOTLIGHT ON: ANNE AKIKO MEYERS, VIOLIN**
>
> **Pressure:** "One time Anne asked, 'What would you think if I quit?'" recalls Yakko Meyers, mother of Anne Akiko Meyers. "I said, 'Absolutely, you can quit if you want to.'" Relocating to New York from California so fourteen-year-old Anne could study at Juilliard Pre-College was not only a big change for her but also for her sister and mother, who moved with her, and for her father, who worked in Oregon. Such a big move, even if the child wants it, can seem like pressure on the child. "I think she wanted to try me out," explains her mother. "It's important for a parent to back off if the child doesn't want to go on." However, Anne's father recalls that at the same time Anne "was also saying, 'I'm living my dream.' Giving her the choice to do what she wanted strengthened her resolve."

However, when she received the offer to study at Juilliard, her father had just accepted a new job as president of a university in Oregon. He didn't move to New York with the rest of the family but visited about once a month. This bicoastal split was hard on everyone. "We thought it would be easy to do, but it wasn't," says Richard Meyers. "We had a family meeting and agreed that we'd do it, but nobody realized it would be for six and a half years. It was a major challenge, but we pulled it off. It gave Anne her chance. Looking back, I might have moved with them and found some other job. I missed critical years of not being with the children in their early teens." However his wife feels that meeting this challenge "made our family bond even stronger."

Performing Arts Schools

Performing arts high schools provide another way to obtain high-level instruction. Some are public schools, such as the one that violinist Adrian Anantawan attended in Toronto. Although he benefited from the instruction he received there, he continued to have lessons with a private teacher. Christian McBride graduated from a public performing arts high school in Philadelphia. Miguel Zenón graduated from one in Puerto Rico. Some performing arts schools are boarding schools, such as Interlochen Arts Academy, the private school in Michigan that Anthony McGill attended for two years of high school.

"We never imagined we would send our son to a boarding school, but Matthew thrived in this environment," says Martha Woodard. Her son, a violinist and composer, attended the Walnut Hill School, a private performing arts school in Massachusetts, after having studied for few years at the pre-college program at New England Conservatory (NEC). "We lived close enough that we could bring him home every weekend. We had always been strong advocates of public schools until we realized his needs weren't being met at our public schools." They received some scholarship help, but she adds, "When we started him on music lessons, we never realized how high the cost would be. But music is such an integral part of our son's life. We have done whatever we could to make it work."

Boarding school costs were also a concern for Cindi Russell, whose flutist daughter spent her senior year of high school at Interlochen. Her Kentucky hometown helped with expenses not covered by the Interlochen scholarship. "Music professors at our local university did a benefit concert to raise money. People donated to help defray some of the costs of sending her to Interlochen," says Ms. Russell.

A chance encounter at a musical instrument exhibit in Beijing led to oboist Liang Wang attending Idyllwild Arts Academy, a performing arts boarding school in California. "I was trying out oboes that were on display at the exhibit. One of the guys selling oboes heard me play and said, 'You're pretty good. Do you want to go to the States to play?'" recalls Mr. Wang, now principal oboist with the New York Philharmonic. At that time, he was a teen studying at the Beijing Conservatory. "I played an audition for him the next day. He was in China recruiting for the school. A month later, I was in Los Angeles with a full scholarship to the school. My mother was OK with me going. She wanted me to pursue my dream."

Summer Networking

The benefits of summer music programs have been mentioned earlier, but for teens considering a musical career, these summer experiences offer the additional advantage of terrific networking opportunities. Valuable contacts, of course, can also be made through music schools, pre-college programs, and youth ensembles, but summer programs often let young people interact with top-level performers they might not otherwise have a chance to meet. Some parent advisors report that the musicians and educators that their sons and daughters connected with during summer programs helped open doors in a variety of ways—either by providing recommendations that helped in gaining admission to a conservatory or university program, or also by suggesting well-regarded teachers for youngsters to approach for sample lessons. "For people who live outside the big metropolitan areas, summer is your best time for making these kinds of contacts," says Brian Zeger, artistic director of Juilliard's vocal arts department.

These contacts helped Laura Vautour's daughter, who attended a summer program at Boston Conservatory after her sophomore year at her Georgia high school. She worked with the head of the conservatory's opera and vocal music department. "Sarah kept in touch with that teacher for the next two years. This teacher has been a great help as far as advice," says Ms. Vautour. "That program was just two weeks long, but when Sarah came home, she knew she wanted to become an opera singer. She even went back to Boston later to have a lesson with that teacher." The next summer, Sarah attended the high school program at Tanglewood where she met the teacher who would guide her the following year and prepare her for college auditions (described in chapter 6).

The networking benefits of summer programs continue past the teen years, according to former artist manager Edna Landau. "Summer festivals are important for all performing artists throughout their careers. I tell conservatory students, where you spend your summers is very important. People see you at festivals," says Ms. Landau.

Student-to-student summer networking is also important. "My daughter made lifelong friends with fellow musicians from all over the world at summer programs and had a network of friends already in place when she arrived at college," says Karen Rile, a Philadelphia writer whose violinist daughter went on to study at Juilliard. "The music world is small. These camp friendships will serve her throughout her life."

Stepping Up the Effort

Higher-level instruction may involve an increase in practice time, although how much of an increase is something for students and teachers to discuss. "The quality is as important as the quantity," advises Joshua Bell. "If you concentrate and know how to practice what you need to practice, and if you know how to structure yourself well, you don't have to practice all day."

Practicing isn't the only thing that needs to be stepped up for teens aiming for music careers, according to saxophonist Miguel Zenón. "Practice is important, but so is listening to music, understanding it, learning about your field, so when you have the opportunity to get that job or recording session, you'll be ready at your highest level. The harder you work, the more you're going to be able to exploit the talent that you have," says Mr. Zenón. "There are a lot of extremely talented kids. I tell young musicians that talent only goes to a certain point. Now that you're young and don't have a lot of responsibilities to deal with, put in the work."

That's why Sandra Shapiro recommends that young people study music theory, which she hadn't studied enough as a child, causing her difficulties as a young performer. She had already started performing professionally as a preteen, but during rehearsals for a concerto she was to play with an orchestra when she was twelve, it became clear that she didn't know how to count the beats in her part. When her playing didn't mesh with what the orchestra was doing, she couldn't count out her part to get back in sync. "I had learned the piece by ear and by looking at shapes in the score but wasn't good at note reading or counting, all things you learn in music theory," she explains. "I was placed with a theory teacher to try fill in those gaps. I've come across this same situation with students who have moved so fast learning new pieces that some things were overlooked. Theory classes, and sight-singing too, need to go hand in hand with private lessons, to develop a well-rounded, complete

Jazz saxophonist Miguel Zenón performing with a student orchestra at New England Conservatory, where he is on the faculty.

SPOTLIGHT ON: MIGUEL ZENÓN, SAXOPHONE

Mind blowing: At his high school in Puerto Rico, Miguel Zenón's saxophone training was classical, but he played in salsa bands on the side. "When I was fifteen, older guys in the band passed around Charlie Parker tapes. That's how I discovered jazz. The way he played saxophone was mind blowing, such technical proficiency, improvising over such an intricate and deep language," he says. "At first I had no idea what he was doing in terms of theory. I kept listening. I started transcribing solos, playing with the recordings, learning the language of jazz on my own. I still transcribe solos. I make my students do it, too. When I write down a Charlie Parker solo, I not only get the notes he plays, but the notes in relation to the chords played by the pianist, what he's doing rhythmically, his motifs. You build your database and can then channel it in your own way."

musician. If you're just taking lessons, you're not understanding music to the core."

Learning about the inner workings of music can make music seem more intriguing to teens, according to string teacher Rebecca Henry. "Teens find this stuff fascinating, comparing chord progressions in Beethoven with those in rock and roll, or other historical comparisons, so they become more sophisticated musicians," says Ms. Henry. A more in-depth understanding of music may improve a student's technique, too. "Just telling teens to make their bows straight is usually futile. It is often better to focus on the music. Once they realize they can't get the sound they want and you help them discover that the crooked bow is the source of the problem, they are eager to take control of trying to fix it."

Academic Choices

In terms of their nonmusic education, most of the pros on our advice panel went to regular schools—mainly public schools, although some went to private or parochial schools. The same was true for the daughters and sons of most of our parent advisors. A few families used alternatives to regular schools, such as homeschooling or cyber schools, both of which are discussed in the next section.

For most of the youngsters who attended regular schools, their private music lessons, practicing, and ensemble rehearsals took place after school or on weekends. However, some parents arranged to have school schedules customized to allow more time for music. Joshua Bell's high school allowed him to do all his academic classes in the morning so his mother could pick him up at about noon and take him across town to Indiana University for violin lessons, chamber music rehearsals, and other music classes. Jonathan Biss, who attended the same high school as Joshua Bell about ten years later, had a similar half-day arrangement. "The high school was glad to consider all my musical studies as fulfilling my elective requirements. I earned grades from the university for my music lessons," he says. "My free periods were marked 'college release.' I went to school for part of the day and then went home to practice." Toyin Spellman-Diaz also had a part-time schedule at her Washington parochial school so she could attend a music school in the afternoon and have lessons with a National Symphony oboist.

Anne Akiko Meyers and Sandra Shapiro used a different kind of academic school when they moved to New York City to attend Juilliard Pre-College. They received their non-musical education at the Professional Children's School, a private school geared to young performers; it is flexible about adjusting class times and assignments to fit a youngster's performance or rehearsal schedule.

Violinist Sarah Chang had a distance-learning arrangement with her Philadelphia private school. The teachers gave her assignments to work on when she performed out of town. "For a short time, I was mailing back assignments," says Ms. Chang, who started doing this before the e-mail era. "Then came faxing assignments, but when e-mail kicked in during high school, that was a lifesaver because it was so much easier to do assignments by e-mail. I would do a concert, then go to a reception and postconcert dinner. I'd get back to my hotel around midnight to do my homework so I could fax it or e-mail it before catching a flight the next day for the next city. That wasn't much fun. For a while I traveled with a tutor because I had so much work to catch up on before coming back to school."

Other parents worked out similar arrangements for their kids. Although their youngsters may not have had such high-powered careers as Ms. Chang, their music involvement still caused them to miss school or be late on finishing assignments from time to time.

Homeschooling and Cyber-Schooling

Some families chose nonschool alternatives: homeschooling, in which the parents make arrangements for children to receive academic instruction; or cyber-schooling, an option provided by some school systems and private companies that let students take academic courses online at home. In some cases, the decision to use nonschool instruction had nothing to do with a child's musical interest but was a choice a family made for educational reasons. Other families turned to homeschooling or cyber-schooling after a youngster became so involved in music that parents felt a nonschool option would allow more time for practicing and performing.

Leslie Curda, who has five children, chose online schooling for her older preteen and teenaged children because she and her kids often travel for certain periods of the year to Los Angeles or New York from their home in Chicago so her youngsters can audition for and perform in musicals and on TV shows. For her elementary school age children, she tried to enroll them in local schools when the family had to do this kind of traveling.

A few families turned to nonschool alternatives when regular schools were not as accommodating to their children's musical studies as Joshua Bell's and Sarah Chang's schools were. This is why Annette Radoff chose to homeschool her violinist daughter toward the end of high school. "We had tremendous support from the elementary school, less at the middle school, and virtually none at the high school," she says, describing the Philadelphia-area public schools her daughter attended. "It became clear that homeschooling was the appropriate option. Elena was homeschooled for the second half of tenth grade and all of eleventh. Then she got accepted early into Curtis for college. Elena wasn't lonely doing homeschooling," says Ms. Radoff. "By then, much of her time at home was spent practicing. Her social life centered around Temple Prep."

Some youngsters handle homeschooling and cyber-schooling quite well, but one mother reports that her teenager became lonely as a cyber-school student and also tended to fall behind in assignments. This young musician decided to return to regular high school. Jiji Goosby suggested homeschooling to her son Randall. "He refused," she says. "He likes the social aspect of school, getting together with friends, being a teenager. He goes to a regular high school in Tennessee." His weekends for several years were spent in New York City, so he could attend Juilliard Pre-College.

States have different requirements for homeschooling and cyber-schooling that parents should investigate carefully before deciding on a nonschool arrangement. Some companies that operate cyber-schools are nonprofit, while others are for-profit businesses. A study by the National Education Policy Center uncovered problems with some online providers and found that students who received their education from certain providers made less progress than students in brick-and-mortar schools. The Bibliography has a link to this report, authored by Gary Miron and Jessica Urschel, which can give parents ideas of what questions to ask when checking out online possibilities.

Keeping Future Options Open

No matter what the educational venue for high school—regular, home, cyber, or boarding—the goal for most of our parent advisors was to make sure their teens finished high school and did well enough to have plenty of future options.

Sometimes teens can be eager to head out and make their mark in the musical world, but as Debbie Chipman discovered, teens can also just as quickly change their minds, making it wise to not let them burn too many bridges along the way. "I remember my daughter saying, 'Why do I even need to finish high school? I'm going to go to a conservatory,'" recalls Ms. Chipman, mother of violist Lauren Chipman. "She had friends in her Chicago youth symphony who were passing their GEDs [high school equivalency exams] during their sophomore year of high school and going to conservatories. We met with her high school guidance counselor, who was amazing at encouraging her to stay in school and do well academically." It turned out that by the time Lauren was a senior, her feelings had changed about what to do after high school. Instead of going to a conservatory, she decided a university would fit her wide-ranging interests better. She chose a university with an excellent music program, the University of Southern California (USC), a choice that wasn't even on her radar in sophomore year. She majored in music but hasn't gone the straight classical route. She performs with rock bands in addition to teaching and playing in classical ensembles. "I'm glad I got a broader education. My favorite classes at USC were not the music classes. They were amazingly cool history and political science classes. I took a lot of French, too, and film scoring."

Susan Raab is also glad her son decided to complete his high school education. "It was important for us to know that he had a solid base in his education," says Ms. Raab, whose son was tempted to audition for a professional musical and go on tour rather than stay in school and continue doing shows at the local community theater. "Musical theater isn't an easy career. We didn't know where life was going to take him and what he might want to do, but we saw that he had broad interests, that there were a lot of things he could do well. He was a strong student. We wanted to make sure that he had options. We saw some kids who left school and went off touring in a show. We said to him that this will be an up and down road, and you need to have other ways to support yourself as this evolves."

Her son, Jeff Raab, notes, "I go back and forth on whether it was a good decision to stay in high school. I think it's good it happened the way it did. You never know what parts of your education you're going to need to call upon." After graduating from New York University as a music performance major, he has been using more than his singing ability. In addition to performing, he is a teacher and a composer, with an interest in having his own performance group and applying for grants to fund it. "Once my parents saw that I was still going to get an education and was pretty well-balanced about it, it was easy for them to get on board and support me in what I was doing," he says. "They let me experience it for myself without imposing any expectations that they might have had about what I would do."

Even the conservatory-bound can benefit from keeping educational options open during high school because of all the curve balls that can head a musician's way, such

SPOTLIGHT ON: ROBERT GUPTA, VIOLIN

Silver lining: Robert Gupta's family felt his upstate New York schools were so unsupportive that his mother arranged for him to enroll at age thirteen in a nearby college. The next year he also began working on a violin degree at Manhattan School of Music. This plan fell apart when his mother became too ill to drive him to both schools. "My parents said I should be a doctor and have music as a hobby. I was devastated, but I didn't rebel," he says. He quit music and earned a biology degree. Then he persuaded his parents to let him earn a master's in violin at Yale. "I thought I would take an orchestra audition, wouldn't get it, and would apply to medical school. But I won a job at the Los Angeles Philharmonic. I was nineteen. My parents were shocked. As was I. They reverted back to finding a way to make things happen. I'm happy they made me get the biology degree. During college, I discovered different kinds of music. When I came back to violin, I developed a greater flexibility in technique." He still likes science and has started a group that brings classical music to mentally ill communities.

as the tendonitis that ended the piano career of Theresa Chong's sister. "I tell my son there's no guarantee," says Ms. Chong. She makes sure her cellist son still does his schoolwork while also studying at Juilliard Pre-College on weekends. "He may change his mind about music. Would he resent me in the future if something happens and I hadn't encouraged him to explore other areas?"

"Musicians who have a wide scope of knowledge and imagination are among the most interesting," says Edna Landau. "There is so much cross-genre programming that brings together musicians, dancers, writers, and other artists." She feels it's important for musicians to "continue their nonmusical education in every way they can, to become truly literate young people. Languages are important, history, literature, and so forth."

To Lighten Up on Academics—or Not

However, keeping options open can be tricky. Some slippage on the academic side may occur for young people who do music fully enough to keep the music option completely open. Some of our parent advisors have children who are all-around high achievers, able to handle lots of practice and lots of homework. Other parents have had to accept some academic streamlining.

After Ranaan Meyer discovered jazz during high school, his mother says, "He practiced all the time, doing jazz bass and classical bass. It was his passion. There was no stopping him. He was also playing gigs in the jazz world. He did OK in high school, maintaining decent grades, but taking only an occasional honors class as opposed to all honors. I thought that was fine. I figured if he changed his mind later in college, he could catch up. There are only so many hours in the day, and I did not want to create a kid with ulcers at seventeen."

Toyin Spellman-Diaz's parents took the same approach. They spoke up for her when her high school gave her a hard time about grades and release time for music. "My grades until high school were good, but I was never interested in academics. It was always music for me," she recalls. "In high school, my grades weren't great, but I wasn't flunking. My mom had a meeting with the dean of my high school and said, 'My daughter is a musician. She's trying really hard to fit into this academic way of thinking, but she needs her space to become the great alumna she's going to be for you.' She helped them back off and let me be myself."

"Some parents give teens mixed messages," notes Rebecca Henry. "They want teens to get all A's and get into Harvard but complain if they don't do well in a competition. I explain that if they want their child to do that competition, the youngster has to spend more time practicing. The parents say there's no time, that their child has to get all A's. Parents have to make peace with who their child is and help the youngster find a balance between music and academics that fits with both the family's values and the child's needs. This is a highly personal process within each family."

Cutting Back on Extras—or Not

As discussed earlier, some musical teens keep up with their nonmusic activities in high school, while others cut back. Kristin Bond's older daughter, a singer, was among those who continued doing sports. She ran track and cross country during high school. "She is also interested in art, but that had to go. In our high school, it's very difficult do both music and visual art," says Ms. Bond. "I think schools do a disservice when they make it impossible to pursue more than one arts elective. My daughter could decide during college that music isn't for her after all. This whole idea of specialization really rankles, that kids should have to decide so young that they want to do music over everything else."

Laura Vautour's daughter cut back on sports. "She swam competitively for seven years, balancing her two interests—swimming and singing. At the beginning of tenth grade, she stopped swim team and focused on her vocal work," says Ms. Vautour. As noted earlier, some teens who dropped team sports kept doing sports informally, as

Randall Goosby (left) and Chase Park (right) studied at Juilliard Pre-College during high school and are shown playing in one of the school's chamber music groups with Valerie Kim.

Alisa Weilerstein did in making time to run every day. But she didn't pursue a lot of other activities. When she began performing professionally as a teen, reporters would ask what extracurricular activity she did. "I would say, 'Mine is music. That's what I love. I don't feel deprived.'"

Ms. Weilerstein didn't perform with her high school orchestra, partly because she was at school only a few hours each day, but other pros did perform with their high school ensembles. Eastman percussion teacher Ruth Cahn encourages her students to play in their school bands and orchestras, both for the performance experience and to support music in the schools, so her students' skills can give a boost to the group. David Grossman notes, "My public high school in New York City had a strong music department, and I played in the school orchestra and jazz band."

"Having time to hang out with friends is important, too," notes one mom, explaining why her son dropped team sports after his sophomore year of high school and cut back on clubs and volunteer work, too. "His interest was music. Since he carried a full course load in high school, including honors courses, his time was limited for extracurricular things."

About Competitions

Competitions are such a big part of the lives of serious-about-music youngsters, that we're devoting several sections to presenting their pros and cons, as well as suggestions for how to handle the pressure. First, here's a general overview of the many kinds of competition-like events for young musicians—along with thoughts from educators concerning the kinds of kids who seem to thrive on these events and those who don't.

Music teacher organizations often sponsor evaluations that are supposed to be low-key but which may seem like competitions to a nervous youngster. These involve a child receiving a written evaluation after playing a piece for a teacher other than the child's regular teacher. Other competitive experiences include auditions for youth ensembles. In addition, there are concerto competitions organized by youth orchestras, summer programs, or professional orchestras, with the reward being a chance to perform as a soloist with the orchestra. Some local, regional, and national competitions that are sponsored by community groups or music organizations may carry monetary prizes along with performance opportunities. For the extremely skilled, there are international competitions. Student ensembles sometimes participate in competitions as a group, such as the competitions that marching bands participate in or Jazz at Lincoln Center's Essentially Ellington high school jazz band competition, which several of our parent advisors' kids participated in and loved.

Some of our advisors' children also participated in the Sphinx competition for African American and Latino string players. "My daughter felt like she had found a family there, a nurturing environment, even though it was a tough competition in every sense of the word," says Annette Radoff, describing the Sphinx competition her daughter Elena Urioste won at age sixteen. This organization keeps in contact with its contestants, has them perform in concerts over the years, offers career guidance, and also provides tuition assistance for summer programs. Parents are equally positive about their kids' experiences with the public radio program *From the Top*, which probably seems like a competition to the kids who send in a taped audition to win a chance to perform on the show. *From the Top* also offers scholarships to excellent musicians who need financial help.

"Competitions aren't for everyone—or not for everybody at every stage of their development," says string teacher Rebecca Henry. "There are times when preparing for competitions can be motivating for goal-oriented students. But it's not a good idea when someone is making technical changes, has recently changed teachers, doesn't enjoy the pressure, or has played in some competitions and become demoralized by not placing well. You have to make sure that it is a positive aspect of their education." Cleveland Institute's Sandra Shapiro agrees, "For me, the educational philosophy has to come first. If a competition comes along and its repertoire works in tandem with whatever the teacher is working on with the student that year, then go ahead and do it."

"I don't send all my students to contests," observes San Francisco Conservatory's William Wellborn. "They don't motivate everyone. The not-winning and the pressure can crush some students. It's all about choosing the right event for each student, whether it's a small local competition or a big state or national one."

His piano colleague John McCarthy observes, "Some kids are drawn to competitions and are ready for the challenge. But for others, competitions are like poison. Competitions are useful for talented, ambitious teenagers who are at a stage of development where they're out to confirm who they think they are. Those ambitious teens eat them up. But younger kids can become burdened by competitions. I tend to go slow with younger kids. I hear all the time from parents who want kids to do this or that competition. I explain to parents and kids that competitions aren't intrinsically evil, but they are absurd. The outcome is not necessarily a reflection of the most talented person in the room that day. There's always the subjective element. It's not a swim meet where you can measure quantitatively who's the best. However, competitions are a fact of life. I've made my peace with them. Competitions can open up good teaching moments, regardless of the outcome. Each one is a dress rehearsal for the next one."

The Upsides of Competitions

On the plus side, there are other benefits to doing competitions besides those mentioned in the previous section. Jennifer Koh liked them as a kid, although, as seen in the next section, she has modified her opinion as an adult. "As a kid, I saw competitions as a way to learn repertoire and have a goal for practicing," she recalls. "At first, it seemed like fun, the little local competitions. I got to meet other kids my age who were playing the same kinds of pieces I was. I didn't even think of it as a competition. Once I started doing international competitions as a teenager, it was like, 'Wow, I can go to these countries.' I would read the literature of that particular country. Even going into the Tchaikovsky competition when I was sixteen, I didn't go in thinking I had to win. Actually, one reason I wanted to do the Tchaikovsky competition was because I was obsessed with Russian literature and history and was taking courses on that in my freshman year at Oberlin."

Payton MacDonald notes a practical benefit of doing well in competitions: It helped with his efforts to change the mind of his father, who wasn't sure music was a wise career choice. "It was useful for my father to see me win concerto competitions, although I never cared much about that and still don't," says this percussionist and composer. Competition wins allowed his father to see that his son's achievements were valued by others.

Our parent advisors offer a few additional good points about competitions:

- **Reality check:** "If you become a professional musician, performing under pressure is what you do every day. The earlier they learn to handle the pressure, the better."—Ann Turner, Ohio
- **Learning tool:** "Competitions can be a bit strange, with the prejudices of the judges affecting the results. But learning that you can't always win, that life is not always fair are good life lessons. Competitions can give a sense of what needs to be improved, especially if the notes from the judges are studied carefully."—Buzz Ballenger, California
- **Confidence builder:** "Competitions built my son's confidence and enabled him to be comfortable performing and speaking in public. Pressure can prepare kids to excel. Music has always been his passion, and he has just picked himself right up and tried again."—Carolyn Sax, Massachusetts

The Downsides

In addition to stress, which was discussed earlier, piano instructor John McCarthy points out other downsides. "Competitions can produce a very artificial and theatrical type of playing. They can also be very disruptive to real skill development" by taking time away from other kinds of practicing. Sandra Shapiro agrees, "When you're preparing for competitions, and recitals, too, things get put on hold. When you're simply learning for the competition—like 'teaching for the test' in school—you may have some success, but there may be holes in your foundation that will catch up with you later."

"Students trash talking each other about getting into all-state, and the imprecise and often random audition process, create a competitive, cutthroat environment, which is exactly what music shouldn't be," says a young veteran of several rounds of all-state auditions during high school. He feels that these statewide competitions, which so many students participate in, can sour the atmosphere in high school band and orchestra rooms. "It should be about making beautiful music and learning to work with others."

Jennifer Koh has philosophical reasons for changing her opinion of competitions as an adult. "I'm ambivalent about competitions. I don't really believe in them now," she says. "When you go into the arts, it's not about who is better than the others. It's about diversity and different points of view. That's what makes music interesting."

"Winning a competition doesn't really launch a career, even as high level a piano competition as the Van Cliburn," observes John McCarthy. Edna Landau agrees that winning a big competition is not an automatic career starter, although she says it helps people become aware of a performer and may make it easier to sign with an agent or manager. She notes that many musicians have successful careers without ever having won a major competition.

Richard Stoltzman is a prime example of someone who has succeeded despite not winning big competitions. This clarinetist admits, "I was terrible in competitions. It made me nervous to play for judges to try to prove myself. I thought maybe I can't be a musician. So I gave up on competitions. I made up my own plan." Instead of auditioning to win an orchestra job, he carved out a new career for himself: solo clarinetist, something other clarinetists weren't doing in the 1970s when he started his career. He began performing as a guest soloist with orchestras and chamber music groups, winning jobs on the basis of performing well for *audiences*, not for judges.

Cellist Adrienne Taylor also had competition-induced doubts. "I did the Sphinx competition during college but was totally incapable of playing well in a competition," she reports. "I realized that this didn't happen when I performed for people who want to be moved by music. If students feel that if they don't win competitions that they might as well throw in the towel, the world might miss out on some great musicians." She has found her way: She is in a chamber music group that performs and also gives free lessons in the South Side neighborhood of Providence, Rhode Island.

Competition Coping

The suggestions in chapter 9 for calming performance jitters can help with competitions. So can the following:

- **Talk it over:** "As a family, we do a lot of talking and processing of things, and I think that helped my daughter who said after her first singing competition, 'I will never do another one.' What was bothering her was the awareness that in this field, it's about competition. This isn't part of her personality," says Juli Elliot. "But once you get past the pettiness about competitions that can happen at the high school level, there are positive things about competing. We talked about the value in doing them for learning new repertoire and performing. We talked about people peaking at different ages, that voices mature at different times, that there's a place for lots of different people and different voice qualities, and not fretting that you're not at a certain place yet. I'm a musician, and it helped that I shared my experiences in competitions with her." Her daughter continued doing competitions and gradually felt better about them. "The competitions were training for the college auditions."

- **Perspective:** Laura Vautour helped her daughter gain a sense of perspective when she muffed her sight-singing in the all-state competition during her junior year of high school and didn't get into the all-state chorus. "We said maybe you weren't supposed to make all-state because you got into Tanglewood instead, which is a better opportunity," says Ms. Vautour. It would have been too expensive to send her daughter both to the all-state festival and to Tanglewood.

- **Trial runs:** "No matter how well they've played the competition piece in the living room, it should not be taken to an audition if you haven't played it yet in public," says Karen Rile. It's also important to practice everything that will be expected at a competition, such as playing scales or sight-reading.

- **Preparation:** "The better prepared they are, the better they'll handle the stress," says Afa Sadykhly Dworkin, artistic director of the Sphinx organization. "Being prepared involves getting plenty of sleep, eating right, taking care of their bodies, and physical fitness."

- **Process—not results:** "Competitions can be good if they're not taken too seriously. Focus on how they played, independent of how they *placed*," says Marilyn Resmini, a Virginia mother of a young flutist.

- **Stay home:** "I had to recognize that I made him nervous," says Carolyn Sax, who noticed that her son did better at competitions if she wasn't there.

Wide-Ranging Exploration

Many pros on our advice panel discovered that the broader their musical experiences, the more opportunities they had in their careers. But not all our pros did that as teens. Many concentrated instead on mastering the classical repertoire for their instrument. Their interests broadened later. Among those who spread their wings as adults are violinists Jennifer Koh and Anne Akiko Meyers, who often perform contemporary pieces now, including ones they commission themselves. Ms. Meyers even played the "Star-Spangled Banner" for 42,000 baseball fans at a Seattle Mariners-Boston Red Sox game. Robert Gupta released an album on which he performs Indian ragas, including one he wrote. Joshua Bell performs in many genres besides classical—playing the soundtrack for the movie *The Red Violin*, releasing a bluegrass-oriented album and also an album with Sting, Kristin Chenoweth, and Tiempo Libre, a Miami-based Cuban band that plays timba music. In addition, as music director of London's Academy of St. Martin in the Fields, he does some conducting.

However, others of our pro advisors filled their teen years with wide-ranging musical explorations. Jazz bassist Christian McBride played jazz and classical bass as a teen and performed with all kinds of ensembles in the Philadelphia area. "Everything about that instrument that I could possibly learn in whatever genre, that's what I was doing," he says. Bassist Ranaan Meyer also did both classical and jazz, while venturing into composing, too.

Taking the prize for most varied musical experience as a kid is violist, singer, and composer Caleb Burhans. "One of the best things my parents did was they weren't dogmatic about me doing just one kind of music," explains Mr. Burhans. He started singing in choirs very young, added violin at age ten and guitar later, dabbled with other instruments during middle school and high school. He even sang backup vocals on Everly Brothers tunes with his father, a guitarist and bass player who performed in clubs. The switch to viola came while earning a bachelor's degree at Eastman. During high school in Wisconsin, he says, "I played in orchestras and rock bands, sang in choirs, played guitar and bass in jazz bands. I started writing music even before I started violin. I would put things down on paper, not really knowing what I was doing. I didn't start using a computer to compose until college.

"Keep your horizons broad," Mr. Burhans advises young musicians. "It used to be that you could just play violin in a string quartet or orchestra, or have a solo career. That has become much more limited in the last twenty years. Put your ear out and become aware of other types of music. It makes you so much more sellable in terms of being able to do any type of gig. Even if you're not going to perform in all those styles, knowing about them can enrich your life and everything you do musically. Another good thing my parents did was to encourage me to perform as much as possible." In addition to recitals, concerts, and youth ensemble performances, he branched out to present other kinds programs. "I performed in nursing homes and churches," he says. "I'd play little romantic gems on violin or jazz standards on piano. I'd talk with the audience about the pieces. It's important to interact with the audience."

Getting used to talking with audiences is wise, according to NEC faculty member Randy Wong, who explains, "Performers are being asked to do more outreach, get out there talking to audiences. But most students don't start doing that until late in college. To feel comfortable with this, start earlier." He helps train NEC musicians for their teaching roles and has found it helps if they have done some volunteer tutoring of younger musicians during high school. "A lot of musicians wind up being teachers. It's good for kids to start going through the thought process of what makes a good teacher."

Gary Ingle, executive director of the Music Teachers National Association, points out another reason to explore a wide range of musical styles. It will help with the teaching side of a musician's career. "Private music teachers are expected to teach more than the classical repertoire," he says. "The broader a musician's knowledge of different styles, the better possibility of having a full studio of satisfied students."

Composition Experience

Quite a few of our pro advisors do some composing and arranging as well as performing. Several of our parent advisors' kids also became involved in composing. Some started the way Caleb Burhans did, by jotting down their own tunes before having any formal composition training. Others produced their first compositions using music-notation computer software. Two of the most popular software programs—Sibelius and Finale—have introductory versions that can be downloaded for free so young people can do some initial exploring before having to buy the full software. There are less-advanced programs, such as Garage Band, and more complex ones, such as Pro Tools or Digital Performer. All the budding young composers of our parent panelists eventually worked with a composition teacher. Parents located composition teachers using the same strategies for finding other music teachers. Some young people also studied composition at summer programs. Several entered their pieces in competitions specifically for teen and preteen composers, including a national competition sponsored by the composer organization ASCAP.

Going Pro—or Not

Whether to let a young musician "go pro" is a decision most music parents won't have to make, but some of our parent advisors have grappled with this. A few of their youngsters signed with professional managers before graduating from high school. So did several professional musicians on our advice panel.

The pro option came as a surprise to most parents, including Shirley Bell. Gradually she began to realize that her son Josh was headed for a professional career when she saw how much he loved violin and performing. After he won several national competitions, including one that had him perform at age fourteen with the Philadelphia Orchestra, it was no long a matter of whether he might have a career. He already had one. She realized she was in over her head. She and her husband signed up their fifteen-year-old with a manager. "I wanted to be careful, because I knew some managers can exploit young people," says Ms. Bell. "So we went with two young teachers who were just getting started in the music management business, Charles Hamlen and Edna Landau. They were young and personable and said they would involve me in making decisions. I needed to be involved, but I didn't want to do all the negotiation that I had been doing. I didn't know how to handle certain things." At first, his managers kept the number of concerts low so he could continue violin lessons.

Three other of our pro advisors signed with managers as youngsters—Sarah Chang, at age eight; Alisa Weilerstein, at age fourteen; and Anne Akiko Meyers, at sixteen. Until all three were eighteen or nineteen years old, they traveled with a parent when performing in other cities or countries. Their parents tried to limit the number of performances.

Emanuel Ax notes, however, that performing as a teenager isn't the only path to success. "You have some kids who thrive on the fact that they play professional concerts at the age of fourteen, fifteen, or sixteen. But you have others who would suffer a great deal from it," he says. "If a student isn't out concertizing at age seventeen, there's still hope for having a good career."

To present more views on going pro as a youngster, here are three personal accounts.

- **Sarah Chang's experience:** "My parents were protective and would turn down offers for me to perform at first," explains Ms. Chang. "They wanted to make sure I had enough breaks in the schedule to come home after performances, go back to school, be a kid, and have proper lessons at Juilliard Pre-College. It was all about balancing the schedule, encouraging the career that was starting, which I was fortunate to have, but making sure that this was good for the long-term, so I wouldn't burn out. The emphasis was to do big high-profile concerts with major orchestras, such as the New York Philharmonic. If you do those, other ones will come. If you can't do them all in one year, do the others later. We program two and a half years in advance." When Ms. Chang was sixteen, she decided, "I needed a break. I had been going, going, going since I was eight, with no long vacations. I didn't have the luxury of slacking off because there was always the next concert coming. My slacking off would be to say, 'Today I don't want to practice. I want to go shopping, but I'll go back to practicing tomorrow.' " She called her managers together and told them she needed more than a one-day break. "They were supportive. But the earliest they could schedule that sabbatical was when I was eighteen. At least I had that to look forward to. I was supposed to have three months off, but conductors started asking for favors. Favorite musicians wanted me to play a chamber concert, but that was fun, not really work. It ended up being about a month-and-a-half break. Now I play about a hundred concerts a year. It's my choice. Nobody is forcing me to do this."

- **The Curda family's experience:** Leslie Curda's five kids have performed professionally in musical theater productions and on TV shows. Ms. Curda signed with one agent to manage them all. "Tying to coordinate multiple agents and schedules would be a nightmare," she explains. Her family's show-biz adventure began when her older children began performing in shows in Chicago, their hometown. "Then they started getting called to audition in New York. That's when I began treating this more seriously," she says. The performance and auditioning opportunities that the agent has uncovered for her older kids have caused the family to move from Chicago to California and New York for certain periods of the year. "It has its ups and downs, and we have our crazy days," says Ms. Curda. "There have been some big disappointments. I let them feel sad about it for a while, but the next day they have other auditions. It's not something they dwell on. None of them has ever gotten so upset that I thought this is not OK. We spend a lot of family time together. My kids are really self-motivated. It makes a huge difference that the kids really want to do this."

- **The Norden family's experience:** The Nordens discovered it's hard to say no to the opportunities a manager uncovers. They knew nothing about the musical theater scene when their daughter Claire started performing in musicals at age six at local theaters near their Pennsylvania home. After Claire appeared at age seven in a local production of *Annie*, her mother, Beth Norden says, "I was getting a lot of cards from people who wanted to manage Claire. It seemed surreal. We met with three managers and chose the one who said she wanted Claire to be a normal kid." But when Claire was in fourth grade, an opportunity came along that posed a challenge for the whole family. She won the role of Baby June in a touring company production of *Gypsy*. "Be careful what you audition for," says Ms. Norden. Claire was too young to go on tour alone and so her mother went with her. "We were away for nine months," she says, although there was a five-week break in the middle when they came back home. "Claire loved it, getting on the bus, doing eight or nine shows a week. She never missed a show. But it was difficult for me and the family, especially for my older daughter, who was in seventh grade. I had to take off a year from my job as a preschool teacher. My coworkers were great, and my job was still there when I returned." During the tour, Claire worked with a tutor provided by the musical and also with her mother, who used materials from their hometown elementary school. Otherwise, Claire has been in regular public schools. She sings in her school choral groups and continues to take voice lessons. Her other shows have been limited runs at nearby theaters, although her manager has had her audition for some Broadway shows. "She has come close a few times," says Ms. Norden. "I take her into New York City to audition. Often the answer is a 'No.' She would love to be on Broadway. That's her goal. It's such a hard life, and she has seen it on the tour, but she's still eager to audition. I want to support my kids in whatever their dreams are because so many people are unhappy in their professions. I ask Claire if she still wants to do this. It's a lot of rejection. I've seen the faces on so many kids that you're not sure who this is for. Make sure it's for them and not for you."

Tips for Going Pro

Here are tips about going pro—no matter when it's done—from Edna Landau, who writes an online blog, "Ask Edna," with career advice for musicians:

- **Don't overhype:** "Avoid using over-the-top superlatives when writing about your youngster. The more you hype them up, the harder for them to live up to the praise. It's always good to play down such things," says Ms. Landau. She cautions against using the word prodigy. "There has to be an emphasis on the talent and ability. You don't want a shallowly built prodigy moment in their career to be all there is, so that once they're no longer young enough to be a prodigy, there's nothing left."
- **Limited repertoire:** "Repertoire should be limited when they start a career. It's perfectly OK to start with a few pieces and play them for a couple of years. They can be studying other things at the same time, but shouldn't be performing a huge range of work because inevitably they can't do everything well if they take on too much. Nobody should play something in an exposed situation without having had multiple opportunities to play it before," she says.
- **Check out managers:** "If you're trying to pick a manager, don't be star struck by being approached by managers. There are managers out there who are not the most qualified. Look at the managers' rosters and at the number of performances their artists have. Try to contact the artists they manage and see what kind of experience they're having. Google the managers' names and read everything you can on them. If they have information on their website that is old and hasn't been updated, or if they have typos and

inaccuracies, that's not good. They have to present a first-class image," says Ms. Landau.

- **Professional know-how:** "All contracts that are to be signed for any purpose whatsoever should be reviewed by a professional—a lawyer or the manager," adds Ms. Landau. "If youngsters are going to perform or be interviewed on television or in other media, they need coaching beforehand by someone who possesses expertise in this area." (See Resources for a link to the "Ask Edna" blog.)

Sibling Strain

It's not easy being the sibling of a young musician who is beginning to achieve success. "My older daughter didn't love it at first, when she saw me doing so much for her sister Claire," says Beth Norden. "Seeing your younger sister get all this applause wasn't easy." During the year of the *Gypsy* tour, "Whenever we were within an hour of home, my husband and my older daughter would drive to see us." They also spent a week together over Christmas and spring break. "Parents need to do something entirely different for the other child. My older daughter took piano for a few years but then got interested in other things. In high school, she became a budding film-maker and writer, and is in the acting group. The older she got, she realized that I cultivated her interests as well."

Supporting the individual needs and interests of each child is part of normal parenting, but sometimes the amazement that parents feel at the blossoming skills of a young musician can lead to things getting a little out of whack. Shirley Bell acknowledges that finding the right balance can be hard because of the time-consuming support that goes with nurturing a young musician. "I've talked this out with my two daughters," notes Ms. Bell. Both of her daughters studied music for a while. One played piano and the other cello, but they ended up quitting and pursuing other interests. Ms. Bell explains that while the attention her son Josh was receiving as a young violinist "was exciting, it did take a toll on the family. Because of the traveling, the phone calls, the performances, and the publicity, the household was concentrating a lot of its time on this one child. Dinner table conversation would revolve around what's going on with Josh. He never flaunted anything about himself. His sisters adore him. They may be angry with me for the way I handled things, but they're close to Josh. The connection they have as siblings made them all survive pretty well in spite of me."

Recent photos of cellist Alisa Weilerstein and pianist Jonathan Biss.

11 College and Career Concerns

COLLEGE-APPLICATION SEASON IS FILLED WITH WORRIES for many parents but can be especially nerve-wracking for music parents. With so many kinds of schools and degree programs to choose among, parents may fear that by choosing one route over another their teenager may close off career options. Alisa Weilerstein and Jonathan Biss made choices at opposite ends of the music-education scale, and yet doors remained opened, which they note in their vignettes that set the stage for this chapter's discussion.

"I decided when I was in eighth grade that I wanted to go to a university, instead of a conservatory. I wanted to meet people from different fields and read a lot," says cellist Alisa Weilerstein, who attended Columbia University. "I knew early on that I wanted to be a musician, and so I had put in many hours of practice already. I still had a lot to learn, of course, but by the time I was eighteen, I had a good foundation and didn't feel I needed to practice six hours a day as a lot of conservatory kids do. Going to Columbia was the best thing I ever did for myself. I met so many interesting people and took such great classes. I took only one music course. I majored in history, which helps me now place things I perform in context." Improving her writing skills with all the papers she wrote during college "helps focus the way I express myself musically, too."

She feels that college also made her a more efficient practicer. "Going to a university was one of the hardest things I ever did because I had to study, practice, and play a lot of concerts. So I had to learn to structure my time, to practice very efficiently. I was used to having a lot of time to practice, but when I found my hours devoured by classes, homework, and writing, I found I could get done in two hours of practicing cello what I used to do in five."

Pianist Jonathan Biss also knew for many years that he wanted to be a professional musician. He, too, had put in loads of practice time as a preteen and teen, but he made a different educational choice. He spent his college years at a conservatory, the Curtis Institute of Music. "I struggled with the decision," he says. "As much as I feel like I missed out on another kind of education, I knew that those were the years of my life when I needed to have all the time in the world to practice. Those are such vitally important years for the physical development of a musician."

He notes, however, that there was another key factor in his decision making. "You go where the teacher is that you want to work with," he explains. "I wanted to study with Leon Fleisher. At that time, he taught at two conservatories. One was Curtis. I auditioned at Curtis and went there when I was seventeen. To fill in some gaps in my academic education, I took a couple of classes at the University of Pennsylvania while I was at Curtis, which has a reciprocal relationship with the university. After Curtis, when I moved to New York, I took some classes at Columbia. It's a compromise."

First, the Worries

Of course, Alisa Weilerstein and Jonathan Biss are special cases, extraordinary musicians who benefited from excellent early instruction and performance opportunities, as well as a leg up from having parents who are professional musicians. Even so, Ms. Weilerstein's experience shows that investing in a liberal arts education for four years can be compatible with a performance career. Mr. Biss's choice shows that it's possible to double down on practicing for four years at a conservatory and still find ways to engage in wider intellectual pursuits, which he has found an outlet for in the thought-provoking essays he writes on his blog, in the scholarly program notes he writes for his performances, and in the teaching he has done online.

This chapter explores the varied educational choices made by other pros and also by our advisors' sons and daughters, both those who hope to have a career in music and those who are preparing for other careers but want to keep music in their lives.

But first, it's time to confront one of the biggest worries, the one that keeps many music parents up at night: Will a student with a music degree be able to earn a living from music?

The news is mixed, according to a jobs forecast from the US Bureau of Labor Statistics (BLS) in its *Occupational Outlook Handbook* issued in 2010. (See Bibliography.) This report concludes that the employment scene is tight for many professions but especially tight for performing musicians, with nearly half of all professional musicians working part time. The BLS study notes that employment for musicians and singers is expected to grow "about as fast as the average for all occupations" but adds that "strong competition is expected for the jobs because of the large number of workers who are interested in becoming musicians or singers." The BLS handbook goes on to warn that musicians "must be prepared to face the anxiety of intermittent employment.... Even when employed, many musicians and singers work part time in unrelated occupations." Those "unrelated occupations" are what career counselor Peter Spellman calls "lifeline careers." These are the temporary jobs that help musicians pay the bills and "supplement what they earn from music," explains Mr. Spellman, who directs the Career Development Center at Berklee College of Music.

The performing-musician pyramid has a broad base, but few musicians reach the very top as Ms. Weilerstein and Mr. Biss have. Ann Turner has seen how tough the competition is in her daughter's part of the music world—symphony orchestras. "We've been lucky that our daughter has an orchestra job, but several friends of hers haven't been able to land one," says Ms. Turner. "At her first French horn audition, there were 150 musicians auditioning for one spot. When you look at the numbers, they're pretty staggering."

About 6,000 students received music performance degrees from conservatories and colleges in 2010–11. There are nowhere near that many openings each year in major US orchestras. In one recent year there were only a few hundred calls for new musicians in those orchestras, according to statistics from the National Association of Schools of Music and the International Conference of Symphony and Opera Musicians. Of course, many young people who earn performance degrees aren't interested in a symphony job, and other performance opportunities are possible. But there were also about 10,000 additional students in 2010–11 who earned either a music education degree or another music related degree. Some of them may have been hedging their bets by earning a nonperformance degree while still hoping to land an orchestra job. Any way you look at it, the competition is stiff.

However, the BLS report offers some optimistic advice that's similar to suggestions made by our advisors in earlier chapters. According to the Bureau's jobs forecast, "Talented individuals who are skilled in multiple instruments or musical styles will have the best job prospects." Seconding this advice are officials at universities and conservatories. "A twenty-first-century musician has to have a broad base from which to draw," says Laura Hoffman, assistant dean for admissions at the University of Michigan's School of Music. "You simply have to be well versed in a variety of spectrums to have the maximum number of opportunities when you graduate." Agreeing with her is Berklee's Peter Spellman, who explains, "Our students come so focused on their music. They need to balance that with adaptability and versatility so they can take the music education they're getting and express it in a lot of different ways and make those ways turn into revenue streams." Conservatories and colleges offer courses for musicians on entrepreneurship, arts administration, freelancing know-how, and other business-related skills that can help musicians carve out more opportunities for themselves.

"There are many more pathways than when I was young," observes flutist Paula Robison, who in addition to being a top-level performer is also a flute professor at New England Conservatory (NEC). "There's not just the path of playing in orchestras. There's chamber music, there are the many performance groups that musicians start themselves, there are many kinds of classical music to play. There's world music—Korean music, African music, Brazilian music, and so on. People are branching out." The US military also provides employment possibilities. With its many bands and other ensembles, the military is actually the largest single employer of performing musicians in the United States.

"What a lot of modern musicians do is a combination of different musical activities," says Payton MacDonald. He has a multifaceted career that includes performing as a percussionist in several new-music ensembles, composing music, self-publishing his compositions, and teaching as a tenured associate professor of music on the faculty of William Paterson University.

The Teaching Anchor

As Payton MacDonald and others have discovered, teaching can anchor a life in music. The possibilities include teaching at the elementary and secondary school level, which usually requires a musician to have earned either a bachelor's or a master's degree in music education. Most musicians who earn music performance degrees—the bachelor of music degree—also wind up teaching at various points in their careers. Some do so without earning an additional music education degree by teaching privately or in schools that don't require education degrees. Others follow up a performance degree with a master's or doctorate in performance or some other area of music, which allows them to apply for university teaching jobs. Singer Jamie Jordan earned a bachelor's in jazz studies and a master's in vocal performance. Then she earned a master's in music education so her "lifeline career" as a voice teacher would keep her involved with what she loves while still allowing time for performing.

"I tell my students that Bach had to do all sorts of things besides play music to support his family," she says. "That's the reality for many musicians."

Some young people know before they enter college that they want music education to be the focus of their careers. Teaching isn't a backup alternative for them, but the main attraction, the aspect of music they like best—introducing it to others. Part of what led band director Matthew Ceresini to choose a degree in music education over one in engineering resulted from the excellent teaching he received during high school when his school jazz band took part in Jazz at Lincoln Center's Essentially Ellington festival. Wynton Marsalis and members of the Jazz at Lincoln Center orchestra served as teaching artists for the students. "There was such a joy in the teaching and in the music," recalls Mr. Ceresini, a trumpeter. "It wasn't just learning how to play the right notes. It was seeing people who could express themselves and get others to feel it just by watching and listening. Music allows us to express our truer selves. Guiding students toward finding that nonverbal voice is very rewarding for me."

Volunteering during high school to tutor music students started Wes Sparkes on the path to teaching. He also taught while earning a performance degree in trumpet at the University of Cincinnati's College-Conservatory of Music. Later, he earned a master's in teaching and became a music teacher at a Colorado middle school. "What hooked me on teaching was to see the progress in young students, to work them through musical challenges, and see the joy in their maturing as musicians. I had intended to be a performer, but I had such rewarding experiences teaching that I found I had a stronger passion for teaching. Performing is a self-gratifying experience. Teaching is the opposite—the focus is on the student. To me, that's more satisfying."

Elizabeth Núñez majored in music education because she already knew she wanted to be a choral director. "I'd always been in choirs. I love the sense of community you

Paula Robison, flutist and professor at New England Conservatory,
teaching one of her graduate students, Adam Eccleston III

get in choirs," says Ms. Núñez, assistant conductor of the Young People's Chorus of New York City. However, after starting work as a choral director, she has continued to do some performing on the side, as have many other music educators.

Budget cutting has curtailed music programs in many public schools, but Eastman and Berklee report that their music education graduates generally find teaching jobs. Gary Ingle, executive director of the Music Teachers National Association, has studied the BLS jobs forecast carefully and found a bright spot for music teachers in the "self-enrichment teacher" category, which is predicted to grow much faster than average. To boost employability, he advises musicians to "embrace nontraditional approaches to teaching. With all the baby boomers retiring, more senior adults are going to be taking music lessons for self-enrichment, to stay active, keep their brains active—the wellness aspects."

Planning for "Plan B"

The tight employment scene for performers may prompt some parents to urge their young musicians to have backup possibilities on hand if needed. Some parents lobby for a university rather than a conservatory education so their teens can take a broad range of electives in addition to their music studies, thus giving them skills in nonmusical fields. Other parents are fine with a sequential approach, having their sons and daughters focus on music training during the college years in order to give them the best possible shot at a performing career, figuring that other skills can be added later in graduate school, if needed.

Conservatory officials note that if a "Plan B" should turn out to be needed, students who earned a performance-oriented bachelor of music degree don't necessarily have to find themselves in a dead-end situation. "I try to make sure that parents understand the flexibility of the bachelor of music degree," says Matthew Ardizzone, associate dean of admissions at Eastman School of Music, a branch of the University of Rochester. At conservatories such as Eastman, which are part of a university, music students can take courses in the university's nonmusic departments. Those extra courses might help prepare a performer for job hunting outside the music world. Career shifting—working in a field other than the one majored in—happens to many college graduates, not just to musicians.

An online essay by Peabody's director of admissions, David Lane—"What Can You Do with a Music Degree?"—presents a positive spin on musical career shifting. The essay notes that a music performance degree gives students transferable skills that can make them attractive hires for nonmusic employers. These crossover abilities include creativity and self-confidence, as well as having good skills in time management, planning, goal setting, and team building. (See Bibliography for a link to the essay.)

The Peabody essay notes that while many Peabody graduates earn a living as performers or music educators, others move on to jobs in other professions. That's the path Anne Akiko Meyers's father followed. He earned a bachelor's degree in clarinet performance, hoping to land an orchestra job. He had a modest amount of success playing in community orchestras and jazz combos. "Those things don't pay much. I decided that there were too many other things I wanted to do. I didn't have the single-minded dedication and determination that Anne has," Richard Meyers explains. So he went to graduate school in psychology and has held a series of college administration posts, most recently as president of Fielding Graduate University. He still plays clarinet in his spare time and has found a way to combine that with his interest in psychology by becoming a volunteer music therapist in nursing homes.

A Rundown of the Choices

Here are different kinds of institutions that offer college-level programs in music and the degrees that can be earned:

- **Conservatory:** A conservatory specializes in intense professional-level training for students who aim for careers as performers, composers, and conductors. Some conservatories also offer programs in music education, musicology, music therapy, and music technology. Students must pass auditions to be admitted. Some conservatories, such as Juilliard or Curtis, are independent institutions. Others, such as Peabody or Eastman, are parts of a university. Conservatory-level training can also be found at some universities, such as the University of Michigan whose music department offers a conservatory program, as well as a regular music major and minor. Some conservatories allow students to apply in only one aspect of music. Others—both university based and independent—offer dual-degree options, permitting students to earn bachelor's degrees in two disciplines, including in a non-music field.

- **College or university:** As noted earlier, some universities offer conservatory-like programs. Other colleges and universities have only a regular music major or minor, although some also offer degrees in music education, music technology, and music business. Many provide opportunities for students to have music lessons and participate in ensembles, often for academic credit.

- **Degrees:** Undergraduates who complete an academic music major usually receive a bachelor of arts (BA) or bachelor of musical arts (BMA). Those who do a performance-oriented program receive a bachelor of music (BM), although at some schools it's a bachelor of fine arts (BFA). Music technology or business students earn a bachelor of science (BS). Students preparing to be schoolteachers usually earn a bachelor of music education (BME) or a bachelor of science (BS). College-level teaching usually requires a master of music (MM), doctor of musical arts (DMA), or doctor of philosophy (PhD). Conservatories also offer an artist diploma for those who focus on lessons but don't complete a full course load; Joshua Bell earned an artist diploma at Indiana University.

Researching the Options

Our advisors' families started college-application season the way many families do when junior year rolls around: talking with teachers and high school counselors, reading college guidebooks, and doing research online.

Music teachers proved an important resource, not only for providing suggestions of schools to consider but also for recommending instructors at different institutions with whom students might study. "I've learned over the years what type of student is going to fit in where, on the basis of their musicianship, their level of maturity, stamina, and demeanor," says band director Scott Brown, who has been handing out college advice for many years at Seattle's Roosevelt High School. "A lot of kids are drawn to the big-name conservatories on the East Coast, and I have a lot of talented, highly motivated kids who go that route. But great teaching goes on at a lot of colleges, too. Those East Coast schools aren't

---

SPOTLIGHT ON: DAVID GROSSMAN, BASS

Focus: In high school, David Grossman did classical, jazz, and composing. He was accepted at Juilliard but turned it down for a new jazz program in Boston. After a few weeks there, he changed his mind. "I was younger than the other students and realized I needed to learn my core curriculum first." The next semester, he enrolled at Juilliard and studied with a bass teacher who "inspired me and made me fall in love with the orchestral literature. A light turned on for classical bass. It wasn't a matter of what did I like most, but what did I want to focus on right then." He won a job with the New York Philharmonic during his last year at Juilliard. He still plays jazz on the side and composes music—just not all at the same time. "I try to focus on one thing at a time."

always the best fit for some students who may not be on that level musically or not ready to handle cities like New York. I try to steer them to a comprehensive college or university where they can get a good music education."

College guidebooks helped Kristin Bond locate possibilities for her older daughter, a singer who wanted to major in music education, but who also wanted a school with a strong vocal program. "I had a gut feeling of the kind of small, liberal arts college that would be good for her. Then I looked at the programs they offered. Some had strong performance programs but not a strong music education department," says Ms. Bond. That helped her daughter narrow the choices. After gaining

David Grossman

acceptance at several schools, she chose the one that seemed to offer the best for both her interests—St. Olaf College in Minnesota.

Many parents also searched online. Marion Taylor, who notes that she "started with zero knowledge," says she learned a lot quickly through the online site College Confidential. It has a "Music Major" discussion forum on which people share what they've learned about different colleges and conservatories. However, it's good to remember that these are just personal opinions. The Taylors tried not to be discouraged by some comments they heard, such as, "Flute is so competitive she won't get in anywhere." That turned out not to be true. "She got accepted at way more places than we expected," says Ms. Taylor.

The Taylors picked up an especially helpful tip from the College Confidential online forum—the importance of visiting schools and having a trial lesson with one of the music teachers. The junior year college tour is a staple of many college searches, but for music students, adding a trial lesson provides valuable extra information. "We visited two schools that were nearby, so they were just day trips," says Ms. Taylor. "We immediately realized the importance of the lessons, not just to see whether she would click with the teacher, but the lessons helped us evaluate where she would be a competitive candidate. We began to understand where she would fall in place."

Dr. Jeanny Park helped her trumpeter son fit in a few trial lessons on the way to delivering him to the summer program he did between junior and senior years. "I looked on the website of the university or conservatory that he was interested in and found the contact e-mails for the trumpet professors. I gave my son the list, and he e-mailed the professors and made arrangements for the lessons," she explains. "My son eliminated some schools after those visits. He had a pretty good idea of what styles of teaching work better for him." Both the Taylors and the Parks had to pay for most of these trial lessons, with fees ranging from $60 to $200. Juli Elliot didn't have to pay for any of her daughter's sample voice lessons. Discuss the fee when arranging a lesson to avoid embarrassing moments later.

Not all families went to the expense of traveling to schools for trial lessons before their teenagers filed applications. They held off until after their sons and daughters were accepted. Sarah Odhner thought it might actually be awkward if her violinist son had a trial lesson with one professor but then requested to study with a different one when he applied. Some applications require students to list a professor to study with at the school. Her son listed professors based on recommendations from the teacher he had in high school and waited until he was accepted for sample lessons, which led him to choose the Cleveland Institute.

Whether sample lessons come before or after filing the application, the University of Michigan's Laura Hoffman stresses their importance. "If you're going to invest four years undergraduate and perhaps two years at the graduate level with a particular teacher with whom you will have an important mentorship relationship, you want to do as much research as possible to know that you'll have some chemistry with that person, that this is going to be a good working and building relationship." She also suggests that students watch an ensemble rehearsal and "sit in on a studio class that many professors hold, a perfect way for visiting high school students to sit in the back of the room, not have the spotlight be on them, so they can gain an idea of how the professor works, the caliber of the music making."

Choosing a Conservatory

Most of the pros featured in this book studied at a conservatory after high school because, like Jonathan Biss, they knew they wanted to be musicians and were eager for a conservatory's rigorous training. That was true also of the sons and daughters of several of our parent advisors.

Pianist Erika Nickrenz notes an additional reason for her conservatory choice. "I felt like I wanted the intense competition that a conservatory like Juilliard could afford," says Ms. Nickrenz. "I'm a pretty competitive person. I knew from my experiences in summer camps that if there are other people around me who are at my level or higher, I would strive for more. I practiced so much at Juilliard. I was in the practice room all day. It was definitely the right situation for me, but I don't think it's necessarily for everybody."

This kind of concentrated music experience appealed to saxophonist Miguel Zenón, who says of his years at Berklee, "The main thing for me at Berklee was the community, being around people like you. People were practicing all day, transcribing, listening to music, playing sessions, writing music. It was inspiring being around people like that. This was my first experience with jazz education. I was filling in a lot of the basic stuff I didn't know."

Bassist Ranaan Meyer credits his conservatory training for helping him become a more versatile musician. "It opened up a world of options and didn't limit me to just one genre," he says. "When I first started thinking about college, I wanted to be a jazz bassist, but I knew a lot of jazz bassists had studied classical bass. That's how they got their chops up." So he studied classical bass first at Manhattan School of Music (MSM) and then at Curtis, while polishing his jazz skills by playing jazz gigs on the side. "The marriage of the two—jazz and classical—has enabled me to play in all the genres I play in today."

Becoming part of a conservatory community also helps in establishing the personal connections needed to build a career. "In the music business, it's all about who you know and who knows you. That is what is really going to propel your career," says Peter Spellman, career advisor at Berklee. Former artist manager Edna Landau agrees, "Teachers, conductors, and administrators at the conservatory see you, they get excited about you, and talk about you. You're part of the publicity that goes out from there."

In addition, students often form lifelong artistic partnerships with fellow students. That's how several of our pro advisors formed the ensembles that shaped their careers. Erika Nickrenz teamed up with two of her fellow Juilliard students—a violinist and cellist—to form the chamber music group she has performed with ever since, the Eroica Trio.

There are other ways to make professional connections besides spending the college years at a conservatory. Many musicians who go the college route attend a conservatory for graduate school and immerse themselves in conservatory networking at that time. In addition, there are many non-conservatory-based networking possibilities that both college and conservatory students can participate in: summer festivals, competitions, or gigging with professional musicians.

Miguel Zenón made the most of the networking opportunities that were available to him as a Berklee undergraduate and later as a graduate student at MSM. "I interacted with the people at the school, but I was also interacting with my jazz heroes by going to clubs and meeting great saxophone players or great piano players, talking with them, playing in jam sessions, and eventually playing with them in paid gigs," he

Erika Nickrenz, pianist (center), with other members of the Eroica Trio

explains. "You build a community that is so important in this field, having people know who you are and the way you play so that when they need a musician, they'll call you." This networking has enabled him to become a saxophonist people call on to perform with a wide range of combos and has also helped him organize his own band and make recordings.

However, the intense music-only atmosphere at a conservatory, while heaven for some students, may be a bit of an adjustment for others. Even Erika Nickrenz, who loved being able to practice all day at Juilliard, says she missed not being able to take courses in a wider range of subjects. "It was a little bit of a culture shock having such a music-driven education," she explains. "I came from an exceptional high school where I had phenomenal English and history classes. The transition was hard. Now Juilliard offers a dual-degree option with Columbia. If that had been offered when I was at Juilliard, maybe I would have tried that, to get the best of both worlds."

Violinist Adrian Anantawan also took a while to adjust to the music-focused conservatory experience. "It was the first time in my life that I was absorbing so much material on just one subject," he says of his experience at Curtis. "I visited the University of Pennsylvania campus while I was at Curtis, wishing sometimes that it would be nice to be a normal college student, taking typical lecture courses, but I never had enough time to take a course at Penn. That was one of my motivations in applying to graduate school in music at Yale after Curtis, because Yale is an academic university with an opportunity to take courses outside of the music school. At Yale, I took a psychology course and an art course, but there was limited time there, too, because there are so many music requirements in the master's program." He made up for missed academics later when he did a one-year Arts in Education program at the Harvard Graduate School of Education. There he worked on gaining skills needed to try to achieve his goal of creating programs to improve music instruction for kids with disabilities.

Choosing a University-based Conservatory

University-based conservatories offer many of the same advantages as an independent conservatory in terms of intensity of instruction and networking but have the added bonus of a wider variety of elective courses. When Laura Vautour's daughter made her postacceptance campus visits, she realized that a small conservatory wasn't for her. She wanted a conservatory environment within a larger university and chose the University of Cincinnati's College-Conservatory of Music. Academic variety played a role in the choice Marion Taylor's daughter made: the University of Miami's Frost School of Music. "Becky enjoys science, and it would be foolish for her not to also be able to take premed-type classes," says Ms. Taylor. Michigan's Laura Hoffman notes, "If a student has genuine interest in additional subject areas, that's someone who should consider studying at a university as opposed to someone without those interests who would be infinitely more happy at a conservatory."

SPOTLIGHT ON: PAYTON MACDONALD, PERCUSSION, COMPOSITION

See what happens: "My father worried whether I could earn a living from music," says Payton MacDonald. When he chose the University of Michigan for college, that gave his dad hope that "I'd change my mind and be an engineering major." Then Payton began to worry, too, and shifted to prelaw. "I was miserable. I decided to make a go at music, and if nothing much happened by my late twenties, I'd go to law school." He earned a master's and a doctorate in music at Eastman, landed a university job, but it wasn't until he became a tenured professor that his father stopped worrying. "Despite my parents' reservations, they were incredibly supportive. I had scholarships, but there were other expenses that they covered. I left school debt free—a huge difference in my ability to build a career."

In some cases the nonmusic electives win out over the music classes. That happened to Kurtis Gruters. As a music theory major at Eastman, he not only kept up his interest in percussion by being part of the percussion studio, he also took neuroscience courses offered by the University of Rochester. He became so fascinated by music's impact on the brain that he changed direction. "I am eternally grateful that I chose a conservatory with an associated college. This gave me the opportunity to take nonmusic courses in neuroscience, which has led to where I am now," he says. After Eastman, he entered a doctoral neuroscience program at Duke to investigate how the brain coordinates information from ears and eyes.

Choosing the College Route

Violinist Jennifer Koh chose the college route for much the same reason as Alisa Weilerstein. Ms. Koh was already deeply committed to music and on track for a professional career when she entered Oberlin—the *college*, not the conservatory. After she won the Tchaikovsky Violin Competition during her freshman year, a lot of people pressured her to transfer to an East Coast conservatory. She stayed put, although she continued violin lessons and spent summers at the Marlboro Chamber Music Festival.

"I'm so happy that I stayed at Oberlin," she says. "I may not have taken the fast track to a career, but I wanted to develop as a person. My emphasis in my major was poetry. In some sense, how to phrase something in music, what the skeletal structure of the piece is, all those things were developed in the way I thought about literature. Every word in a poem signifies something much greater than just that word or the components of the letters. Music is similar. It's not quite right to say that music is a language, because it's much more, but there are parallels. A lot of my programming ideas and the way I think about music are informed by my time at Oberlin." After Oberlin, she packed in a solid dose of conservatory training by earning an artist diploma at Curtis. Her circuitous path puzzled her parents. "After I graduated from Curtis, my parents suggested that medical school is still a possibility," she says. Soon they realized that she was well on her way to a successful career in music.

Other pros on our advice panel also used the two-stage approach—first college and then a conservatory. Richard Stoltzman majored in both music and math at Ohio State, not sure whether to be a band director or a dentist. After college, he applied both to dental school and to a graduate program in clarinet performance. Clarinet performing won out. Trumpeter Mark Inouye made his two-stage transition before finishing college. He spent his first two years as a civil engineering major at the University of California at Davis and then transferred to Juilliard, with the encouragement of the Davis trumpet teacher, "who was convinced I could have a career in music and got me to audition at Juilliard," says this San Francisco Symphony principal trumpeter. Conductor Marin Alsop also made a midstream switch, transferring to Juilliard after two years at Yale.

The two-stage approach can pose difficulties, however, as flutist Alice Jones discovered. She was an academic music major at Yale and then went to the conservatory at Purchase College to earn a master's in flute performance. She found that her flute playing wasn't at the same level as students who spent their undergraduate years at conservatories. "But when it came to writing assignments, doing program notes, researching composers, I was more prepared than my conservatory peers because I had done that kind of work at college," she says. "I was able to step up my flute playing. Then I realized I love teaching." That led her to a doctoral program at the City University of New York, where she is preparing to teach at the college level, with the goal of continuing to perform, too.

Students who plan to major in music education face a similar choice, whether to study at a conservatory or at a university. "I loved music in high school, but I was also into math. I had thought I would probably be an engineer," says Michael Ceresini, now a Pennsylvania high school band director and music teacher. He was accepted at some colleges for engineering but also applied to the music-education program at a school near his home, Lebanon Valley College. "I realized I wasn't ready to make music only a side part of my life," he says and chose the music education program, although he took extra courses to earn a BA at the same time and later earned a master's in music education online from Boston University.

The college versus conservatory choice was especially tough for Richard Zhu, who had two loves: violin and science. He won a scholarship to a university-based conservatory but turned it down to do premed at Duke, leading to medical school at the University of Maryland. "I chose college because I wasn't sure I wanted a career in music. College allowed me to explore nonmusic opportunities as well as continue to study music," he says. He was in the Duke orchestra and played with a community orchestra during medical school. "Studying music gave me an appreciation for detail and doing something at a high level of expertise. It also gave me a source of inner strength for times when I have struggled."

Students like Richard Zhu who want to participate in music during college need to make sure the college they choose offers challenging enough private lessons and performance opportunities to hold their interest. Zachary Rayfield continued to study music and participate in a piano ensemble and several informal bands throughout his years of college and graduate school as a science and engineering major. He also was able to continue studying composition, which he had begun during high school.

Some parents report that their teenagers' musical backgrounds strengthened their college applications, especially if they submitted recordings of performances as an "arts supplement." Jamie Raudensky Doyle's viola playing earned her a special scholarship earmarked for arts-oriented students at Wake-Forest University. "I didn't have to major in music to keep the scholarship but had to be involved with music. I did orchestra and played chamber music," says Ms. Doyle, now a research scientist in Boston.

The Dual Degree Option

"A lot of schools seem to discourage the idea of the dual degree," says Mei Carpenter. Even so, her younger daughter took the plunge and has enjoyed the Oberlin dual degree program, working on a BM degree in cello performance from the conservatory and a BA in psychology from the liberal arts college. This will take her five years, which is typical of dual degree programs. Her older sister, a violinist, went the conservatory route at the Cleveland Institute of Music, both for undergraduate and graduate school, which helped her land a job performing with the Cincinnati Symphony Orchestra. "We're worrying a little less about her," says Ms. Carpenter. "But we felt our younger daughter should do the double degree program, to have something else in case music doesn't work out."

"The dual degree is the most rigorous path a student can choose. Some students will be up for it, but others not so much," says Laura Hoffman, assistant dean at Michigan. Eastman's Matthew Ardizzone warns, "It's quite a course load. If you're not equally dedicated to both subjects, it's hard. If you're doing the academic side because of a need to have something to fall back on or because your parents told you to, that often doesn't work out so well. I look for students who have just as much light in their eyes when they talk about physics as when they talk about music. We also have students who do a dual major in music education and music performance." About 10 percent of Eastman students are in a dual degree program, although each year some drop the academic portion and become straight conservatory students, while others add an academic major to their music studies.

Martha Woodard's son is doing the dual degree program at Bard, which requires that all music students earn two degrees, a bachelor of music and a bachelor of arts. Toyin Spellman-Diaz's parents urged her to earn two degrees at Oberlin, an oboe degree and a music education degree. "She dropped music education her sophomore year. Her oboe teacher said she had to make a choice," says her father. "We knew that with talent and discipline something would work out, that she'd find her way." After Oberlin, she earned a master's in oboe performance at MSM and is now on its pre-college faculty, while also performing with the Imani Winds.

Hit the Road—or Not

"I thought about skipping college, but Mom and Dad weren't into that," says Ranaan Meyer. He was tempted to just keep doing jazz gigs. "I'm glad that's not what I ended up doing. I never would have done what I do now if not for the journey I had," says Mr. Meyer, who, as noted earlier, chose the conservatory route.

Christian McBride also played jazz gigs during high school. After starting at Juilliard to study classical bass in 1989, he began performing with famous jazz musicians in New York City. "It was hard to maintain this unexpected dual career of being a student and a professional musician," he explains. "It was too hard to work at a club until three o'clock in the morning and be at orchestra rehearsal at 8:00 a.m. and try to study in between. Toward the end of that first school year, I spoke with my bass instructor, and he said he'd support my decision if I didn't come back to school. Then I had to run it by my mother. I was too chicken to present this to her in person. I called from a pay phone." He explained to her why he wanted to leave school, told her about the great jazz musicians he was performing with, and the "good money" he was earning. "There was a long two-minute pause that sent a chill up my back. I said, 'Mom, are you there?' She said, 'I'm thinking.' She asked where I was going to live. Another two-minute pause. Then she said, 'If I taught you to be anything like me, I know you're going to make the right decision. I trust you.'"

He felt confident about his chances. "I had a grand plan," explains Mr. McBride. "I was thinking of things to do that would separate me from the rest of the pack." He set out to learn the music of all the bands and musicians he wanted to perform with one day. He got their albums and learned their tunes. Then, if he had a chance to meet them and sit in with their bands, he would be ready to make a good impression. Before long, he was performing in the bands of his jazz heroes.

Leaving school early also worked for Wynton Marsalis, who made that choice ten years before Mr. McBride—heading out on the road with a top jazz band after one year at Juilliard. When he and Mr. McBride were students, Juilliard didn't offer a degree in jazz. Now Juilliard and many other conservatories and universities have started jazz programs, bringing in top jazz performers to serve as instructors. Some observers report that jazz students are now staying in school and doing their apprenticeships with the jazz greats who teach there. "School becomes a lab in which you can experiment," says Berklee's Peter Spellman. "But some students still have this urgency, this drive to get out of school and go do it. If someone has a passion, feels they're ready, and has something feasible to work with, then go out and orbit. You can always come back to finish the degree." Finishing the degree "is a sign of completion in our society and can be a door-opener. Not having the degree can be a door-closer."

"Having a doctorate or a master's doesn't mean you're going to be a successful performer or composer," says Miguel Zenón. "School is definitely not for everyone, but what it did for me—meeting people, building a network—I wouldn't have gotten that if I had stayed home and practiced by myself."

Rock musicians are also tempted to skip college. That's the choice made by Keith Fertwagner, who performed in a series of bands and had success as a songwriter and recording artist before becoming music director of Omaha's School of Rock. However, some famous rock bands actually got their start when their members were in college, such as Arcade Fire, Animal Collective, R.E.M., Radiohead, Queen, and Pink Floyd. A few universities now offer degree programs in rock and pop music.

Financial Aid

The financial aid process for music programs is similar to that for regular colleges, although two conservatories are tuition free: Curtis and Colburn. The Yale School of Music, which is only for graduate students, is also tuition free, as is the Thelonious Monk Institute of Jazz Performance. Some conservatories and universities offer merit scholarships in addition to need-based assistance. Our parent advisors found a big difference in the financial packages that their sons and daughters received at different schools. It pays to shop around.

The low in-state tuition for the University of Missouri's bachelor's degree program in music education "was a factor in deciding where to go," says Missouri native Kirstin Cash, daughter of one of our parent advisors. "It would have been a lot more expensive to go to the University of Illinois or a private college in another state." Also important were the rave reviews about the Missouri program that she heard from the band directors at her St. Louis high school. "All of them went there. I visited the university and really liked the faculty,"

SPOTLIGHT ON: MIGUEL ZENÓN, SAXOPHONE

Proud parent: "My mom was happy about my music until I decided to be a jazz musician," says Miguel Zenón. "I was a good student, interested in math and science, got good grades. I was already admitted to a good engineering school when I decided to follow a musical career. Berklee seemed like the place to go, but my family couldn't afford to send me there. I applied and was accepted but didn't have a scholarship. I spent a year and a half playing gigs in Puerto Rico, saving to buy a ticket to Boston. Once I got there I was able to get some scholarship help and student loans. Mom was worried, but she didn't say not to do it. After a while, she realized I was happy and making progress. She stopped worrying and was just proud of everything."

says this clarinetist. On her visits to other schools, including some out of state, "I didn't click with the faculty as well." She chose the University of Missouri, loved it, and hopes to spend her career as a middle school band director in the St. Louis area.

Audition Advice

Auditions are usually required for admission to conservatories, as well as to college or university programs in performance and music education. Applicants for other music-related programs often have to audition, too. In many ways these auditions are similar to competitions, and thus the tips offered in chapters 9 and 10 for handling competitions and performance jitters can help with college auditions.

Juli Elliot notes, however, that college auditions differ in an important way from competitions. Becoming aware of that difference proved very helpful for her daughter who used to hate competitions, but with a little attitude adjustment was able to shine at college tryouts. "What helped was she had a keen awareness that people at college auditions were judging her on her *potential*, not on where she was right at that moment. So she could think, 'I'm auditioning for these people to train me, to bring me along.'" She was accepted at several schools and chose the conservatory at a small liberal arts school, Wheaton College.

Also important is the choice of an audition piece. Some schools require certain pieces, but if there's any leeway in the audition repertoire, a showy piece that's a bit of a reach may not be the best choice, according to Michigan's assistant dean, Laura Hoffman. Her advice for young auditioners: "If you choose something that's at the edge of your technical capacity, that may not be wise because in an audition setting maybe you'll be nervous or the travel may have made you more tired than you expected. Choose pieces that are very secure and that reveal the highest degree of artistry that you have." Eastman's Matthew Ardizzone gives similar advice. "It's more important *how* you play than *what* you play," he says. "The faculty is better able to judge applicants as developing artists when they're playing repertoire that's well within their reach, so the students can show off their phrasing, their musicality."

"We want people to show up with a beautiful sound and a sense of who they are as performers and as communicators," says Brian Zeger, head of Juilliard's vocal arts program. "If they sing with musicality, heart, and a sense of real beauty, that's better than trying to sound like a thirty-year-old opera singer, doing pieces that are much too difficult for them. It's better to choose a song within their range. People have actually gotten into Juilliard singing 'Danny Boy.'" Flutist Paula Robison, who watches a lot of auditions at NEC, notes, "What I look for is a kind of intelligence in the playing and the possibility of the player being able to think for him or herself and not be a copycat."

Audition policies differ from school to school. "A live audition is the ideal way to audition," Mr. Ardizzone recommends. "That gets you to the campus. You get to know the school so in April when you're trying to make a decision, you have more information as to whether it's going to be a good fit. But we recognize that not all students can fly to different schools to audition. We do regional auditions at various urban centers throughout the country, and we also allow recordings to be submitted." At some schools, before students are invited to audition they have to submit a prescreening recording.

Many schools now require that recordings be submitted as digital files uploaded online to the school's server. "We recommend that they make a decent-sounding, unedited recording," says Mr. Ardizzone. "If you set up a video camera in the living room, that leaves very little question that you are who you say you are, and we're getting an honest representation of your playing. If you use a professional studio, it's hard for us to tell how doctored the recording is. That may raise red flags. Digital cameras do such a good job now of capturing sound that the faculty aren't too concerned about sound quality with home recordings." Several parents report that their kids made audition recordings at a local music school that has recording equipment. Dr. Park decided to record her son's trumpet prescreening auditions herself. She used a camcorder for the visual, recorded the audio with a microphone hooked up to a computer, and then combined the two using special software.

No matter what the recording method, "You want to be as prepared as you can be, as if you were doing a live audition," says Mr. Ardizzone. "There's a tendency if you're setting up the camera in the living room to treat it informally. The student needs to take responsibility to give the best possible performance."

Marion Taylor offers additional audition-season advice. "There's so much traveling to auditions that the kids invariably get sick. We let Becky sleep in some days and miss a little school," says Ms. Taylor. "Another thing that we found that was critical: Earplugs for the hotel rooms, because my husband snores." Lauren Chipman had a similar problem when she went on her audition trip with her dad. "It was the night before my first audition, and my dad snored so loud. I said, 'Dad, I can't sleep!' He went down to the lobby and sat there until nine in the morning so I could get some sleep. After that we had two hotel rooms," says Ms. Chipman. Her mom didn't go on the audition trip. "I would get too nervous," says her mom. "My husband is very mild mannered."

Creating Opportunities

Many of the professional musicians on our panel have varied careers. Quite a few perform more than one genre of music and do more than perform. A sizable number have been entrepreneurial—organizing and managing new ensembles and music festivals; producing their own CDs or videos; and marketing their own compositions, CDs, and videos online. Some create new music as composers and arrangers or by commissioning new pieces. Like most musicians, many also teach—as faculty members at conservatories, music schools, and summer festivals or by giving master classes, private lessons, and workshops.

"These are good times for musicians because the control of the music industry is increasingly decentralized," says San Francisco Conservatory's John McCarthy. "The few managers on 57th Street in New York City, who used to control who played what with every orchestra, have to contend now with people who want to play repertoire that isn't marketed by those managers. With the rise of the Internet, there's a new entrepreneurial spirit."

The musicians' personal websites listed in the Resources section of this book provide an idea of the range of activities that keep them busy. Some of their ventures have been mentioned earlier. Here are more details on a few of them:

- **Toyin-Spellman Diaz:** In 1997, she joined a group that flutist and composer Valerie Coleman was creating—Imani Winds, a woodwind quintet of African American musicians. One goal was for the group to serve as role models. "At first, it was something we did because we liked to play music together. Most of us were still thinking we would win orchestra jobs," says Ms. Spellman-Diaz. "After a while, we realized we had something special to say and decided this was better than an orchestra job." The quintet performs a mix of classical and jazz. In addition, they commission new works, teach in educational residencies and master classes, and hold a chamber music festival each summer.

- **Ranaan Meyer:** He met two violinists at Curtis who introduced him to bluegrass music. "I thought it was one of the most joyous things I'd ever heard," he explains. While in their early twenties, the three of them formed a string trio, Time for Three, which plays a blend of bluegrass, classical, jazz, and pop. "At that age, you can go up to someone and say, 'We have a video of what we do. Can we have ten minutes of your time to play it for you?' They'd see the video and give us a gig." He composes a lot of the group's music and runs his own summer institute for bass players.

- **Lauren Chipman:** "I always thought I'd play in a major orchestra, but in 2005, I got a call from Matt Sharp asking if I wanted to play viola in his rock band, the Rentals. I had never played rock but said, 'Yeah, sure,'" she recalls. "I like rock music, but it never occurred to me that classical and rock could intersect. I dropped out of the master's program at USC to join the band." She has continued to perform with this band and with a string quartet that plays rock songs with a classical twist. She also teaches, is principal violist of two California orchestras, coordinates a community outreach program for the Colburn School, and runs an online business called Baroque Bling, which sells string instrument accessories encrusted in Swarovski crystals.

- **Caleb Burhans and Payton MacDonald:** They started playing contemporary classical music with other students at Eastman. "In 2001 when a number of us were graduating, we realized that we had the beginnings of a core ensemble and decided to turn this into a professional group, Alarm Will Sound," says Mr. MacDonald. "It started slow, playing just one concert the first year, then two or three the next. Now we do about fourteen concerts a year. About half of us have jobs as professors; the rest are freelancers."

- **Randy Wong:** While earning a performance degree at NEC, he took courses in its Music in Education (MIE) program. "I was interested in how to use music to teach other subjects," he says. That led to his earning a master's degree at the Harvard Graduate School of Education and then to a job at NEC supervising MIE students doing internships around the country, something he does online via video from his home state of Hawaii. His parents were upset at first that he didn't make more use of his classical training, but they came to accept what he calls his "multidimensional situation." He combines the NEC job with being executive director of the Hawaii Youth Symphony Association; playing double bass with the Hawaii Symphony; and leading his own band, Waitiki, which performs "exotica" music, a blend of Hawaiian and jazz styles.

- **Marin Alsop:** Despite a Yale education and two violin degrees from Juilliard, she wasn't accepted at any conducting programs in the late 1970s and early 1980s. So she took private conducting lessons and formed her own orchestra to showcase her conducting skills. Finally, at age thirty-two, she spent a summer studying conducting at Tanglewood, which led to a series of conducting jobs, culminating in her becoming the first woman to lead a major US orchestra when she landed the Baltimore Symphony Orchestra job in 2005. She has continued creating opportunities, this time for others, when she used money from her MacArthur "genius" award to start Orch-Kids, the first El Sistema program in the United States.

Beyond Performing

There are many nonperformance-centered music careers besides teaching that might appeal to teens who aren't sure of their chances as performers. "I was interested in psychology in high school but had no idea how that could be combined with music," says Brian Jantz, a guitarist who started as a performance major at Berklee. Then he took an introductory class there in music therapy and realized it would merge his two interests. Music therapists use music to enhance the social, emotional, educational, and behavioral aspects of the lives of people who need extra support, such as the patients he has worked with at two Boston hospitals—Children's and Dana Farber Cancer Center. Sometimes he leads music activities with groups of patients or works one-on-one with children to relieve stress and provide them a means for self-expression. Music therapists also work in mental health centers, schools, correctional facilities, and other settings.

"Music therapy requires someone who is very solid musically and has an interest in helping others," says Suzanne Hanser, who directs Berklee's music therapy program. Another of her graduates, singer Rebecca Vaudreuil, worked for a while at the Naval Medical Center in San Diego, using singing and songwriting to help veterans cope with post-traumatic stress disorder and traumatic brain injury. She and Mr. Jantz do a little performing on the side. Adam Sankowski, another music therapist, has a more active performing life. He works in a Boston school for children with multiple special needs and uses the school's summer break to tour with an indie-folk band, The Grown Up Noise.

Speech pathology offers another career alternative. Mary McDonald Klimek, the speech pathologist quoted in chapter 6, was a music teacher and singer before earning a degree in speech-language pathology. For many years, she was a speech pathologist at Massachusetts Eye and Ear Infirmary, helping people (including some famous singers) heal after damaging their voices or after having vocal surgery. She still finds time to perform.

Tech-savvy teens might be attracted to degree programs that offer training for careers as recording engineers, music software developers, acoustics technicians, and other technical specialties. Some schools offer degrees in music business. Arts administration provides another alternative, as does working as a musician's manager or publicist, music lawyer, or music editor. (The Resources section has more on music-related careers.)

Spare-Timers

"There's a renaissance of serious amateur music making," declares piano teacher John McCarthy. "There are people who don't want to earn their bread and butter as professional performers but choose to have a day job so they can keep performing. The quality level of playing by serious amateurs is astoundingly high." Quite a few of our parent advisors are spare-time musicians, playing with community orchestras and bands, singing in choirs and other choral groups, taking music lessons, or forming their own ensembles. There are also summer music camps for adult amateurs, including Rusty Musicians, started by Marin Alsop, which lets amateurs study with Baltimore Symphony musicians. For pianists, there's even a competition—the Van Cliburn International Piano Competition for Outstanding Amateurs.

Dr. Gene Beresin, the child psychiatrist on our advice panel, is a spare-time musician. He took piano lessons as a kid and toyed with the idea of being a professional musician, but his interest in medicine and psychiatry prevailed. Several years ago, he began taking jazz piano lessons and now plays piano with other child psychiatrists and physicians in a jazz band—Pink Freud and the Transitional Objects—that performs at medical conferences. "I'm not good enough to play solo piano like my jazz icons," says Dr. Beresin. "My strength is to play as part of a band and make other people sound good. This unites my passion for music with my professional career."

Research scientist Jamie Raudensky Doyle plays viola with a community orchestra, the New England Philharmonic, which has professional and amateur musicians. "We rehearse Sunday nights, so I don't have to rush there from work," she says. "It's such a nice break, my time to relax and use a different part of my brain. Because I put in a lot of hard work practicing when I was younger, I can just enjoy playing, absolutely no pressure."

Some spare-timers eventually cycle back to music as a career, as baseball slugger Bernie Williams has done. He studied classical guitar growing up in Puerto Rico and continued playing guitar in his free time during sixteen years with the New York Yankees. After retiring from major league baseball in 2006, he has focused on music. He performs, composes, and has written a book, *Rhythms of the Game,* on the links between musical and athletic performance. (See Bibliography.)

College Wrap-up

Our parent advisors worried a lot during the college-application process. But most wound up supporting their kids' decisions, whether to go on with music or keep it as a part-time hobby. As Sue Jones noted when she was interviewed for this book: "We were worried when our daughter decided to major in music. I did try to get her to think about music from a practical standpoint. But at the same time, I felt that it was not my place to destroy her dreams. Dreams are never realized unless you try them. She had convinced me that she had enough love of music that I would be doing her a disservice by trying to discourage her." Here's what other parents had to say about their kids' choices:

- "I didn't feel it was up to us to tell our son what his love should be. I've spent my career working with people who did something else for thirty years because that's what they felt they were supposed to do and later, after a big struggle, doubled back to what it was they really wanted to do," says Susan Raab, who works as a marketer for people in the arts. She was comfortable with her son's decision to earn a degree in musical theater and grateful that he has been able to cobble together a career.

- "Music is great for kids. Not all of them are going to wind up being like Renée Fleming or Andrés Segovia, but they can have fun along the way," says Buzz Ballenger. His daughter is pursuing a performance career in opera, but his son decided not to continue in the music field after earning a bachelor of music in classical guitar performance. "He saw his teachers struggling to make ends meet and didn't want to do that. He did a minor in business during college and that helped him find jobs with Internet start-ups. They appreciate him because he's a creative type. He still plays guitar on the side."

- "Any field is going to be tough, whether it's being a medical doctor, lawyer, teacher, or engineer. You need to be creative, juggle lots of things, have a get-out-and-do attitude," says Yoko Segerstrom, whose daughter studied violin at a university and whose son studied composition at a conservatory. "I feel my children should do what they are passionate about. It is all up to how they do it."

Tess Fagan playing keyboard in a student performance at Boston University.

12 Moving On

AFTER SOWING THE SEEDS of musical interest and nurturing it in their kids, some parents discover that this interest may lay dormant for a while but can blossom later in unexpected ways, as it did for the music mom whose reminiscence opens our final chapter.

"My daughter was kind of coasting with her piano lessons during high school," says Janice Fagan, whose daughter, Tess, had been taking piano lessons in the preparatory division of New York's Manhattan School of Music school since she was five years old. "There were days when she wouldn't practice at all or just a half hour. I was constantly reminding her, but after a while it wasn't worth the battle. She is very strong-willed. She was involved in so many things at high school, pulled in a lot of directions—school plays, clubs, AP classes, a cabaret production every year, school choir, and a special choir that went on tour to Italy. She didn't want to miss anything. She played piano but wasn't serious about preparing her pieces or performing more often. I wanted to stop the lessons, but she never wanted to quit. I didn't want to push so she would never touch the piano."

Then everything changed—*after* her daughter started college at Boston University, as an economics and environmental science major. "Over the summer before college, she realized she wanted to take piano lessons at college," explains Ms. Fagan.

Her daughter, on her own and without help from mom, found an instructor in the university's music department to give her private lessons. Once those lessons began, "The light bulb went on. She realized that in order to stay with this university instructor, she needed to step up to the plate. She needed to practice at a certain level if she wanted to play at a certain level. It hit home with her in college. It never did when she was in middle school and high school." Maybe it was having a new teacher, a fresh start in a new city, or being away from home on her own that caused the change. Ms. Fagan's conclusion: "She grew up a little."

Her daughter had to relearn some things with the new instructor. "She says she would never have been able to do it if she hadn't attended music school all those years," adds Ms. Fagan. "I feel good that I gave her a good foundation. Isn't that what it's all about? I'm not disappointed that she's not becoming a professional musician. That's not the end-all. Some kids have a talent for sports, others for art. Hers was music, and I wanted to support it. Wherever it was going to lead, so be it. I think her interest in music kept her grounded. Attending music school every Saturday, music helps define who she is."

"We became closer," Ms. Fagan says of her relationship with her daughter during Tess's first year at college. "When I went up to visit her that year, she said to me, 'Thank you for giving me this, that you never gave up on me.' She says she practices about an hour or two every day in one of the school's practice rooms. She likes being part of the music world there. Her friends are people who play an instrument or have a passion for music. Part of it came naturally from her, and part of it was brought out through her music school education. She wants to keep music in her life." She added music as a minor, joined the university's symphonic choir, and looked into starting jazz piano lessons. Different kids, different timetables.

Seeds Sown

A few other examples of musical seeds blooming in unexpected ways have already been mentioned, but Sarah Odhner recounts two others. "All through high school, biology and music were the dual loves of one of our sons, who was very involved with French horn and singing," she says. At first, biology won. But after earning a degree in biology, he decided against a science career, worked in construction for a while, went to back to school to earn a degree in music education, and became an elementary school music teacher. Her oldest son, the one who dropped piano before she figured out how to be a more hands-on music mom, took up guitar and singing during high school. After earning a doctorate in engineering, he works in robotics but still plays guitar and sings in a choir. One of Juli Elliot's sons also had a post-college career change. He had piano lessons as a child, took up guitar and singing during high school, and majored in psychology in college, with a minor in sacred music. He decided not to continue with psychology but enrolled in Middle Tennessee State University's master's degree program in recording arts and engineering.

Paula Robison's daughter also found a way to keep music in her life, although not as a professional musician like her mother or her father, who is a violist and concert organizer. "She has the most beautiful voice and was always with us at concerts and festivals, but classical music just wasn't her thing," says Ms. Robison. "She got into the folk-rock scene and is a wonderful songwriter. She earned a PhD in comparative human development and still sings in a band on the side. As a child, she was gifted in several areas. We just wanted to prop her up, water her like a plant, and wait to see what she would like to do."

Sometimes those seeds can take generations to blossom. Ann Turner's daughter, Catherine, a French horn player with the Montreal Symphony Orchestra, performs on a horn that belonged to her grandfather. He wasn't a professional musician, had stopped playing horn long before he became a father, and died before his granddaughter was born. But the family kept his French horn. It was a part of family lore. When a wind quintet came to Catherine's preschool, she liked the sound of the French horn best. When her elementary school gave students a chance to choose a band instrument to play, she picked French horn. The family cleaned up grandpa's horn and Catherine has played it ever since. Her mother observes, "I love the fact that my dad's horn is still making music. It has been a connection to my parents. I know he'd be thrilled that his granddaughter is probably playing that horn better than he ever did."

Even if a young person drops music and never comes back to it as a performer, being deeply involved with music as a young person leaves a mark, according to Wynton Marsalis. In comments he gave to high school musicians who were taking part in his Essentially Ellington band competition one year, he spoke about the lasting impact that jazz would have on them. The same is true of classical, rock, pop, folk, or any kind of music that a young person invests a good chunk of time

---

WORTH IT REPORT

Noah Nathan: "Learning to improvise, the core of jazz, was incredibly important for building self-confidence. You stand up in front of an audience, open yourself up and go, while reading the crowd, seeing if it's going well. That has made me more comfortable speaking to audiences, giving opinions in seminars," says Noah Nathan, a political science graduate student who played saxophone in jazz bands through high school and college. "What's going to stay with me is that I love this music. It's a passion that's never going away. From playing jazz, I've learned so much about how to listen to it. Even if I do something else in my career, have no time to practice, I'm going to be a listener of jazz the rest of my life."

studying and playing. Mr. Marsalis, in comments that are available as a podcast online, told the students:

> The deepest value that is in jazz is that it teaches you how to listen and how to be empathetic about what you are hearing.... It's a way to listen so deeply into something, that you hear far deeper than what's being said or what's played.... As you all go to college, as you all go through your lives, you will always be ambassadors for this music on a certain level. You will always be a part of it. You will always be jazz musicians because you played it. That will never change.... If you end up not playing music at all, you still are a jazz musician your entire life.

New Roles

"I was totally unprepared to let my child go at seventeen when she started at Curtis, living on her own," says Annette Radoff. "I knew that Elena had to be completely immersed in her world and I couldn't be hanging on looking over her shoulder, but it took a while to get used to the quiet house. I had been hearing her practice for hours each day and loved every scale. I missed that so intensely. I still do. Nothing makes me happier than when she spends a little time at home with us and does some practicing."

A quiet, empty-nest house takes all parents a while to adjust to, but the silence can seem especially jarring for music parents. Along with the absence of those familiar warm-up exercises there is also a winding down of the supportive organizing that music parents grew used to doing for so many years. Ms. Radoff lets professional managers and agents do the organizing now. She and her husband have adjusted to their new role as enthusiastic audience members at their daughter's performances. That's the role taken on by other parent advisors whose kids have finished college and are performing, whether as professionals or as spare-timers pursuing other careers. Sarah Chang notes, "My mom hears my concerts when I'm a drivable distance from her home. She doesn't like to travel much anymore. I think she overdid it going to all those performances with me as a kid. But she still goes to Korea with me when I perform there."

Years of music parenting leave other imprints on the lives of the parents. It gave many an opportunity to learn more about music, inspired some to start playing instruments or sing in choirs, and turned quite a few into regular concertgoers. Music parenting also opened career avenues for some parents. Shirley Bell earned a degree in counseling and psychology while raising her three youngsters. Before her retirement, she specialized in working with teachers who were being trained to teach gifted children, a logical outgrowth of raising her own gifted child, violinist Joshua Bell. On occasion, she still gives workshops for music teachers and parents on the

The informal playing that Vivian and Donald Weilerstein did with Alisa when she was young led them to form the Weilerstein Trio.

social and emotional needs of gifted children. Sarah Odhner turned volunteering at her kids' youth orchestras into a paid job for a few years by becoming the personnel manager for two of the youth orchestras. When her kids' youth orchestra days ended, she became an accompanist at an elementary school.

Vivian Weilerstein and her husband turned something they did for fun—playing chamber music at home with their daughter Alisa when she was very young—into a professional sideline for all three of them. They formed the Weilerstein Trio when Alisa was about thirteen. "We play fewer concerts now because Alisa's solo career has expanded. It adds another layer to our relationship," says Vivian Weilerstein. Norma Meyer has started performing with her son, bassist Ranaan Meyer. "I've been playing piano with him since he was a kid. In high school, when he was learning new bass pieces or playing them for auditions, I would play the piano part with him," she says. Now he writes pieces for bass and piano and performs them in concerts with his mother. "I keep pinching myself. It's incredible that he still wants to play with me," says Ms. Meyer.

End Notes

"The thread that I weave through my teaching is that there is inherent worth in studying an art—and to keep that at the forefront. It's not merely a steppingstone to acceptance at a good college. I spend time with my students to sort out the place of music in their life, regardless of professional aspirations," says John McCarthy of the San Francisco Conservatory piano faculty. "Arts education is essentially a reflective process. Students must ask, 'Who am I? Why do I want to do this?'"

Throughout this book, our contributors have cited many reasons why they wanted to become involved with music—academic, emotional, social, and artistic. "What I have enjoyed most is to share with my kids on the very deepest level a love for and understanding of some of the greatest achievements of humankind," says Jocelyn Stewart. For others, it was the sense of connectedness that music provides. "Playing music can give you a feeling that you're part of something larger than yourself," says guitarist and music therapist Adam Sankowski, who notes that what he always liked best about music as a child was "playing music with other people." That sense of community carries special benefits for a family. "Music has helped us stay connected," says Gary Borkowski, father of a teen percussionist. Kyle Todd, father of two young adults who are pursuing nonmusical careers, says that music remains "something that we hold in common. It continues to provide us with activities for shared experiences."

Theresa Chong loves how music helped her forge "a close connection with my kids through our shared passion for music and our shared experience of music making." She planted the seed for this book by suggesting the idea of tapping into the huge reservoir of helpful advice that experienced music parents can offer. As she predicted, the music moms and dads who joined our advice panel have indeed offered an abundance of good ideas and useful insights. So did all the educators and professional musicians who joined the team—everyone pitching in to help keep music in our lives.

WORTH IT REPORT

Helen Jones: "I took piano lessons in elementary school. My parents allowed me to stop the lessons when I was tired of them. This, to me, is just as important as encouraging a child to continue," says retired schoolteacher Helen Jones. Those early lessons taught her to read music, which helped years later when she found her real musical love—choral singing. She fell in love with it during college when she joined her school's Chapel Choir. Since then, she has spent nearly forty years singing during her spare time with a chorus in Baltimore that performs choral masterworks. "Music has been the mainstay of my life. It has always been there for me. Bad days at work, personal problems, or exhaustion could be forgotten and magically transformed by going to a rehearsal and working on a beautiful piece of music with my fellow singers. The best thing parents can do is provide children the opportunity to have music in their life, but let the decision to take that opportunity be the child's. My parents encouraged me but never pushed. I explored on my own, in my own time, and discovered one of my life's greatest joys."

The author's older son, composer Eric Nathan, sharing his love of music with some young friends of the family.

About the Advice Panel

A big round of applause goes to the professional musicians, music educators, music parents, spare-time musicians, and others who shared their advice for this book by filling out questionnaires, doing phone interviews, or contributing comments via e-mail. Several musicians and educators interviewed by the author for her earlier book for young people—*The Young Musician's Survival Guide*—agreed to allow information from the earlier interviews to be used in this new book as well. In addition, the following orchestras helped arrange for some of their musicians to be interviewed: Cleveland Orchestra, Los Angeles Philharmonic, Metropolitan Opera Orchestra, New York Philharmonic, San Francisco Symphony Orchestra, and St. Louis Symphony Orchestra.

THE PROS

The author conducted interviews by telephone with thirty-five professional musicians: Adrian Anantawan, March 31, 2012; Emanuel Ax, November 19, 2011; Joshua Bell, April 3, 1998; Jonathan Biss, December 5, 2011; Lawrence Brownlee, August 11, 2011; Caleb Burhans, October 5, 2011; Sarah Chang, September 21, 2011; Lauren Chipman, February 21, 2012; David Grossman, October 21, 2011; Robert Gupta, July 23, 2011; Shachar Israel, December 7, 2011; Alice Jones, September 27, 2011; Jamie

Jordan, September 30, 2011; Jennifer Koh, July 21, 2011; Payton MacDonald, September 30, 2011; Ellis Marsalis, June 21, 2011; Wynton Marsalis, May 20, 1998; Josh Marcum, January 11, 2012; Christian McBride, December 23, 2011; Anthony McGill, December 29, 2011; Ranaan Meyer, December 12, 2011; Anne Akiko Meyers, October 3, 2011; Dana Myers, September 18, 2011; Erika Nickrenz, June 16, 2011; Jeff Rabb, November 19, 2011; Paula Robison, April 11, 2011, February 13, 1998; Toyin Spellman-Diaz, October 21, 2011; Richard Stoltzman, October 29, 2011, March 26, 1998; Adrienne Taylor, November 29, 2011; Isabel Trautwein, November 13, 2011; Liang Wang, September 28, 2011; Alisa Weilerstein, April 29, 2011; Larry Williams, September 14, 2011; Randy Wong, October 20, 2011; Miguel Zenón, April 1, 2012. The author conducted in-person interviews with Eric Nathan on December 27, 2011, and January 26, 2013, and received a completed questionnaire from Noah G. Palmer in early 2011. The following musicians contributed their reminiscences and suggestions by e-mail: Marin Alsop, July 20, 2011; Stephanie Blythe, October 21, 2011; Gloria Cheng, September 17, 2011; Mark Inouye, October 8, 2011; Ali Jackson, November 12, 2011; Kelli O'Hara, August 17, 2012; Brent Samuel, August 9, 2011.

PARENTS

The following schools and organizations helped the author assemble the advice panel for this book by providing access to parents of some of their students: Baltimore Symphony Orchestra's OrchKids, Baltimore, MD; Boston University Tanglewood Institute, Boston, MA; Children's Orchestra Society, Manhasset, NY; College-Conservatory of Music of the University of Cincinnati, Cincinnati, OH; DC Youth Orchestra Program, Washington, DC; Community Music and Dance Academy of the University of Missouri Kansas City, Kansas City, MO; Eastman's Community Music School, Rochester, NY; Face the Music, New York, NY; From the Top, Boston, MA; Jazz at Lincoln Center, New York, NY (through its Essentially Ellington and Middle School Jazz Academy programs); JCC Thurnauer School of Music, Tenafly, NJ; Lindbergh High School, St. Louis, MO; Longy School of Music, Cambridge, MA; Los Angeles Philharmonic's Youth Orchestra (YOLA) and its community partners (HOLA and Harmony Project), Los Angeles, CA; Peabody Preparatory, Peabody Institute, Baltimore, MD; People's Music School, Chicago, IL; Portland Youth Philharmonic, Portland, OR; Pre-College Division, Manhattan School of Music, New York, NY; San Francisco Conservatory of Music Preparatory Division, San Francisco, CA; School of Rock, Montclair, NJ; School of Rock, Omaha, NE; Special Music School, New York, NY; St. Louis Symphony Youth Orchestra, St. Louis, MO; The Sphinx Organization, Detroit, MI.

The author received questionnaires from 130 parents (completed between January and September 2011), and conducted in-depth interviews with more than fifty-five parents. Thirty-one of these interviews were follow-up telephone interviews with parents who had completed questionnaires; twenty-one of the interviews were phone interviews with parents contacted through other sources. The author also did in-person interviews with three parents and held a group discussion with parents at Manhattan School of Music's Pre-College Division on February 5, 2012. Parents interviewed by phone include: Buzz Ballenger, March 28, 2012; Shirley Bell, April 21, 2011, January 29, 2013; Joe Bianchi, December 18, 2011; Kristin Bond, November 9, 2011; Cindy Buhse, November 4, 2011; Gail Caiazza, October 18, 2011; Mei Carpenter, November 21, 2011; Charlsie Cartner, November 9, 2011; Debbie Chipman, February 21, 2012; Diane Cornelius, November 7, 2011; France Couillard, October 24, 2011, January 14, 2013; Leslie Curda, December 6, 2011; Brad and Charlotte Detrick, September 15, 2011; Andrew Elliot, September 24, 2011; Juli Elliot September 19, 2011; Janice Fagan, August 5, 2011; Heather Gange, October 14, 2011; Jiji Goosby, October 29, 2011; April Hansen, September 16, 2011; Thanh Huynh, November 1, 2011; Sue Jones, November 1, 2011; Ellis Marsalis, June 21, 2011; Betsy McCarthy, November 7, 2011; Anne and David McCollough, September 17, 2011; Judy Merritt, September 23, 2011; Norma Meyer, December 20, 2011; Richard and Yakko Meyers, October 3, 2011; Beth Norden, December 19, 2011; Sarah Odhner, September 19, 2011; Jeanny Park, September 12, 2011; Susan Rabb, November 19, 2011; Cindi Russell, November 8, 2011; Annette Radoff, October 27, 2011; Annette Ramke, September 28, 2011; Karen Rile, October 11, 2011; A. B. and Karen Spellman, November 4, 2011; Yoko Segerstrom, September 28, 2011; Marion and Paul Taylor, September 13, 2011; three parents from the YOLA program at HOLA, June 9, 2011; Melissa Tucker, September 15, 2011; Donald and Vivian Weilerstein, June 8, 2011; Martha Woodard, October 5, 2011; Susie Wuest, September 14, 2011; Lydia Zieglar, October 4, 2011. Parents interviewed in person include: Rodney Brewington, April 25, 2012; Theresa Chong, May 7, 2011; Lynette Fields, April 25, 2012. Parents who took part in the Manhattan School of Music group discussion on February 5, 2011, include Julia Castro, Anya and Michael Steger, Jocelyn Stewart, and several others. Two additional phone interviews were conducted during 2011 and 2012—one with a parent and one with a musician, who is also a parent, both of whom prefer to remain anonymous.

EDUCATORS AND OTHER EXPERTS

The author conducted interviews by telephone with the following fifty-two music educators and other experts on music and young people: Barbara Wilson Arboleda,

January 13, 2012; Matthew Ardizzone, February 22, 2012; Paul Babcock, November 4, 2011; Gene Beresin, December 4, 2011, September18, 1998; Scott Brown, December 1, 2011; Ruth Cahn, October 12, 2011; Kristin Cash, August 28, 2012; Matthew Ceresini, November 11, 2011; Mark Churchill, December 19, 2011; Amy Dennison, October 18, 2011; Jill Dew, November 3, 2011; Hiroko Dutton, May 11, 2012; Afa Sadykhly Dworkin, June 1, 2011; Robert Edwin, November 29, 2011; Keith Fertwagner, September 20, 2011; Cheryl Goodman, June 16, 2011; Suzanne Hanser August, 2012; Allen Henderson, November 11, 2011; Rebecca Henry, June 20, 2011, September 17, 2007, February 5, 1998; Laura Hoffman, March 1, 2 012; Gary L. Ingle, August 29, 2012; Laura Jekel, October 26, 2011; Nanette and Tom Jordan, November 7, 2011; Mary Klimek, December 30, 2011; Robyn Lana, September 10, 2012; Edna Landau, December 19, 2011; Yeou-Cheng Ma, July 20, 2011; Ralph Manchester, January 29, 1998; Kraig Marshall, December 2011; Roberto Marti, Jr., February 15, 2012; John McCarthy, July 26, 2011; Cheryl Melfi, June 15, 2011; Stephanie Meyer, July 18, 2011; Vanessa Mulvey, September 19, 2007, March 18, 1998; Elysabeth Muscat, December 13, 2011; Julie Novak, November 6, 2011; Elizabeth Núñez, September 10, 2012; Carol Prochazka, July 8, 2011; Dorothy Kaplan Roffman, July 12, 2011; Jennifer Roig-Francolí, October 24, 2011; Ellen Schertzer, October 21, 2011; Larry Scripp, October 26, 2011; Sandra Shapiro, October 13, 2011; Esther Spadaro, January 23, 2012; Wes Sparkes, November 3, 2011; Peter Spellman, August 14, 2012; Bridget Steele, September 7, 2012; Dan Trahey, July 25, 2011; Jenny Undercofler, July 12, 2011; Willliam Wellborn, August 31, 2011; Brian Zeger, July 16, 2012.

SPARE-TIMERS

The author interviewed by telephone the following individuals who studied music as youngsters but are not primarily full-time performers, pursuing other careers instead: Jamie Raudensky Doyle, September 26, 2011; Catherine Getchell, November 4, 2011; Brian Jantz, August 16, 2012; Kevin Powers, April 19, 2010; Adam Sankowski, August 16, 2012; Kaji Spellman, November 14, 2011; Rebecca Vaudreuil, August 20, 2012. An in-person interview was conducted with Noah Nathan, December 27, 2011. The following people contributed their comments for the advice panel via e-mail: Meara E. Baldwin, March 10, 2012; Kurtis Gruters, February 15, 2012; Helen Jones, November 3, 2012; Richard Zhu, December 24, 2011.

Resources

These organizations have useful information on their websites about music education and the value of participating in music. In addition, the Orchestras Canada and the League of American Orchestras websites have listings of youth orchestras.

American Composers Forum
www.composersforum.org

American Music Therapy Association
www.musictherapy.org

Association for Popular Music Education
http://www.popularmusiceducation.org/

American Orff-Schulwerk Association
www.aosa.org

American Society of Composers, Authors and Publishers (ASCAP)
www.ascap.com

American String Teachers Association
www.astaweb.com

Chamber Music America
www.chamber-music.org

Chorus America
www.chorusamerica.org

College Music Society
www.music.org

Dalcroze Society of America
http://www.dalcrozeusa.org

El Sistema USA
http://elsistemausa.org

Estill Voice Training
www.estillvoice.com

From the Top
www.fromthetop.org

International Alliance for Women in Music
www.iawm.org

International Conference of Symphony and Opera Musicians (ICSOM)
http://www.icsom.org

Jazz at Lincoln Center
www.jazzatlincolncenter.org

Kindermusik
www.kindermusik.com

League of American Orchestras
www.americanorchestras.org

Music-in-Education National Consortium
http://music-in-education.org

Music Teachers National Association
www.mtna.org

Music Together
www.musictogether.com

The NAMM Foundation (National Association of Music Merchants)
www.nammfoundation.org

National Alliance of El Sistema Inspired Programs
www.elsistemaalliance.org

National Association for Music Education
www.nafme.org

National Association of Schools of Music
http://nasm.arts-accredit.org

National Association of Teachers of Singing
www.nats.org

National Guild for Community Arts Education
www.nationalguild.org

Orchestras Canada
http://orchestrascanada.org

Organization of American Kodály Educators
www.oake.org

Performing Arts Medicine Association
www.artsmed.org

Suzuki Association of the Americas
http://suzukiassociation.org

The Sphinx Organization
www.sphinxmusic.org

VH1 Save the Music Foundation
www.vh1savethemusic.com

INSTRUMENT ORGANIZATION WEBSITES

American Harp Society
www.harpsociety.org

American Pianists Association
www.americanpianists.org

Guitar Foundation of America
www.guitarfoundation.org

International Clarinet Association
www.clarinet.org

International Double Reed Society
www.idrs.org

International Horn Society
www.hornsociety.org

International Society of Bassists
www.isbworldoffice.com

International Trombone Association
www.trombone.net

International Trumpet Guild
www.trumpetguild.net

International Women's Brass Conference
http://myiwbc.org/

Internet Cello Society
www.cello.org

National Flute Association
www.nfaonline.org

North American Saxophone Alliance
www.saxalliance.org

Percussive Arts Society
www.pas.org

International Tuba Euphonium Association
www.iteaonline.org

Violin Society of America
www.vsa.to

ORGANIZATIONS THAT LEND STRING INSTRUMENTS

Anne-Sophie Mütter Foundation
http://www.anne-sophie-mutter.de/stiftung-hochbegabte.html?L=1

Rachel Elizabeth Barton Foundation
www.rebf.org/home.html

Stradivari Society
www.stradivarisociety.com

Virtu Foundation
www.virtufound.org

WEBSITES FOR MUSICIANS QUOTED IN THIS BOOK

Marin Alsop— www.marinalsop.com

Adrian Anantawan— www.adriananantawan.com

Emanuel Ax— www.emanuelax.com

Joshua Bell— www.joshuabell.com

Jonathan Biss— www.jonathanbiss.com

Sarah Chang— http://sarahchang.com

Gloria Cheng— www.gloriachengpiano.com

Stephanie Blythe— http://www.opus3artists.com/artists/stephanie-blythe

Lawrence Brownlee— www.lawrencebrownlee.com

Caleb Burhans— http://www.calebburhans.com/wordpress/

Lauren Chipman— www.laurenchipman.com

David Grossman— www.davidjgrossman.com

Robert Vijay Gupta— www.laphil.com/philpedia/robert-vijay-gupta

Mark Inouye— www.inouyejazz.com

Shachar Israel— www.clevelandorchestra.com/about/israel-shachar.aspx

Ali Jackson— http://alidrums.com

Alice Jones— http://www.alicehjones.com

Jamie Jordan— www.jamiejordansings.com

Jennifer Koh— www.jenniferkoh.com

Payton MacDonald— www.paytonmacdonald.com

Ellis Marsalis— www.ellismarsalis.com

Wynton Marsalis— http://wyntonmarsalis.org

Christian McBride— www.christianmcbride.com

Anthony McGill— www.anthonymcgill.com

Cheryl Melfi— http://cherylmelfi.wordpress.com

Ranaan Meyer— www.ranaanmeyer.com

Anne Akiko Meyers— www.anneakikomeyers.com

Dana Myers— http://www.stlsymphony.org/bios/first-violins/dana-edson-myers.aspx

Erika Nickrenz— www.eroicatrio.com

Kelli O'Hara— www.kelliohara.com

Jeff Raab— www.jeffreymichaelraab.com

Paula Robison— www.paularobison.com

Jennifer Roig-Francolí— http://www.artoffreedom.me/

Brent Samuel— www.laphil.com/philpedia/brent-samuel

Adam Sankowski— www.thegrownupnoise.com

Wes Sparkes— http://www.wessparkes.com/

Toyin Spellman-Diaz— www.imaniwinds.com

Richard Stoltzman— www.richardstoltzman.com

Adrienne Taylor— http://www.communitymusicworks.org/staff.htm#Adrienne

Isabel Trautwein— www.clevelandorchestra.com/about/trautwein-isabel.aspx

Liang Wang— http://nyphil.org/about-us/ArtistDetail?artistname=liang-wang

Alisa Weilerstein— www.alisaweilerstein.com

Donald and Vivian Weilerstein— www.weilersteintrio.com

William Wellborn— www.williamwellborn.com

Larry Williams— www.peabody.jhu.edu/preparatory/faculty/williams.html

Randy Wong— http://randywong.net/bar

Miguel Zenón— www.miguelzenon.com

MUSIC BLOGS

Alex Ross, the *New Yorker* music critic, has an excellent blog that also lists many other music blogs. http://www.therestisnoise.com/

Musical America. This website hosts several blogs, including "Ask Edna." http://www.musicalamerica.com/mablogs/

Pianist Jonathan Biss's blog. http://www.jonathanbiss.com/writing

Violinist.com blog. http://www.violinist.com/blog/

Voice teacher Barbara Wilson Araboleda's blog. http://blog.voicewize.com/

ORCHESTRA WEBSITES

Many symphony orchestras have blogs, podcasts of performances, texts of program notes, videos, games for kids, and other educational materials on their websites. Among the orchestras that offer these online extras are the New York Philharmonic (www.nyphil.org), Boston Symphony Orchestra (www.bso.org), Los Angeles Philharmonic (www.laphil.org), National Symphony Orchestra (http://www.kennedy-center.org/nso), and San Francisco Symphony Orchestra (www.sfsymphony.org), Carnegie Hall also offers a wide range of online educational material on its online Resource Center (http://www.carnegiehall.org/ORC).

EDUCATIONAL CDS AND DVDS

Famous Composers; and *More Famous Composers*. Naxos AudioBooks, 2007.
These two CDs for kids, available for purchase online or in bookstores, introduce six classical composers each, narrated by Marin Alsop.

Keeping Score: Revealing Classical Music. PBS. Produced by SFS Media, San Francisco
   Symphony.
Highlights several classical composers, with commentary by Michael Tilson Thomas
   and performances by the San Francisco Symphony Orchestra. These programs
   can be viewed online on the PBS website and are available for purchase as separate
   DVDs. Available: http://video.pbs.org/program/keeping-score/.

The Kid and the Singing Teacher. Produced by Voicewize, An Entertaining Diversity
   Production, 2008.
This instructional video from Robert Edwin and Barbara Wilson Arboleda presents
   their teaching methods for working with very young voice students. Available for
   purchase at: www.voicewize.com.

PODCASTS, ONLINE VIDEOS, AND OTHER HELPFUL WEB-BASED RESOURCES

College Confidential—here is the link to this online site's Music Major Thread.
   http://talk.collegeconfidential.com/music-major/

"Gallaudet Fight Song"
Shows a pep-rally song developed by deaf students at Gallaudet University. Posted
   Aug. 24, 2010. Available: www.youtube.com/watch?v=1fH1FW421MM.

Jazz Stories
A wealth of information about jazz is available in this series of audio podcasts of interviews with famous jazz musicians that can be listened to on the Jazz at Lincoln
   Center website, which also has an archive of Jazz at Lincoln Center NPR radio
   broadcasts. Available at these two web addresses: http://jalc.org/multimedia;
   http://jalc.org/multimedia/browse?filter_toggle[category]=11.

National Public Radio
NPR's archive has many stories, interviews, and commentaries on music including
   several that feature Marin Alsop and Wynton Marsalis. Available: http://www.
   npr.org/series/100920965/music-articles/.

"The Pianist: Harriet Wingreen of the New York Philharmonic." WQXR
   Classical.
Presents a brief overview of her career (which is also described in *Meet the Musicians* by Amy Nathan). Posted Jan. 26, 2011. Available: http://www.youtube.
   com/watch?v=OPN74D-2lZk&sns=fb.

"Time for Three–Stronger"
Video on bullying created by the string trio Time for Three. Posted Oct. 10, 2011.
   Available: http://www.youtube.com/watch?v=OnzAWPlM470.

"When patients have 'music emergencies.'" CNN. A program on music therapy, featuring the work of Brian Jantz and Rebecca Vaudreuil. Posted Aug. 23, 2013. Available: http://www.cnn.com/2013/08/23/health/music-therapy/

"Wynton Marsalis in Conversation." Interview by Elliott Forest. WNYC-FM. Aug. 17, 2012. Podcast audio. Available: http://www.wnyc.org/shows/specials/2012/ aug/17/.

YOLA RESOURCE LIBRARY

This website for YOLA (the El Sistema program sponsored by the Los Angeles Philharmonic) includes helpful suggestions and materials for how to "bring an El Sistema-inspired program to your neighborhood." Available: http://www.laphil. com/education/yola/resource-library.

Bibliography

BOOKS ON MUSIC OR MUSIC EDUCATION

(*) Books with an asterisk include suggestions that can help with practicing

Beeching, Angela Myles. *Beyond Talent: Creating a Successful Career in Music.* New York: Oxford University Press, 2005.

Bloom, Benjamin S., ed. *Developing Talent in Young People.* New York: Ballantine Books, 1985.

* Breth, Nancy O'Neill. *The Parent's Guide to Effective Practicing.* Milwaukee, WI: Hal Leonard, 2007.

* Bruser, Madeline. *The Art of Practicing: A Guide to Making Music from the Heart.* New York: Bell Tower, 1997.

Colvin, Geoff. *Talent Is Overrated: What Really Separates World-Class Performers from Everybody Else.* New York: Penguin Group, 2010.

* Cutietta, Robert A. *Raising Musical Kids: A Guide for Parents.* New York: Oxford University Press, 2001.

Gladwell, Malcolm. *Outliers: The Story of Success.* New York: Little, Brown, 2008.

* Green, Barry. *The Mastery of Music: Ten Pathways to True Artistry.* New York: Broadway Books, 2003.

* Green, Barry, with W. Timothy Gallwey. *The Inner Game of Music*. New York: Doubleday, 1986.

* Johnston, Philip, and David Sutton. *Not Until You've Done Your Practice!* Pearce, Australia: Future Perfect, 2000.

* Lang Lang. *Journey of a Thousand Miles: My Story*. New York: Spiegel and Grau, 2009.

Levitin, Daniel J. *This Is Your Brain on Music: The Science of a Human Obsession*. New York: Penguin Group, 2006.

* Marsalis, Wynton. *Marsalis on Music*. New York: Norton, 1995.

* Miller, Richard. *Solutions for Singers: Tools for Performers and Teachers*. New York: Oxford University Press, 2004.

* Nathan, Amy. *Meet the Musicians: From Prodigy (or Not) to Pro*. New York: Henry Holt, 2006.

* Nathan, Amy. *The Young Musician's Survival Guide*. New York: Oxford University Press, 2000, 2008.

* Ristad, Eloise. *A Soprano on Her Head: Right-Side-Up Reflections on Life and Other Performances*. Moab, UT: Real People Press, 1982.

* Romeo, Nick. *Driven: Six Incredible Musical Journeys*. Boston: From the Top, 2011.

Ross, Alex. *The Rest Is Noise: Listening to the Twentieth Century*. New York: Macmillan, 2007.

Sacks, Oliver. *Musicophilia: Tales of Music and the Brain*. New York: Random House, 2008.

Spellman, Peter. *The Self-Promoting Musician: Strategies for Independent Music Success*. Boston: Berklee Press, 2008.

* Suzuki, Shin'ichi. *Nurtured by Love: The Classic Approach to Talent Education*. 2nd ed. Translated by Waltraud Suzuki. New York: Alfred. 1983.

Tunstall, Tricia. *Changing Lives: Gustavo Dudamel, El Sistema, and the Transformative Power of Music*. New York: W. W. Norton, 2012.

* Tunstall, Tricia. *Note By Note: A Celebration of the Piano Lesson*. New York: Simon and Schuster, 2008.

* Westney, William. *The Perfect Wrong Note: Learning to Trust Your Musical Self*. Pompton Plains, NJ: Amadeus Press, 2006.

* Williams, Bernie, Dave Gluck, and Bob Thompson. *Rhythms of the Game: The Link Between Musical and Athletic Performance*. Milwaukee, WI: Hal Leonard, 2011.

BOOKS ON PARENTING

Aldort, Naomi. *Raising Our Children, Raising Ourselves*. Bothell, WA: Book Publishers Network, 2005.

Chua, Amy. *Battle Hymn of the Tiger Mother*. New York: Penguin Press, 2011.

Dweck, Carol S. *Mindset: The New Psychology of Success*. New York: Random House, 2006.

Faber, Adele, and Elaine Mazlish. *How to Talk So Kids Will Listen and Listen So Kids Will Talk*. New York: Harper, 1980.

Elliot, Andrew J., and Carol S. Dweck, eds. *Handbook of Competence and Motivation*. New York: Guildford Press, 2005.

Grolnick, Wendy S., and Kathy Seal. *Pressured Parents, Stressed-Out Kids: Deal with Competition While Raising a Successful Child*. Amherst, NY: Prometheus Books, 2008.

Levine, Madeline. *Teach Your Children Well: Parenting for Authentic Success*. New York: Harper Collins, 2012.

Solomon, Andrew. *Far from the Tree: Parents, Children, and the Search for Identity*. New York: Scribner, 2012.

Stipek, Deborah, and Kathy Seal. *Motivated Minds: Raising Children to Love Learning*. New York: Henry Holt, 2001.

Tough, Paul. *How Children Succeed: Grit, Curiosity, and the Hidden Power of Character*. Boston: Houghton Mifflin Harcourt, 2012.

ARTICLES ON MUSIC EDUCATION AND MUSIC'S VALUE

Kraus, Nina, and Bharath Chandrasekaran. "Music Training for the Development of Auditory Skills." *Nature Reviews Neuroscience* 11 (Aug. 2010): 599–605.

Roden, Ingo, Gunter Kreutz, and Stephan Bongard. "Effects of a School-based Instrumental Music Program on Verbal and Visual Memory in Primary School Children: A Longitudinal Study." *Frontiers in Psychology* 3, article 572, Dec. 21, 2012.

Scripp, Larry. "Critical Links, Next Steps: An Evolving Conception of Music and Learning in Public School." *Journal for Learning Through Music*, 2nd issue (2003): 119–40.

Scripp, Larry S. "Music-in-Education Research Case Study: The Conservatory Lab Charter School—NEC Research Center 'Learning Through Music' Partnership (1999–2003)." *Journal for Music-in-Education* 1, no. 2 (2007): 202–23.

Scripp, Larry, and David Myers. "Evolving Forms of Music-in-Education Practices and Research in the Context of Arts-in-Education Reform." *Journal for Music-in-Education* 1, no. 2 (2007): 381–99.

Scripp, Larry, and David Reider. "New Ventures in Integrated Teaching and Learning: Working Toward a Model of General Symbolic Literacy Based on the Growing Understanding of Fundamental Literacy Skills Shared Between Music and Language in Grades K-2." *Journal for Music-in-Education* 1, no. 2 (2007): 337–79.

Scripp, Larry, Devin Ulibarri, and Robert Flax. "Thinking Beyond the Myths and Misconceptions of Talent: Creating Music Education Policy that Advances Music's Essential Contribution to 21st Century Teaching and Learning." *Arts Education Policy Review* 114, no. 2 (2013).

Skoe, Erika, and Nina Kraus. "A Little Goes a Long Way: How the Adult Brain Is Shaped by Musical Training in Childhood." *The Journal of Neuroscience* 32, no. 34 (Aug. 22, 2012): 11507–10.

Trahey, Dan. "Teaching Sistema Style." *The Ensemble: A Newsletter for the U.S. & Canadian El Sistema Movement,* Dec. 2013.

Wakin, Daniel J. "The Juilliard Effect: Ten Years Later." *New York Times*, Dec. 12, 2004.

White-Schwoch, Travis, Kali Woodruff Carr, Samira Anderson, Dana L. Strait, and Nina Kraus. "Older Adults Benefit from Music Training Early in Life: Biological Evidence for Long-Term Training-Driven Plasticity. *The Journal of Neuroscience* 33, no. 45 (Nov. 6, 2013): 17667–74.

Winn, Marie. "The Pleasures and Perils of Being a Child Prodigy." *New York Times Magazine.* Dec. 23, 1979.

ONLINE ARTICLES, BOOKLETS, MAGAZINES, AND REPORTS

"Career Center—Glossary." National Association for Music Education. N.d. Available: http://musiced.nafme.org/careers/career-center/glossary/.

"Careers in Music." Berklee College of Music. N.d. Available: http://www.berklee.edu/careers/.

Deasy, Richard J., ed. *Critical Links: Learning in the Arts and Student Academic and Social Development.* Washington, DC: Arts Education Partnership, 2002. Available: http://www.gpo.gov/fdsys/pkg/ERIC-ED466413/pdf/ERIC-ED466413.pdf.

Edwin, Robert. "Teaching Children to Sing." Nov. 2002. Available: http://www.robertedwinstudio.com/downloads/aats.pdf.

The Ensemble: A Newsletter for the U.S. & Canadian El Sistema Movement. A monthly newsletter, available by e-mail. For a free subscription, e-mail: theEnsembleNL@gmail.com.

Lane, David. "Admissions Tips," "The Double Degree Dilemma," "Comments on College Guides," "Understanding Music Conservatories," "What Can You Do With a Music Degree?" and "Music for Accountants." N.d. Peabody Institute. Available: http://www.peabody.jhu.edu/conservatory/admissions/tips/.

Miron, Gary, and Jessica Urschel. "Understanding and Improving Full-Time Virtual Schools." National Education Policy Center, Boulder, Colorado, July, 2012. Available: http://nepc.colorado.edu/publication/understanding-improving-virtual.

Rile, Karen. "Never Mind Talent: Practice, Practice, Practice." Philly.com, Dec. 3, 2012. Available: http://articles.philly.com/2012-12-03/news/35550138_1_violin-lessons-suzuki-method-practice.

Occupational Outlook Handbook. Bureau of Labor Statistics. 2010. Available: http://www.bls.gov/ooh/.

"Scholarship Resources for Music Students." National Association for Music Education. N.d. Available: http://musiced.nafme.org/resources/scholarship-resources-for-music-students/.

"Serving the Nation Through Music." US Army. N.d. Available: http://www.music.army.mil/careers/.

"Thinking of a Career in Music?" National Association for Music Education. N.d. Available: http://musiced.nafme.org/careers/.

"What Is Music Therapy?" Musicworx. N.d. Available: http://www.musicworxinc.com/therapy/definition.php.

"What It Takes to Be a Music Major." National Association for Music Education. N.d. Available: http://musiced.nafme.org/careers/what-it-takes-to-be-a-music-major/.

Author's Note

As explained in the first chapter, I have tried to be an objective narrator, but personal experiences can influence even the best efforts at being objective. This Author's Note presents the basic paths our two sons took, after the initial missteps described in chapter 1. Both took music-and-movement classes as preschoolers. They began piano lessons during first grade with an excellent neighborhood teacher, Judy Gutmann, who taught in her home; they continued to study with her through high school. For their band instruments—trumpet and saxophone—they started with group lessons in elementary school. At the suggestion of their school band director, Peter Kanyuk, we soon found the boys private teachers recommended by him. Our older son, Eric, stayed with his private trumpet teacher from fourth through tenth grades. For his last two years of high school, he took trumpet and composition lessons with faculty members at Juilliard Pre-College but continued with his neighborhood piano teacher until she suggested he move on to a teacher with expertise in the advanced repertoire he was learning. Our younger son, Noah, had a few different saxophone teachers and added on jazz improvisation lessons at a local community music school, Hoff Barthelson in Scarsdale, NY, during high school.

From elementary school through high school, both of our sons performed with their public schools' concert and jazz bands. They also played in all-county and all-state groups, pit bands for musicals, and in jazz bands and wind ensembles at a local music school. During high school, Eric performed with two youth orchestras and formed his own chamber music group. Both attended a day camp at a local music school through elementary and middle school, moving on during high school to the sleepaway variety: Eric spent four summers at the Boston University Tanglewood Institute and attended a program at Eastman one summer; Noah attended Jazz in July at the University of Massachusetts for several summers. Eric also performed on From the Top during his senior year in high school.

As for their post–high school experiences, Eric, now a composer, was a music major at a liberal arts college, earned an MM in music composition at a university-based conservatory and a DMA at a university with a strong composition program. Noah, now a political scientist, chose a liberal arts college with a terrific jazz band, in which he played saxophone. Eric's website tells more about his musical journey: www.EricNathanMusic.com.

Neither my husband nor I are musicians, but my husband's father was an amateur pianist who loved to play ragtime and show tunes for our sons. I took piano lessons as a child but never gained a sense of fun from those highly structured lessons and quit at age sixteen, although I loved singing in my high school's glee club and played trumpet in my all-girl public high school's band. In my mid-twenties, I returned to music through singing, taking lessons for several years from a teacher who empha-sized the joy of music making. When my sons began piano lessons, I asked Judy to give me lessons, too, for a few years to revive my skills, which are still pretty rusty but which give me a lot of pleasure when I find time to sit at our upright piano and work my way through pieces I love.

Acknowledgments

Warm thanks go to all the musicians, parents, educators, and others who took time from their busy lives to be interviewed for this book or to fill out questionnaires, and who, in some cases, also searched through their files to find photos to share in the book. Although about ninety parents are quoted in this book, there are so many other parents who filled out questionnaires—too many to quote directly or to list— but all the comments and suggestions that parents jotted down on their question- naires helped define the issues to be covered in this book and the nature of the dis- cussion. Thanks also go to the DC Youth Orchestra Program, Interlochen Center for the Arts, Jazz House Kids, St. Louis Symphony Youth Orchestra, JCC Thur- nauer School of Music, and the Young People's Chorus of New York City for making available beautiful photos of their students.

In addition, I am very grateful to the following individuals for their help with ar- ranging for parents, educators, musicians, and others to be part of the advice team or for making photographs available for the book: Lindsey Adams, Judah Adashi, Ingrid Arnett, Dan Bernstein, Melody Blythe, Edith Bolton, Matt Buttermann, David Campagna, Antony Catlin, Jane Covner, Amy Dennison, Eleanor Dowling, Barbara and Virginia Doyle, Angela Duryea, Brent Edmondson, Gwilym Evans, Bob Fiedler, Erika Floreska, Cheryl P. Guess, Jane Günter-McCoy, Adalberto Guti- errez, Suzanne Hanser, Rebecca Henry, Ellen Highstein, Jessica Ingraham, Lisa Jaehnig, Virginia Johnson, Nancy Klein, Shirley Leiphon, Maegan McHugh,

Zakiyah Munashe, Peggy Neilson, Jana Nelhybel, Francisco J. Núñez, Clayton Okaly, Kathleen Perez, Liza Prijatel, Michael Reingold, Matthew Sandoski, Ellen Schertzer, Joshua Simonds, Ava Spece, Peter Spellman, Genevieve Stewart, Sean Samimi, Joshua Simonds, Erica Tuchman, Lou Tutt, Jean Young, Melissa Walker, and Christine Witkowski. I want to send special thank-yous to Judy Gutmann, the piano teacher who gave both of our sons a good start in music, and to all the wonderful music teachers and band directors they had throughout their years in the Mamaroneck public schools. Warm thanks also go to the music teachers they had at Hoff-Barthelson Music School and at Juilliard Pre-College, as well as to all the teachers who gave our boys private lessons, including Julius Sposato, Stephen Christos, and Hiroko Dutton. Thanks also go to the terrific editorial team at Oxford University Press—Suzanne Ryan, Norman Hirschy, Todd Waldman—and to the many members of the production team.

Without our two musical sons and their glorious music that has filled our lives, this book would never have happened. Nor could it have come to life without the encouragement, support, love, and gentle editing from my husband, Carl.

Credits

QUOTED MATERIAL

Other than the quotation references listed below, all other direct quotes from individuals in this book come from questionnaires they filled out for this book, from personal telephone and in-person interviews conducted by the author, or through e-mail communications with the author. Full citations are in the Bibliography.

The quotes from Wynton Marsalis on page 230 come from the following podcast posted by Jazz at Lincoln Center: http://hwcdn.net/j3u8s7y7/cds/podcasts/jazz_stories_podcast/JS_Wynton_One_on_One.mp3.

The quote on page 20, "music is a resource that tones the brain for auditory fitness," comes from page 599 of Kraus and Chandrasekaran, "Music Training for the Development of Auditory Skills."

The quote on page 20, "adults who received...music lessons," comes from page 11507 of Skoe and Kraus, "A Little Goes a Long Way."

The quote on page 20, "whether these structural...auditory fitness," comes from page 227 of Levitin, *This Is Your Brain on Music*.

The quote on page 8, "No one reached...to excellence," comes from page 509 and the quote "a long and intensive...of capability" comes from page 3 of Bloom, *Developing Talent in Young People*.

The quote from the alphabet book on page 31 comes from page 50 of *Dr. Seuss's ABC* by Dr. Seuss, published in 1963 by Random House, New York, copyright renewed 1991 by Dr. Seuss Enterprises.

The quote from Deborah Stipek on page 117 comes from page 168 of Stipek and Seal, *Motivated Minds*.

The quotes from Isaac Stern on pages 126 and 137 come from Winn, "The Pleasures and Perils of Being a Child Prodigy."

The quotes in chapter 11 from the Bureau of Labor Statistics (BLS) come from "Occupational Outlook Handbook," http://www.bls.gov/ooh/.

The quote from Larry Scripp on page 21 "Music should be taught…." comes from pages 375–6 of Scripp and Reider, "New Ventures in Integrated Teaching and Learning."

PHOTO

Cover (top), 22, 120—© Sarah Carmody; Cover (bottom), 17, 89, 91, 150—Courtesy Young People's Chorus of New York City, Artistic Director/Founder Francisco J. Núñez, photograph by Stephanie Berger; 2 (both)—Courtesy the Nathan family; 6—Courtesy Christian McBride and Jazz House Kids, photo by Ed Berger; 9—© Colin Bell, under license to EMI Classics; 12 (top), 42 (bottom), 172 (top)—Courtesy Interlochen Center for the Arts; 12 (bottom)—Courtesy Toyin Spellman-Diaz; 23 (both)—Courtesy the Goosby family; 25—Courtesy DC Youth Orchestra Program; 26 (top two), 166 (both)—Courtesy Joshua Bell and Shirley Bell; 26 (bottom)—Courtesy Joshua Bell, photo by Lisa-Marie Mazzucco; 31—Courtesy Alisa Weilerstein and Vivian Weilerstein; 33, 177—Courtesy Anne Akiko Meyers; 36—Courtesy the Marsalis family; 42 (top)—Courtesy the Couillard family; 47—Courtesy Payton MacDonald, photo by Dave Kerzner; 49, 69—© Richard Holland, October 7 Productions; 59, 75, 188, 233—© Amy Nathan; 61—Courtesy Adrian Anantawan; 62 (top, bottom L)—Courtesy Jennifer Koh; 62 (bottom R)—Courtesy Jennifer Koh, photo by Fran Kaufman; 70—Courtesy Imani Winds, photo by Matthew Murphy; 84 (all)—Courtesy the Vautour family; 93—© Derek Blanks, all rights reserved; 101—Courtesy Kelli O'Hara, photo by Laura Marie Duncan; 102—Courtesy Stephanie Blythe; 104—Courtesy Stephanie Blythe, photo by Kobie van Rensburg; 106—Courtesy Paula Robison, photo by David V. Robison; 112—Courtesy Erika Nickrenz; 123, 153—Courtesy the McCarthy family; 128 (both)—Courtesy Theresa Chong; 140—Courtesy Erika Nickrenz, photo by Laurie Newton; 144—© Mark Silverberg; 146—© Rob Waymen; 159—Courtesy Ranaan Meyer; 164—Courtesy Richard Stoltzman; 172 (bottom)—Courtesy Anthony McGill, photo by David Finlayson; 181, 205—© Andrew Hurlbut/New England Conservatory; 200 (top)—Courtesy Alisa Weilerstein, photo by Lucio Lecce; 200 (bottom)—© Benjamin Ealovega; 209—Courtesy David Grossman, photo by Henry Grossman; 212—Courtesy Eroica Trio, photo by David Bean; 226—Courtesy the Fagan family; 231—Courtesy the Weilerstein family.

Index